Praise for *No Matter What*

'If you've ever wondered what it's like to adopt, this book holds the answer: it's hard, sometimes traumatic, and far from "normal family life". It's also special, joyful and utterly transformative – for parents as much as children. Yes our families are different; this book explains in both a moving and matter-of-fact way why we are proud to be so.'

– Baroness Oona King, adoptive mother

'I found this book almost unbearably moving and, ultimately, uniquely uplifting. I have never before read, in a single book, such a compelling portrait of the horrors of child neglect and its consequences, alongside a portrait of the historical inadequacies of adoption assessment and post adoption support. This is a staggeringly vivid account of a heroic struggle by heroic adopters to heal the deep scars of neglect and abuse. I cannot recommend it warmly enough.'

– Sir Martin Narey, Government Advisor on Children's Social Care and Visiting Professor, Durham and Sheffield Hallam Universities

'Honest, refreshing, heart-breaking, thought-provoking and inspiring – this is a valuable insight into adoption and the devastating effects of trauma.'

– Lorraine Pascale, TV Presenter, Chef and former Model, adoptee and TACT patron

'This book is sheer therapy for an adopter and enlightenment for anyone who comes into contact with adoption in any way. A must-read for parents, schools and authorities.'

– Carrie Grant Vocal Coach/TV Presenter, adoptive mother and BAAF adoption champion

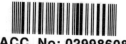

'Sally Donovan has written a warm, humorous, hard-hitting and compelling story about her own adoption journey. What she says will resonate with the majority of those who have adopted children from care. Ultimately this is an overwhelmingly positive celebration of the transformation that adoption can bring to society's most damaged and vulnerable children, but it also clearly sets out the realities of parenting children affected by early childhood abuse and neglect. Every adopter will be able to recognise some aspect of their own experiences in Sally's story and I would urge every professional working with adopted children – including health visitors and teachers, as well as social workers – to read this so they know what understanding and support those parenting adopted children need.'

– Hugh Thornbery, Chief Executive, Adoption UK

'*No Matter What* is by a long way the best account ever written of the experience of being an adoptive parent and carer of children traumatised by maltreatment. With heart-wrenching candour, it tells the story of a couple's journey through the pain of childlessness, the adoption process, and the lived experience of caring for Jaymey and Harlee whose early lives were "almost unbearable to read about". Sally Donovan evokes brilliantly the commitment, energy, therapeutic skill and humanity required to care for and heal children whose past abuse has left them distressed, feeling unworthy and acting out in often chaotic ways. This remarkable book is not only a major contribution to work on child welfare; such is the sheer power and brilliance of the writing that it triumphs as a work of literature, as art. Utterly compelling and humane, *No Matter What* is essential reading for all those who care for and about vulnerable children, adoption and fostering and who are open to being inspired by the healing power of love.'

– Harry Ferguson, Professor of Social Work, University of Nottingham

'Everyone should read this funny and deeply moving account of modern adoption: the highs, the lows, the risks and the rewards. Sally's writing is honest, insightful and beautiful to read.

I am, and will remain, totally in awe of Sally and her husband Rob. Their empathy and resilience is sure to inspire anyone who reads this book, particularly those thinking about adopting a child.

In the most modest, refreshing and unassuming way, Sally gives a voice to everyone struggling with infertility or learning to parent traumatised children. This book is a triumph in so many ways.'

– Camilla Pemberton, Children and Families Editor, Community Care

'With great humility Sally shares her journey of courage, hope and persistence in boldly loving her children despite the odds, no matter what... Throughout the book I laughed and cried, experiencing the highs and lows of loving children who have lived the unthinkable. For too long adopters walked this journey very much alone. We must now accompany them on this journey, in our neighbourhoods, communities and cities, and within our education, social care and health services. Together we can make a difference; each life is precious, however fragile and different. *No Matter What* communicates this truth, and is an important contribution at this time of policy change.'

– Louise Michelle Bombèr, Adoption Support Teacher for Brighton and Hove, Attachment Support Teacher Therapist for The Yellow Kite Attachment Support Service

'*No Matter What* pulls no punches in describing Sally and Rob's moving journey of adopting two siblings and the challenges of parenting them in great detail. It is beautifully written with humour and understanding.

We learn from Sally that adopting children who have suffered neglect and abuse, requires not only resilient parents but expert advice, support and understanding from a range of professionals and from family and friends.

This book is required reading for professionals such as social workers, health professionals, teachers and early years staff. It is also a must for those who want to adopt and for their families as it provides an honest account of the challenges but also the joys of falling in love with your adopted children. We can all learn so much from Sally and Rob's story.'

– Sherry Malik, Director of Children and Adult Services in Hounslow

'In *No Matter What* Sally has written about her adoption journey in a way which enables us to walk in her shoes and those of her children and which is informative and humbling. Anyone associated with children in the care system in any capacity could only benefit from reading this outstanding book.'

– Jane Evans, Trauma Parenting and Behaviour Skills Specialist and Trainer

NO MATTER WHAT

Sally Donovan

AN ADOPTIVE FAMILY'S STORY OF HOPE, LOVE AND HEALING

Jessica Kingsley *Publishers*
London and Philadelphia

First published in 2013
by Jessica Kingsley Publishers
116 Pentonville Road
London N1 9JB, UK
and
400 Market Street, Suite 400
Philadelphia, PA 19106, USA

www.jkp.com

Front cover image source: iStockphoto®. The cover image is for illustrative purposes only, and any person featuring is a model.

Library of Congress Cataloging in Publication Data
Donovan, Sally (Adoptive mother)
No matter what : an adoptive family's story of hope, love and healing / Sally Donovan.
pages cm
ISBN 978-1-84905-431-7 (alk. paper)
1. Donovan, Sally (Adoptive mother) 2. Adoptive parents--Great Britain--Biography. 3. Abused children--Great Britain--Biography. 4. Adoption--Great Britain. I. Title.
HV874.82.D66A3 2013
362.734092'2--dc23
2013005856

British Library Cataloguing in Publication Data
A CIP catalogue record for this book is available from the British Library

ISBN 978 1 84905 431 7
eISBN 978 0 85700 781 0

Printed and bound in Great Britain

CONTENTS

Acknowledgements 9

Author's note 11

Part 1 Revelations: In the Bad House

Chapter 1. 15

Part 2 Keeping Secrets: Hope and Disappointment

Chapter 2. 21

Chapter 3 41

Part 3 Planning a Future: Flip Charts and Handouts

Chapter 4 55

Chapter 5. 75

Chapter 6. 95

Part 4 In the Family Way: Early Days

Chapter 7. 115

Chapter 8. 139

Chapter 9. 155

Part 5 Extreme Times: Life and Loss

Chapter 10 175

Chapter 11 197

Part 6 Getting Educated: Learning the Hard Way

Chapter 12 225

Chapter 13 245

Chapter 14 259

Part 7 A Time for Healing: No Matter What

Chapter 15 285

Chapter 16 303

Chapter 17 323

Chapter 18 345

ACKNOWLEDGEMENTS

To my children for allowing me to write this book. Your strength and courage have taught me so much. It is my love letter to you both.

To my sister and her family for their generous support, intuitive understanding and trashy magazines.

To my parents for their continued and generous support, cake and breakfasts.

To S, K and I for catching us when we needed to be caught.

To Mel for her brilliant social work, expertise, time and empathy. We are lucky to have you.

To N for guiding us through the darkest times with the lightest touch.

To R for putting up with the worst of me, for not ever flinching and for being an unwavering advocate for the children of trauma.

To Dr Dan Hughes, the godfather of therapeutic parenting, for tirelessly and patiently educating us all with such warmth and wit. I can't imagine doing this without him.

To Louise Bombèr for writing her books on supporting children with attachment difficulties at school, which gives the subject the gravitas it deserves.

To Rachel for nurturing the writer in me with care and insight and for her friendship.

To my agent Genevieve Carden for sticking with me through the nearlies and the not so nearlies.

To all at Community Care for their encouragement, particularly Camilla Pemberton.

To all my friends, particularly K, K and S for the tissues and the tea, for Friday evenings, for the terrible sushi and the wonderful bread.

To J, S, J and E because you deserved better.

To Mathew, my fellow traveller, to whom I never have to explain.

To all the teachers who have taken the time to understand trauma and attachment and who have listened and been the very embodiment of 'every child matters', particularly Mr R, Mrs H, Miss H, Miss S, Miss A, Mrs B and the two Mrs Ws.

To all my Twitter and blog companions. We may not recognise each other in the street but we are all 'doing it differently'. I thank you heartily for your black humour, which has eased the difficult times.

AUTHOR'S NOTE

This story is based on real events, but names have been changed to protect the identity of those involved. Some characters and situations are composites or fictitious, and some timings have been changed.

PART 1

Revelations

In the Bad House

CHAPTER 1

I watch as Jaymey systematically arranges treasured teddies, dogs, rabbits and monkeys along the gap between his bed and the wall. It takes time; every gap must be filled, checked and if necessary refilled more securely. He is frightened of dark, unknowable spaces, where the terrifying might be lurking.

We have endured another traumatic day of struggle, shouting and upset and we are both worn out. Any attempts I make to hurry him will only delay the process so I try to remain calm and cheerful.

'Your animals look very comfortable. Are they all in the right places now?'

He continues rearranging and doesn't answer. I stifle the half-sigh half-yawn that rises up from my lungs and pass him the last few soft toys.

'All ready now,' he says and curls down on to his pillow with his little collection of silent protectors. I lean over to stroke his soft hair and as I kiss his cheek, his eyes suddenly snap open.

'Mummy, Mummy, I want sit up, now, sit up.' It is as though he has been switched on, electrified. He is agitated, urgent.

'Jaymey, what's the matter?'

He looks straight into my eyes. He never looks straight into anyone's eyes. It stops me still.

'In the bad house, Ellie, him had long pole with sharp bits on the end. Him push it into my mouth, hard like this.'

His speech is rushed and jagged. He jabs into his duvet with a little balled up fist.

'And my tooth it did come out.' He pulls down his lower lip and points to the gap in his milk teeth.

His eyes do not veer from mine but drill into them and I hope I do not betray the wave of cold panic that flushes through me. My beautiful son, four years old, who has been mine for such a short time, is entrusting me with a precious secret. I want him to trust me, to have no doubt that I am on his side.

'Jaymey? How long was the pole?'

Such a stupid question but I am all at sea and don't know where to begin. He stretches his little arms out as wide as he can. His Bob the Builder pyjama top rises up.

'Was it done on purpose, or by accident?' I ask, mindful that Jaymey, given two options of anything, will nearly always choose the last.

'It was done by purpose and Ellie and the people are in prison now and Ellie was my friend and now him isn't anymore.'

The names and the information are unfamiliar but he is animated with certainty in a way I have never seen him before – reaching into his memory, desperate to explain, to make me understand.

'There was blood, a lot of lot of blood and it hurt very, very much so I couldn't eat anymore. I could not even eat biscuits, for long, long time.'

He goes over the events again and again, with the ever-present, saucer-like eyes, reaching into mine, asking me to believe him. This is a test of me; a brave test of whether I am going to have the mettle to last the course with him.

'It must have been very scary and very frightening for you,' I venture.

'And and Ellie and the people, they are in prison now?' he asks.

Ellie is not a name I recognise from the information we have been given, so I have no idea. But I sense that what Jaymey needs from me is to feel reassured and safe. So I lie to him. 'Yes, they are in prison, because what they did to you was a very bad thing.' He agrees with me, so emphatically.

'Will I have to see them again?'

'No, you will never have to see them again. You are with me and Daddy and Harlee forever and nothing like that is ever going to happen to you again.' His face changes. Relief washes over it.

'I want play bin lorries with you tomorrow.'

We chat about bin lorries; the grinding change of gear troubles me but soothes him. I tuck him in amongst his teddies again and kiss him goodnight.

'I love you, Jaymey.'

I check that the night light is on, leave his bedroom door open the required amount and creep downstairs.

He sleeps all night. I lie awake for most of it, sick and numb. I think of the force needed to knock out a tooth, the blood and the pain. He would have been not quite two years old. A baby. My shock mixes with anger. How could someone inflict that on my baby? My beautiful boy. And no one was punished for this crime, carried out in the dark cocoon of violence and neglect created by his birth family. Evidence not robust enough, witnesses too young and too scared to speak out, the benefit of the doubt, second chances, third chances. And the act was no doubt covered up. Jaymey was never taken to the doctor or to the dentist. The event was recorded in the paperwork as another 'unexplained incident'. And he was left in their care for a further six months.

The following morning, over breakfast, I refer to our conversation of the previous evening, anxious that Jaymey knows his act of bravery has been remembered and valued. I try to get some more detail from him.

'Is Ellie a lady or a man?'

'A lady.'

'Is Ellie a girl or a lady?'

'A lady.'

'Is Ellie a big lady or a small lady?'

'A big fat lady.'

'Does Ellie have blonde or dark hair?'

'Dark hair. Him wear grey tracksuit t-shirts and grey tracksuit trousers.'

The previous weekend, I had been choosing some new pyjamas for myself in M&S. Jaymey was naturally uninterested until I briefly considered a pair made from a grey, stretchy, cotton fabric. He grabbed my arm and shook it. He said he really did not like them and that I was not to buy them, that they were horrible and I would look horrible in them.

I will never know for sure who Ellie is. She could be Trudy, Jaymey's birth mother, another relative or a friend. Whoever she is, he is frightened of her still, of having to go back to her, of me becoming like her. I tell Jaymey that I love him and that I appreciate him telling me about his tooth. I dash upstairs to get changed – something bright today, I think.

PART 2

Keeping Secrets

Hope and Disappointment

CHAPTER 2

The car journey to the takeaway is the perfect duration: long enough for me carefully to introduce this much-rehearsed strand of conversation and not so long as to leave us trapped together awkwardly if it is not well received.

'Shall we start trying then?' I finally say, as we are within sight of the car park, cursing myself for leaving it so late. I try to sound casual but do not succeed.

'Trying for what?' Rob replies, trying to come across as though he has no idea what his 30-year-old, happily married wife might be alluding to. He is going to make me say it in full, to buy himself some thinking time no doubt and, I suspect, so it appears as though I'm suggesting we do something totally bizarre.

'You know, a baby.'

He clearly hasn't bought himself quite enough thinking time and needs some more.

'I'm only 28,' he pleads, as though his adolescence is barely over.

'And I'm 30. I don't want to be an older mother and I would like more than one child…' It's now obvious I have rehearsed this conversation in my head, as well as mapped out the timeline, so I drop all efforts at sounding casual. We park and sit beside each other in the dark.

'Our food will be getting cold,' says Rob.

We are jovial with the lady who hands us our white paper carrier bag of curried joy and silent with each other as we head back to the car. The baby conversation hangs over us on the journey back as we talk inconsequentialities.

Goodness, it's chilly tonight. There's ice forming on the windscreen already. This takeaway is hot against my legs. I wonder if we'll get back in time for Have I Got News for You.

Over the next few days I nudge Rob again. He resists, which is the usual pattern, and then just as I'm starting to think he'll never agree, 'OK. OK. Let's start trying.' I resist the temptation to ask, 'Trying for what?'

Distant conversations with university friends come to mind. We were going to do such marvellous things with our careers that there would not be time for children until we were at least 35. We did not give our biological clocks room back then. Ageing was something we could hold back through sheer willpower and positive thought. We looked down on school friends who had had children in their early 20s and who had sacrificed their careers as a result. Yes, motherhood was definitely something menial and we were not cut out for menial work. But then we graduated in a recession and our glittering careers took a little longer to materialise than we had planned. I ended up temping for a big company and clung on there for a few years. Despite doing reasonably well there, it was plain that I was not a natural at the politicking and the schmoozing. I despised writing reports that no one ever read, fighting the bureaucracy for tea and coffee requisitions for important meetings and travelling to foreign trading estates, and I somehow always knew that I wasn't meant to do a job that required the wearing of tights. I did, however, meet Rob there, so as a step on life's journey it did me well. We worked in the same office, rubbed shoulders on the same projects and that was the start of a beautiful thing. We bought a house together, got married.

Rob always knew that I was an outdoor girl, but I think it came as a bit of a shock to him when I handed in my notice, cut up all my tights and enrolled on a horticulture course. Within a year I was working full time in a historic garden doing one of the most menial jobs there is. Now I dig, weed, prune, plant and water and love every minute of it. I love the camaraderie, the visitors, the history, the exercise and the visual delights that every day brings. I also like having a job that I can explain to other people in a single, short sentence: 'I am a gardener.'

'Wow, that's so interesting. Where do you work? What do you do exactly? I'd love to do that,' is the usual response. After a rambling explanation of my previous job I was usually met with a chasm of uninterest.

And now it just feels like the right time to start a family. My second career is well established and we haven't left it too late. I am a fertile 30. It is exciting. I'm almost consumed with the excitement of what might be in a few months' time. I will have to start thinking about which room will be the baby's room, what the baby will be called, what I'm going to wear, how long I should take as maternity leave. I wonder what sort of parents we will be – overprotective, pushy, indulgent, strict? I think about what sort of children we will have. Will they inherit Rob's dark colouring and height or my fair skin? Perhaps my blonde hair and my artistic streak and Rob's mathematical ability? Rob says that most of all he hopes that our children inherit his beautiful feet and don't flap about on my ugly ones. I say I hope that the feet don't come as a job lot with the Donovan ears. We joke that if the dice fall favourably we will produce the most gorgeous and talented children the world has ever seen.

*****

Amongst our excitement we get on with our lives. We work, socialise with our friends, meet with our families and lead quite unremarkable lives. It probably won't be too long before our baby comes along, so we go to art exhibitions, spend a few weekends in European cities and do the things that young expectant couples do. We talk casually about babies' names, add them to our surname, check for awkward rhymes, make sure the initials don't spell something crude. My sister Alice, my friends are having babies. All our babies will grow up together, we will be parents together, a neat circle of maternity. Our lives are planned to perfection.

The news of Alice's pregnancy is met with much excitement in our family. Her baby will be the first grandchild for my parents and for her husband Mark's parents and the first nephew or niece for Rob and me. The Golden Child. It is a long time since there has been a baby around in any of our lives and I can hardly wait to be an aunty. Aunty Sally. I am close to Alice and we live in neighbouring towns. We will be able to spend so much more time together when we have children and I feel glad that the cousins we bear will be able to grow up together.

At work, the early arrival of the warm weather dictates that we start the summer tasks. We brush off the mowers, plant out the summer bedding and welcome the visitors back. It has been dry so I haul the hose out from the back of the shed and hook it up to the old brass tap. Watering is one of the few more static activities in the garden. It enforces a slow-down and with that comes time for contemplation – the opportunity to look up for a change, at the bigger picture. I slowly make my way up the steps, watering each of the large planters in turn. I gaze at the water gushing on to the compost. There is something hypnotic about watching the water fill to the rim of the pot, then reaching the hose to the next pot and repeating the process. At the top of the steps is the terrace, which overlooks the garden – the geometric flower beds, the sharp yew hedging and the wide drive heading off into the parkland. It is early morning, silent, the warmth is just coming through, but within a couple of hours the gardens will bustle with coach parties. I wonder if this will be the last summer season that I will experience here for a while. Surely by next summer I'll be sitting in my own garden, on a blanket, under the apple tree, my baby next to me. I had hoped to be pregnant by now, not to be anticipating the autumn jobs. I read in magazines that it can commonly take six months to get pregnant.

*****

One September night I go to bed late knowing that my sister Alice has been in labour all day and that she will ring me sometime after the birth. I slip in and out of sleep, my worry for Alice tainting my dreams with frights and imagined pains. The church bells ring out midnight, one o'clock, two o'clock; I miss three o'clock and then hear four. Then the phone wakes me in a half-panic, the ringing momentarily being incorporated into the dream. I race downstairs, grab the phone and jab at the green button.

'It's me.' Alice sounds terrible, exhausted, upset. Then she bursts into tears. 'It was awful.'

'Alice. I wish I was with you. But it's all over. You'll be home soon.'

There is a long silence filled with sobbing.

'What did you have – a girl or a boy?'

'A boy. We had a boy. Luke William.'

'Is he alright?' I ask, worried that there may have been complications.

'He's fine. Eight pounds, twelve ounces.'

'A big bouncing boy. I'm glad to hear he's following in the family tradition.'

Another long pause.

'I'll come and see you all, OK? Do you want me to contact anyone else?'

'I've rung Mum and Dad. Mark's going to ring everyone else.'

'OK. I'll see you later.'

Alice says goodbye through choked tears.

I feel a cheat offering platitudes when I don't know what she's been through. I scan back through everything I said to her. Maybe the last thing she needed was me promising to visit or my stupid reference to the baby's weight. I also feel a little shard of sharp jealousy wrapped up in shame. How can I feel jealous at a time like this, when a new life has come into the world, my own sister's baby? I know that I need to bundle up my piece of jagged jealousy and hide it where no one will see it. I climb back into the warm bed and curl up next to Rob.

'What did they have?' he croaks.

'A boy. Luke William.'

'That's fantastic news. Everyone OK?'

'Yes, fine,' I say.

We visit Alice, Mark and baby Luke. Alice looks pale, puffy and exhausted, but relieved. She hands me the warm bundle of baby and as he settles from the movement he shifts in his babygro with a catlike satisfaction. He had grown inside my sister, but until this very moment I had never thought of him as a reality. But with his shimmer of strawberry blonde hair, his little rounded chin and the gentle movements of his mouth, he has arrived – appeared into the family. He vaguely opens unfocused eyes and I say to him, 'We have been waiting for you. It is lovely to meet you. Yes, it is so lovely to meet you.'

I stroke him on the side of his cheek and on his forehead. His skin is so soft I can hardly feel it. I bend my head to brush a kiss against him and a warm smell of pure baby hugs me to him. I am in love. It is aunty love and it is delicious.

During our visits over the months we see Luke focusing his big blue eyes and flashing his long eyelashes.

'The girls aren't going to be able to resist you batting your long eyelashes like that,' we all say.

Over the first few months of his life we see Luke balling up his tiny hands around our little fingers, we hear him discovering the sounds his voice can make and gradually we find some little games, some rhymes, silly noises that make him laugh. Rob seems to have a particular skill at helping Luke to sleep on his chest. Everyone marvels at this talent, at the calmness that Rob must be communicating to this baby. One afternoon, we drop in at the end of a visit by Mark's parents. His mother wonders at Rob's innate ability.

'That'll be a useful talent to have with your own, when the time comes,' she says.

'Yes, yes, hopefully,' Rob manages.

The atmosphere in the room is perceptively awkward. Alice quickly moves the attention back to Luke by bringing his new bouncy chair out from behind the sofa. Everyone exclaims how wonderful the bouncy chair is. They gush, going overboard in their hurry to escape the minefield we have stumbled into.

Later on, I join Alice in the kitchen.

'I'm sorry about her comment. Your face said it all. You and Rob have been trying,' she says.

'For about a year. We didn't want to tell anyone, but I didn't think it would take this long.'

'A year isn't so long. Maybe give it a bit longer?'

'I know she didn't mean to be insensitive and I don't want you to think I feel anything other than complete happiness for you and Mark.' I am anxious not to be cast in the role of bitter, jealous, childless woman.

'I would never think that.'

The jagged piece of jealousy catches inside me, making itself known.

*****

We give 'It' longer. A lot longer. I read about hormone cycles, fertile times, the subtle ways in which my body is telling me when to procreate. I become tuned into these signs, learn to read them really quite well – maybe too well, become a little obsessed by the signs. Over time 'The Trying' takes on a seriousness that it has never had before and it does feel like trying. Like trying to learn some French verbs or trying to cycle up a long, steep hill. The word itself doesn't indicate any success. It suggests tedium. Now our previously carefree and satisfying lovemaking has to happen around certain times, which are not always convenient, perhaps when Rob is away on a business trip or Match of the Day is on. Increasingly, one of us isn't in the mood and so the word 'chore' has become associated with the word 'sex', which takes away a little of the magic.

I read too much 'advice' in too many women's magazines. The 'advice' generally follows the same pattern. First, you absolutely must 'not get stressed'. Just like the 'don't think of an elephant' test, 'do not get stressed' brings on immediate stress. And this is bad for your cells, your partner's cells, your relationship – everything. Second, whilst not getting stressed you must find out when your most fertile time is and you must then have sex as much as possible during that time and preferably outside that time as well. Third, whilst not getting stressed, you must live a very healthy lifestyle, which must exclude alcohol – curious advice indeed when alcohol is the only substance in the store cupboard that renders choresex marginally more enticing than cleaning the oven. Even though I take myself for a sensible woman, not accustomed to getting anything other than a bit of superficial diversion from magazines, I soak them up, hopeful that they are going to contain the secret of the holy grail. Just maybe, the key to conception will be contained within those glossy pages. The micro-nutrient my womb is lacking, the phase of the moon that will give those sperm a little extra kick, the positive affirmations that will allow me to accept that I really do want to become a mother

– all this (plus a free make-up bag) may be discovered for just £4.95.

The lack of success increasingly weighs on my mind. It starts as a little worm of a niggle that surfaces occasionally and that I can push back down. Then it becomes less easy to ignore, catches me suddenly when I am least expecting it, squeezes my heart with a cold fist. I need to break my silence and decide to talk to Alice again. She is three years my junior, but senior to me in common sense and practicality. Verbalising the situation fully, putting my worry – the lack of a baby – into words makes it feel much more real. My sister says it is time we went to the doctor. It has been three years now. She is right. I have been avoiding going, not wanting to force the situation out of my head and into the real world. I also tell my mum, who comforts with words. It took a long time for her to fall pregnant with my sister, so it will happen, just give it time.

*****

Working outdoors makes the simple task of making a private phone call to the doctor's surgery very tricky. The gardeners – a team of three of us plus the head gardener Andy – share a single phone in the bothy: an old stone building that doubles up as our office and staffroom. I trek from one end of the garden back to the bothy, only to find that someone is working in there or having a tea break and then have to walk back to the border I'm working in. I repeat this for two days, finally giving in and convincing Rob that although I understand his 'talking to strangers on the phone' phobia, he's going to have to suck it up. I will be entering menopause before I can make a doctor's appointment. Rob reluctantly agrees, as long as he can make it in my name.

In the days leading up to our appointment with Dr Coburn I am kept busy at work clearing leaves and planting the winter bedding and so don't really think about what the outcome might be. Occasional breaks between tasks provide me with just enough time to convince myself I am not worried about the appointment. The glossies tell me that the un-pregnant are usually far too impatient and that a doctor's first advice is to go on trying for a bit longer. I lie to my boss, Andy, so that I can leave work early to get to the doctor's – my sister is ill and I am looking after my nephew, Luke. I wash my hands before I leave but figure that if I change out of my work clothes it may betray my lie.

We meet in the doctor's car park – Rob looking smart in his dark suit and tie, me feeling like a tramp. Rob seems cheerful, an edgy kind of cheerful. I am happily ignoring why we are here until we are shown into the waiting room and then we wait. And wait. And wait. The time is like prison time. Silent time to consider your crime. You are failing to procreate. The most natural thing, the reason for existence, to spread your selfish genes. You can't do it. The eyes of the other patients are on us. They are thinking what I would have thought in the past – that couples only go to visit the doctor together when terminal illness or mental illness is suspected. We must look odd. A smart, handsome man in a suit and a scruffy, not-quite-grown-up-looking woman in khakis. It's going to look like mental illness. No wonder I can't get pregnant: I play around in the soil, don't have a proper grown-up job. Awkward, tense, quiet, too much time to ponder what might happen in the consulting room. God alive, I might have to undress, take off my work boots, my trousers, my underwear. My heart sinks into my dirty boots.

We are called and watched by every pair of eyes as we make our way to the consulting room. Dr Coburn is businesslike.

'How long have you been having unprotected sexual intercourse?'

'Three years.'

'You will need to have a series of sperm tests at the hospital, Mr Donovan. Mrs Donovan, you will need to have a blood test, around day 14 of your cycle, for the next three cycles. Our practice nurse will carry those out. And in the meantime try to have as much sexual intercourse as possible.'

And that is it. We exit quickly through the waiting room and into the fresh late afternoon air. We go to the coffee shop nearby, to shoehorn a bit of enjoyment into what remains of the day. The busy, sociable atmosphere is a change of gear that relieves us of our tension for a while. The background noise allows us to chat, without an audience, about how at least now we have something to focus on – some action is being taken. We laugh at the mechanical, basic reality of having to take a sperm sample to the hospital, still warm. I feel comforted in this environment, not only because of the warmth and milky coffee, but also because there are no children here. Some situations are becoming difficult to face – situations where there are families, playing together, having fun. I love going to the park or lying on a river bank and used to be quite contented on a deckchair reading the paper, swimming, going for a walk. But now I feel at a loose end, restless – I need someone to play with; I need a child to play with. Luke laps up my need for a playmate and I love being his aunty. But it feels like time I was promoted to Mummy, with a capital M. We finish our coffees and head out into the dusk, the Christmas displays in the shops unsettling me – 'You will be childless again this Christmas,' they say.

*****

A week later I endure Rob's office Christmas meal. I have forgotten how to dress for these occasions and Rob is no help. Smart/casual he thinks but the casual side of smart, although not to worry – I always look nice. I go for my interpretation of the casual side of smart and enter the pub/ restaurant to be faced by a glisten of sequins, velvet, satin and high heels. I am immediately introduced to a very well-spoken man and his wife. They are attentive and interested in what I do. Their politeness is charming but practised and there are hints of good breeding and a solid military background, but I like them. They talk about their garden and their roses and ask jokingly if I could come and do their gardening for them. The well-spoken man makes his excuses to work the room and I am left with his wife.

'Do you and Rob have children, Sally?'

My response is well rehearsed, but her question still punches me in the stomach, leaves me feeling winded.

'No, no we haven't, not yet, how about you?'

Whilst she talks about boarding schools and Sandhurst, I search for Rob in my peripheral vision. He is holding my glass of wine, making his way to me, surrounded by a group of women.

'Sally, here's your drink – sorry it took so long. Let me introduce you to Lisa, Ros and Karen.'

I say, 'Hello, nice to meet you,' and they look me up and down. They say they've heard a lot about me. How to take this is not obvious. They clink their bracelets, pat their solid hair, rearrange their silk scarves, drink from their glasses leaving gloops of bright pink lipstick on the rims. Despite their apparent confidence, they shift from cramped foot to cramped foot, fiddle with earrings and shift tiny sparkling clutch bags from underarm to hand to underarm. They talk about people I don't know, places I haven't been to, events that were so funny I should have been there. They occasionally touch Rob, tease him. This display is deliberate in its exclusion of me. They are reminding me that they spend more time with my husband than I do, that he has a whole life of which I know very little. They are gossipy, squawky, bosomy and I've met their type before. Sadness fuels my unkind judgements. There is a break in the guffawing and then Karen looks at me and Rob.

'So when are you two going to get down to it then, or are you firing blanks, Rob?'

Everyone laughs, loudly. I laugh half-heartedly and, I hope, rudely. I catch the hand grenade she has so casually lobbed and throw it back.

'Do you have children, Karen?'

'Yes, I've got Liam who's nine and Erin who's seven. Right little shit Liam was tonight, right up till his dad came to get him.'

She launches into a long drivel of drunken meanderings about her children. Lisa and Ros join in. Their children are messy, rude, annoying and expensive. I put on a sweet, attentive smile.

My own work Christmas meal is a different affair altogether. We pack up our tools early. In the gloom of the midwinter afternoon it is so dark inside the large shed that none of us can see our hands in front of our faces. I try to hang the forks on the rack but keep missing the hooks. Then from somewhere in the darkness Dean shouts 'Rat!' I hear something scuttling near my feet and go into pure panic. With every breath comes a screeching noise I don't recognise. I drop the fork I am holding, it tangles in my bootlaces, I trip out of the shed and on to the muddy grass. Andy, Jon and Dean all stand around me, laughing like hyenas – laughing so they can't breathe, can't stand up straight.

'Got you,' Dean just about manages to say.

It could go either way – I get stupid, girly, angry and stomp the very long distance back to the bothy or I laugh with them. I laugh and laugh and laugh. Painful, uncontrollable, drowning laughter. There are tears in my eyes; it is like laughing-crying, as though something is being expelled. Out-of-my-control hysteria. Just as it ebbs, I catch the eyes of one of the others and it starts up again. We eventually start the walk back, across the lawn, up the steps, to the terrace.

'Man you were so funny.' Jon does an impression of my screaming and we are all off again. It is brilliant. The sound of pure, of-the-moment laughter.

We go back to the bothy and Andy puts the kettle on.

'Camellia sinensis anyone?' he asks, smiling.

We all raise our eyebrows at each other.

'I hope Santa brings you some new jokes for Christmas,' Dean says. 'Yours are all worn out.'

We get changed in the visitors' toilets and head for the pub. We drink beer, eat fish and chips and finish off with Christmas pudding, coffee and an After Eight mint. We laugh a bit more – remember with amusement some of the strange visitors we've encountered over the year. Andy tells some more bad jokes that we've heard before and I feel happy. We are a strange, tight little team and I value being part of it.

We have Christmas lunch with my parents. It is lovely, sedate, quiet. We exchange a few presents and then Rob watches the Queen's speech. I flick through the pages of the gardening book my parents have given me, look at the lush colour combinations and make sure I know the plant names. Then we get into my dad's Ford Fiesta – Rob and I squashed in the back.

'Are you children alright there in the back?' my dad jokes.

'Yes, I'm becoming reacquainted with my knees though,' replies Rob, almost folded in half.

We are sitting on the back seat of my parents' car on Christmas Day; we are like children.

It is a short drive to Alice and Mark's house. We enter Christmas chaos. Mark's parents are there plus his sister, her husband and their two children. The floor is covered with a wriggling mass of children, toys, cardboard boxes and wrapping paper. The noise is deafening, the central heating is turned up high and the television is on. As I perch on the end of the sofa, my smart Christmas outfit feels too tight and my smart shoes squeeze my feet. I take my shoes off and the fibres from the carpet cling to my black tights. I try to locate Luke through the noise and the stuff – my little blonde two-year-old nephew. He is being bounced on the knee of one of his grannies, whilst under the keen watch of his other granny.

'Can I have a go now?' my mum asks.

Luke is given up to her, rather begrudgingly. My mum then bounces him on her knee whilst his other granny adds in useful tips. 'He likes it if you do this, don't you Luke, you love it when Granny does that.'

She reaches across my mum, clicking and clapping in front of Luke's face.

'Shall we play with the Thomas that me and Gramps, sorry, Father Christmas, got you, shall we Luke?'

Luke scrambles down from my mum's knee but en route to Thomas, sees the bag of presents I am carrying. He has a good look inside.

'Mine? Mine?' he asks me pleadingly.

'Look Luke, here's Thomas, here he is, choo choo Luke choo choo. Sally, you wouldn't believe how much he's played with it today. We had an awful job finding it. In the end my cousin had to buy one in London and send it down to me.'

I make some 'goodness me' type noise of the appropriate wonderment. Meanwhile Luke has practically stuck his head in the carrier bag of presents.

This sets off a ripple of granny panic. They are on him and me, pulling him away from the bag.

'My, that was close,' they pant as though they have outrun an avalanche.

This dance of the grannies goes on for the entire time we are there. Something weird has happened to trigger some ancient strand of Granzilla DNA to kick into action. I hardly recognise either of them as their previously relaxed and sane selves.

I have a short time with Luke and pretend to throw him in the air. He knows this game and laughs but the grannies make it clear that I am being too rough. I give him back without complaint. Alice comes in from the kitchen and breaks the tension.

'Hi everyone. Happy Christmas. Luke, you've found the presents then? Shall we open them now before he bursts?'

We negotiate the seating possibilities. Rob and I sit on the floor. Alice, five months pregnant, sits in the buffer zone between the grannies. The granddads sit on chairs. Luke is all over me. I know that as the hander-out of the presents I hold the power. All eyes are on me. I have already received instructions about the order that certain presents should come out in. I hand Luke his first present – Bob the Builder's tractor – from Rob and me. The grannies sit tensely with their hands in their laps. I help Luke take off the wrapping. 'Travis. Is Travis. Is Travis. Mummy, is Travis.'

Alice quickly releases Travis from his box. The faces of the grannies show barely disguised disappointment that my present has been such a hit. They try to sound enthusiastic: 'Oh isn't that wonderful,' they say flatly, 'a tractor.'

I sit back, leaving the rest of the presents to my mum. I feel bloated, tired and depressed. And strangely lonely.

*****

A new year and a new list. I should go to bed earlier, read more, eat less, but all I can think about is whether this year will be the year we have a baby.

I write, 'Ten things I am looking forward to doing with our children:

1. waking up on Christmas morning
2. throwing stones into the sea

3. cycling along the old railway line
4. baking fairy cakes
5. making pictures with autumn leaves
6. flying kites
7. reading stories
8. going camping
9. singing around the piano
10. growing sunflowers.'

The path to conception is not what I had imagined – white Egyptian cotton bedding, pillow fights, a cafetière of fresh coffee, laughter and then a shared moment with a pregnancy test, the two blue lines singing out a happy future. The years are drifting by and I feel an obsession with my menstrual cycle engulf me, like some big, mad, ticking monster. I develop a secret set of symbols that I use in my diary – spotting is one star, proper start of period two stars, calculated start of fertile time is a circle, which is extended using arrows to the end of fertile time, which is a square. Order bulbs, have sex. Sow hardy annuals, have sex. Scarify lawns, have blood test. Plant out summer bedding, Rob's sperm test. Working amongst a group of men is some sort of relief. Andy has children and talks about them sometimes, matter-of-factly and proudly. Dean is 45, single, shy and lonely. We share a lift to and from work and talk about the invasion of Iraq and listen to Jonathan Cainer read out our horoscopes on Radio 2. Dean wears his loneliness heavily. Jon is a very well-read manic depressive. We talk for hours every week about our latest reads and the music we are into and we swap books and CDs. His illness has dominated his life, has stolen away his life choices. He will never be well enough to parent children and is quietly tortured by this. Dean and Jon remind me that I am lucky – that I have a husband whom I love and who loves me, that I don't have to survive on just my small salary and that I am, as far as I know, healthy and basically happy.

They also just get on with things – they don't have a need to chew over their emotional lives, like my female friends and me. I can chew over life's difficulties with the best of them, but I find their male company refreshing.

But my obsession slowly takes me over. Even when I'm talking about turfing and mulching, all I'm really thinking about is conceiving. I eagerly anticipate ovulation, then beg shamelessly for sex and am then unable to concentrate on anything for two weeks whilst I convince myself I am pregnant. I do a test far too early, don't believe the results and then start my period and feel depressed. In the middle of the depression I may then discover that one of my friends has just got pregnant on their honeymoon. I feel locked into this lonely cycle of fragile hope and crashing disappointment whilst my friends are getting on with their lives, meeting partners, getting married, having children.

To avoid the further piling on of pressure, we have decided not to tell our friends about our difficulty in conceiving and to limit the family publicity to my mum and my sister. I suggest to Rob that we tell his father. He is adamant that he doesn't want any of his family to know – that they would worry and couldn't do anything to help anyway. Rob's mum passed away some years ago and Rob is anxious that we don't introduce any more sadness into his dad's life.

So the secret is kept from wider family, who would worry too much and are too polite to make comment about the passing of time and the desire for grandchildren, nieces and nephews. The secret is kept from employers and colleagues at work to avoid burning one's career bridges. And the secret is kept from friends who then unknowingly torture us with endless conversations about babies, childbirth, childbirth, babies, sleepless nights, vomit, crap. It is a private turmoil, and turmoil is such an appropriate word for the feeling that swamps me. My guts turn over and over – a twisting and falling, turmoil of emotions with little relief.

*****

Eventually the tests are complete. Rob has worked the logistical challenge of delivering several vials of young, warm sperm through a small letter box somewhere in the depths of the hospital, by nine o'clock in the morning. I have woven a web of lies at work to ensure that my blood tests take place on exactly the right day of my cycle.

We are again sitting silently and nervously in the doctor's waiting room. Christmas has been endured, the summer bulbs are planted and it is the end of February. We sit waiting for the punchline – the resolution of the cliffhanger. I think over the scenarios. Maybe there isn't a measurable problem, maybe my body is not producing something. It's likely to be me – I know that from the magazines. Women are far more biologically complicated, more finely balanced than men. We can fall foul of a myriad of gynaecological problems that reduce our fertility.

We sit opposite Dr Coburn. He shuffles papers, looks shifty. Then he launches the bombshell. Fewer than 1 per cent of the sperm are considered healthy. One per cent: a crushingly low number. They are malformed, broken, immobile. We are to be referred to a consultant at the hospital. This time we don't go home via the coffee shop – we drive home in the dark, shocked, in silence. Rob withdraws into the computer room, the HQ of male problem-solving in our house. I want to talk it all through immediately and sort everything out but I have to back off and let him come to terms with the news. The doctor had tried to be optimistic – 1 per cent of a large number is still a large number and all that. He talks of maybe improving the proportion of healthy sperm, but we all know that things are not looking good.

CHAPTER 3

A franked, white envelope welcomes me home from work. It is from the Women's Hospital. The appointment is in four long months' time: a whole season away. I am 34 now and despite the long drag between appointments, birthdays flash past me like unused railway stations en route to the last few fertile years.

We make plans for holidays and weekends away to fill the time and to acknowledge to ourselves that we cannot put our lives on hold any longer. Alice gives birth to another boy, Harry, who is beautiful. Meanwhile I secretly entertain the old wives' tale that promises that once you stop focusing on something you really want, it will sneak up on you quietly. Stop watching the pot and it will boil. Stop looking for a boyfriend and get on with being you, and when you least expect it you will meet the man of your dreams. The magazines concur and have lots of personal accounts to verify the old wives' tale. As far as advice to the desperate goes though it's right up there with 'don't get stressed!'

Eventually the day of the hospital appointment crawls into view. We sit and wait for an hour in a waiting room full of pregnant women and babies. I feel like an intruder. We are eventually called in by a nurse with a gentle manner and a barely disguised look of pity. The doctor is a kind man and gently tells it as it is. One per cent is a very low number. He explains that the hospital may provide a free cycle of IVF but he has a suggestion that could negate the need for this.

Eat healthily for six months and we may be rewarded with a percentage bigger than one. As a lentil-eating vegetarian, married to a carnivore who is partial to more than the occasional burger meal, I am content with that. It means I can bully my husband into eating well because it is on doctor's orders and for the greater good. And so it is brown rice, oily fish, broccoli, zinc supplements and no alcohol. It is right up my street (apart, perhaps, from the lack of alcohol), it is free, it is healthy and it makes sense.

We leave the hospital and the waiting room full of pregnant women and head for the supermarket. Yes, now we are to try to find the answer to our lack of conception in the fruit and vegetable aisle of Tesco. Every little helps. We trawl around the green stuff trying to identify the vegetables that Rob can bear to eat. The selection in our trolley doesn't contain much variety.

'Are you sure you can't stomach mangetout, or courgette, or how about peppers?' I venture.

'Absolutely no to mangetout or peppers. I might try a courgette.'

Rob has a look of revulsion on his face. This is going to be a long six months and I know that I must try not to get frustrated or sanctimonious with him. Finally we settle on a big bag of stir-fry vegetables with a few carrots, one courgette and a red onion, which I promise I will chop up into barely detectable pieces. We buy chicken and prawns for Rob's stir-fry and tofu and chickpeas for mine. We bypass the fizzy aisle and the crisp aisle although Rob looks longingly down their snacky lengths.

The Donovan Diet goes quite smoothly. The courgettes present a small challenge until Rob discovers that he can stomach them lightly fried in curry powder (mild). We eat a lot of stir-fry, some trout and salmon with sweet potato secretly mashed into the acceptable potato and Rob discovers he likes broccoli. We lose a bit of weight and then use this to put our friends off the scent. It is mildly disconcerting to them that we are off the alcohol and I know that they probably suspect that I am pregnant. But publicly at least, they seem to accept that we are 'having a health kick'.

Rob repeats his sperm test and we ready ourselves for the next appointment. We are both really quite pleased with ourselves – we have been set a challenge and we have risen to it. Rob has extended the list of vegetables he will eat without gagging and I have managed to maintain a reasonable level of patience with him.

*****

We again sit in the waiting room of the Women's Hospital. This time it is empty of pregnant women and we are promptly led into the consultant's room. I expect him to ask how we have got on with the diet and for us to have the chance to boast about how brilliantly we have done. Instead, he goes straight to the point. The diet has made no difference whatsoever.

The sperm remain stubbornly distorted. They are so hopeless that we do not even qualify for the NHS IVF treatment, which would shoot the substandard sperm in the general direction of my ovaries. The sperm are too weak to find their own way to the target so we need special, expensive treatment, which plucks out a single healthy sperm from amongst the detritus and injects it directly into one of my harvested eggs. It must all take place under a microscope in a test tube. It is called 'ICSI' and it will be expensive. The consultant delivers this information carefully and sensitively but directly.

The prospect of IVF had travelled around my mind in a roundabout way. I tended to avoid thinking about it too deeply because when I did, it filled me with fear. I feared the hospital visits, the procedures, the drugs, the hormonal chaos, the cancer scares and the secrecy. It scared me so much that I had expected to feel relieved at not being eligible for the free IVF. I had been fooling myself. My reaction is instantaneous, gut-tearing devastation. Tears spring from nowhere, prickling my eyes. My throat narrows and strains. My heart has been dropped into the depths of my stomach. I am keenly aware though that this is not the place for unguarded displays of emotion. We are shown awkwardly out of the consulting room and into the vast waiting area. I fix my eyes on the floor, head down in sorrow and shame. I sweep my hair forward to cover my face and my embarrassment. I swallow down tears as we emerge out of the hospital and into the busy street. We are intruders and now we are cast away.

*****

It is a worn out pacifier, but life does indeed, sometimes cruelly, go on. We drive home, gather ourselves, get changed into our glad rags and go to our friends', Steph and Keith's wedding. It is a shotgun wedding.

Weeks later I look at the photographs we took that beautiful July afternoon. The wedding ceremony went well. Everyone was on time. All roles were performed. No one tripped. I dabbed my eyes a few times, because I always cry at weddings, and then slapped on a smile as we emerged into the bright sunshine. Rob and I, each holding a glass of fizzy wine, stand awkwardly in the grounds of the lavish, Georgian hotel. We look dazed and in need of comfort.

The day had been almost comical in its cruelty. Steph had got pregnant accidentally and was bursting at the seams. Apparently it wouldn't have been right to marry after the birth of the baby so we endured the endless jokes about the groom's epic fertility. Steph gave birth to a baby boy shortly after the wedding. She had desperately wanted a girl and was vocal about the devastation she felt at the arrival of a baby boy into her life. It was very hard to take.

*****

Ongoing, low-level grief weighs me down, presses the energy, the joy out of everything. It is a secret, shameful grief, patched over with shallow smiles. I feel a cheat for grieving when others are overcoming much worse. But there is no funeral, no 'With Deepest Sympathy' cards, no allowances given. And perhaps a public carry-on would be inappropriate. However, the feeling of the loss of the unknown carriers of my genes – whom, for most of my life I had unthinkingly anticipated giving birth to, nurturing and growing old with – is great and deep. I would never have believed I could grieve so strongly for what I'd never had – a missing piece of the future.

Some months after Steph and Keith's baby is born, I endure a night out with Steph and several other friends. Everyone has children but me. We haven't been lifelong friends, but have socialised over the past few years. Where I used to enjoy catching up on their news and telling them mine, through my grief they seem self-absorbed, blinkered and insensitive. Is it socially acceptable to spend the entire evening talking about one's own children? And in such detail? Or am I just too raw and oversensitive, feeling everything too deeply?

'And then I heard her cry for the fourth time and I recognised that the cry wasn't just for milk because Thomas used to make that cry when he was a baby and it sounded exactly the same, well not exactly the same, because when he did it he made a louder sound at the beginning before the proper crying started…'

'Well, Jessica has always liked peas and carrots, not so much carrots, but anyway so when I got back from toddlers this afternoon I thought I'd cook peas and carrots for her tea and you wouldn't believe it, she screamed every time I tried to feed them to her…'

And I want to talk about my work and about Rob and me, but there is no room to do so. My weak attempts at interjection are met with glazed expressions that say, 'Whatever are you talking about? Can't you see that we have far more important things to discuss?' My meagre conversational chips are cleared from the table and we return to the dominant topic. I try hard to show interest in the minutiae of mothering but the grief weighs heavier and heavier as the evening goes on and I feel myself sealing up, separating off. I wonder to myself, would I have been like this if I had sleepwalked into motherhood like my friends have? Then I know I have to go – I have no resources left to endure the remainder of the evening. I need to go home to Rob and wallow in my misery and my anger at my friends' self-indulgence and blindness. I make my excuses – I've got work tomorrow, up early, etc.

'Come on, Sal, we're all staying, we'll be up much earlier than you will be, you lucky devil.'

'Fuck off the lot of you,' I think as I reach into my bag for my car keys and smile and make a polite exit.

I walk out of the pub and immediately into the foggy, still, silent winter air. The silence jolts me but it is peaceful and soothing. I start the car, defog the windscreen and choose a CD. Tonight I need something that will understand how I'm feeling, not something that tries to coax me out of it. I choose foggy music for a foggy night. During the short distance home I gradually turn the music up louder and louder. The tightly packed rage bubbles out of me. It is not only rage at my insensitive friends, but also rage at the whole fucking thing. Rage at the need. Why do I need to? Why can't I just be happy as I am, grateful for what I've got and put my life to a purpose other than having children? I pull into the drive, switch off the ignition and sit for a moment in silence, composing myself. Rob is used to seeing my sadness but not my rage. He will think that I am blaming him for everything and I am not. I don't even know what or whom I am really cross with.

'You're home early. Lots of baby talk?'

'Exclusively baby talk.' I just look at Rob, raise my eyebrows and swallow hard. The tears force themselves out nevertheless.

'Don't go out with them anymore, if it makes you upset. They are unbelievable, really.'

Rob is always so practical. Your friends upset you, friends are to have fun with, friends are not performing correct function adequately, drop friends. I think in this situation he may be right, for now at least.

I lie in bed and set myself the task of contemplating life without children, to see if I can do it, where it would lead. Growing up, Alice and I were particularly close to our next-door neighbours. They would be the first people we would show off a new pair of shoes to, or play a recorder tune. As a young child it never struck me as bizarre that they didn't have children, maybe because they seemed so ancient. But as we grew older, my mum made it known to Alice and I that the couple next door couldn't grow their own baby, just like Aunty Barbara and Uncle Vince couldn't and that it was something that they were a bit sad about and we weren't to be insensitive around them. So I gradually became aware of older childless couples and associated them with sadness and things that one must not say. I don't want Rob and I to become like this – the perpetually sad, the pitied. I try to think positively. Maybe we should learn to look at being childless as an opportunity to do great things in our careers, to travel more, to entertain, to learn new skills, to bake our own bread, to grow our own vegetables. But I just don't think it would be enough. It may keep us happy for a few years, but it would be tragic then to feel the need for children again when it was too late to do anything about it. And we've been to nearly every European capital, seen nearly every impressionist painting there is to see. So I know we must go back to the doctor.

The infertility train goes towards one destination only and it's anyone's guess whether it will actually get there. It's an expensive ticket and sometimes the conductor will ask you to buy your ticket several times over for the same journey. I know right from the start that I am on the wrong train.

Rob and I visit Dr Coburn again. He can't push us on to the train quickly enough.

'We send our infertile couples to Birmingham. We've had a lot of success there. I'll give you the details and you can arrange for a first consultation.'

'Oh god,' I think, 'How do I tell him? How do I tell Rob?'

We are given leaflets, lots of leaflets. It's all quite easy, maybe a small chance of side effects. Chances of success: 25 per cent. Cost: around £4,000.

We start to confide in a few close friends. They all have the same view. What are you waiting for?

I have a terrible tendency sometimes to go along with something that I really don't want to do. I convince myself it's never really going to happen and then it gets closer and closer and I could kick myself for not having said something earlier. Then it becomes much more difficult to get out of the thing because it's obvious that I've been a coward and should have been honest from the start. This occasionally happens to me with an inadvisable New Year's Eve party or a trip to a West End musical and those are embarrassing enough to wriggle out of, but to say to your husband, parents and doctor, 'You know that IVF thing that's been arranged, well I don't think I'll bother if that's all the same,' is a really big deal. Numerous ideal opportunities for the conversation slip through my fingers. I get my words prepared, I am sitting next to Rob on the sofa, right I'm going to say it now, say it, my god just get on and say it, you bloody coward, what's the worst that can happen? (He'll divorce you.) Oh no, can't say it now, Top Gear's just about to start.

And another day, then a week slip by.

Eventually I blurt it out in the middle of Newsnight, 'Rob, I don't want IVF, I think maybe we should consider adoption,' and immediately burst into tears.

It wasn't well handled. But my fears are not borne out at all and I feel ashamed that I have misjudged my husband so badly. He takes it as though I said I don't want to shop in Morrisons anymore. OK, he is more sensitive than that and he is probably in shock, but he takes it calmly and well.

My negative feelings towards IVF are difficult to articulate, partly because they are not completely logical and because I'm aware that for lots of couples IVF has offered them the chance to have a family they would not otherwise have had. For many it is important that they have their own biological children – children who carry and in turn hand on the historical package of familiar family DNA. For me the quest for a family has never fundamentally been about our genes but about the experience of raising children. I consider myself lucky that I feel like this. It is not something that I have had to work at too much and it is freeing, as it opens up other opportunities for building a family. It also means that the price that many pay for their own flesh and blood, for me is too high. All I can focus on is the hormonal chaos, the medical procedures and the likely disappointments. I am just not committed enough to the furtherance of my genes.

*****

During my visits to the doctor's surgery for the many blood tests, I have got to know the nurse a little. We had talked about IVF and I had shared my reservations about it with her. She suggested that I talk to a patient of hers who had undergone successful IVF. She also suggested that I talk to another patient of hers who had adopted two boys. The following day she rang me – both women had agreed to talk to me. The woman who had had IVF mysteriously didn't want me to have her phone number, or her name, but said that she would call me. The adoptive mother, Jan, said that she would be very happy for me to ring her.

I nervously call Jan. She is enthusiastic and warm and tells me she has been expecting my call. My story tumbles out and then she tells me, 'We had unsuccessful IVF over about six years and we've had our boys now for two.'

'How old are they?' I ask.

'Five and seven now, we got them when they were three and five.'

I realise that I have not prepared adequately for this conversation and in falling over myself not to come over as prying, I cannot think of another sensible, constructive question. Jan rescues me.

'Would you like to meet up? I guess that your husband will have lots of questions as well. It might be worthwhile him meeting my husband Patrick.'

I am bowled over by her insight and kindness. We arrange to meet one evening the following week.

Then I receive a phone call from the IVF woman.

'Hello, may I speak with Sally Donovan, please?' She sounds guarded. 'I was asked to call you by the doctor's surgery, about my experience.'

'Yes. We are considering our options at the moment and I'm not really sure that I want to go down that road. Your IVF was successful, I understand?'

'We had a son ten months ago.'

She is disconcertingly cold about it. I try to offer some warmth. 'Congratulations.'

'It wasn't easy at all. In fact it was very, very difficult. We went to Birmingham for our treatment, which was difficult to fit in with work. We kept it confidential. Then I suffered side effects and was hospitalised for three weeks. I was quite dangerously ill. My husband took as much time off work as he could, but I still spent a lot of the time there on my own.'

'But you're alright now?'

Her voice is unnerving. 'I'm fine now and I fell pregnant, but I would never do it again.'

'It was that bad?'

'It was that bad. And please, we still haven't told anyone that we've had our son through IVF so I really need you to keep this conversation to yourself.'

I assure her that I won't be talking to anyone other than Rob about our conversation and thank her for speaking to me.

I could hear her voice loaded with hurt, upset and shame. The shame unnerved me most. Is the shame in wanting a child or in the lengths that we may go to have one? Rob and I had told virtually no one about our difficulties in conceiving. Was that because we were ashamed? Is it just considered bad manners to want something desperately?

*****

We pull up outside Jan and Patrick's house, in a narrow street, opposite a chip shop. The smell of fish and chips is delicious and comforting. Jan comes to the door and invites us in.

We go into their sitting room. Patrick stands up and we all shake hands. It feels odd to come to a stranger's house to talk to them about something so intimate. We break the ice over where we have travelled from, how convenient it must be for them to live opposite a chip shop. It is Patrick who brings us to the real reason we are here.

'Have you reached a decision to adopt?'

'We're still considering it,' Rob responds quickly.

'I'm more sure than Rob,' I add.

'It's often the way. I was more cautious than Jan; she had to pull me most of the way, wait for me to catch up occasionally. But it's honestly the best thing I've ever done. I wouldn't have things any other way.'

'What gave you the final push, made you go for it?' asks Rob.

'Sometimes in life, you just have to take a leap of faith.'

On hearing this, Rob changes his whole demeanour. I can't pinpoint exactly what it is at first and then I realise that a look of relief has spread across his face and his body has relaxed. Here is another man, much like him, who'd had to gather his courage to become a father to someone else's children and whose courage had been rewarded.

We spend most of the evening talking about Jan and Patrick's experiences of adopting their children. I have one burning question for Jan and Patrick, which I leave until the end.

'Your boys, do they feel like your children?'

'Without question,' they both answer, without pause, without having to think.

PART 3

Planning a Future

Flip Charts and Handouts

CHAPTER 4

Andy's desk is covered with papers – some yellowing and crispy, some with faded teacup rings pressed into them – all are coated with a light dusting of soil. He is researching some bedding schemes and the work of many generations of head gardener is strewn around in interlocking layers. He has the day off so I have grasped the opportunity presented by an empty office to make a phone call. Once I've cleared a small space I retrieve the folded piece of notepaper from the depths of my pocket on which is written the telephone number of a children's charity. I've rehearsed what I'm going to say but it's not easy as far as conversational openers go and there is no gentle way in.

'Oh yes, hello, I wonder if I could speak to someone about adopting a child?'

Part of my courage has come from knowing that mine cannot be an unusual request to an organisation such as this. However, it is as though I have asked the most unreasonable and unheard of question and must be treated with maximum suspicion.

'Are you a birth family member?' a lady's voice fires back brusquely.

'Uh no, I'd like to speak to someone about adopting a child.'

'You need to speak with the social worker and he's not here at the moment.' I can imagine her eyes rolling up into her head as she steers me into this conversational cul-de-sac.

'Oh-kay… '

I am having one of *those* conversations that I well recall from my time working in a large company. The disgruntled in a position of tiny power – the keeper of the part numbers, the processor of the purchase orders, whose personal challenge is to put as many obstacles as possible in the way of some innocent who just needs to get their job done. The rules are clear. This woman, the holder of the information, will only give me what I need if I drop on my knees and plead. In this pecking order of two I am, without question, at the bottom. If I am rude to her I could fall at the first hurdle. I grovel and silently show her the V sign.

'Would you please be so kind as to tell me when he might return?'

'In about half an hour.' It is clear from her iced tone that I am keeping her from something much more important.

'I will call back then; thank you very much for your help.'

She puts the phone down just half a second before I've finished speaking, just to hammer the pecking order home. I give it 40 minutes before I ring back and, of course, the social worker has not returned and I endure another awkward conversation. Unwillingly she takes my phone number. I try to explain that I will only be available on this number today. I might as well be howling like a dog.

The social worker rings back, four days later. I am taking a tour group around the garden at the time and when I get back Andy gives me the message. He is desperate to know what's going on and doesn't make any effort to hide his curiosity. Without sufficient warning to construct a cover, I have to tell him the truth. So much for keeping our plans a secret.

The social worker very kindly and patiently explains to me that I should start by approaching our Local Authority first. They place children who are in their care and then refer any children who they find hard to adopt to specialist agencies, such as the one he works for, which are better able to find adoptive parents for them. A part of me is a tiny bit offended by this man's assumption that I may not be up to the job of parenting the 'difficult to place' child. But he does sound as if he knows what he is talking about.

I wait until Andy is in a meeting and hijack his telephone again. I can't find a telephone number for the adoption bit of social services so I ring the county council switchboard.

The recorded message clicks in, 'Press one if you have a query about rubbish collection, press two if you have a query about potholes, press three if you have a query about composting, press four if you have a query about cycle paths…'

Social services comes in at number eight. I then listen to a further list of options before going for 'children'.

The telephone rings and rings; I start to do jobs with my spare hand, sweep the floor, rearrange books. I daren't ring off – I'll never navigate my way back through the calling system again. I imagine the telephone I am ringing; an old, black Bakelite model, in an empty room with grey walls lit by flickering strip lighting. Then a voice.

'Hello, I am ringing to enquire about possibly adopting, do I have the right number?' I decide to employ a half-grovel from the outset.

'Yes you do. You need to speak to Margaret. I'm her assistant. Margaret's on holiday for a week. Can I take your number and she will ring you back?'

Disappointment floods through me. A week. Another whole slow week. I make myself a mug of strong tea, trudge back out to the garden and give myself a pep talk. Be patient. It will happen. Stick with it.

A week later Margaret rings back and is nice and doesn't require grovelling from me. She takes my details and says that the first step we must take is to attend an adoption information session. She holds them every six weeks. We've just missed one. She will put the pack in the post, with the map of where to find the venue and some leaflets.

It is going to be two months since the big decision to adopt was made before we can even get our feet in the door. Two months.

I drift in some sort of middle place. Plans and hopes, a holiday with friends and an interesting research opportunity at work still steer life positively onwards but the emotional commitment is missing. The uncertainty is excruciating. It would almost be a relief to know for sure that children, a family, were never going to happen for us – if that part of the map were torn up, if we were forced to travel somewhere else and make the best of it.

*****

A dusty, musty church hall, on a dark November morning. The weather, the room, nothing indicates exciting new beginnings. We select our seats, not at the back, which may make us appear uninterested, nor right at the front, which could scream 'desperate', but safely in the middle. We chat self-consciously and watch the room fill up. Couples and single people creep in quietly and nervously. We look noticeably younger than most of the other people there. And after ten minutes of arrivals, there must be at least 50 of us. I see leaflets arranged on a table at the side of the room alongside some cups, a bowl of teabags and two urns of hot water. Then a television with an inbuilt video player is wheeled awkwardly into the room.

Margaret introduces herself to the group – welcomes us all here on this cold day. She is not what I was expecting. What was I expecting exactly? I am ashamed to acknowledge to myself that I have unwittingly taken on board the stereotype – long mud-coloured skirt, sandals and woolly tights, portly stature, kind of useless. But Margaret is smart, businesslike, safe.

She gives a short presentation about the sorts of children who come up for adoption, the numbers of children placed every year and the adoption process. She takes a breath before stressing that very few babies are adopted. A little ripple of reaction spreads through the room. A woman whispers angrily into the ear of the man next to me, 'I told you that, didn't I tell you that?' A baby, the most desired gift this Christmas, like a living Cabbage Patch Kids Doll. Would we be camping outside in the street and elbowing each other in the ribs if Hamleys had a surprise delivery? I check my feelings. Baby? Baby? No, I think I've always known that teenage mothers are allowed to keep their babies these days, which has dented the supply somewhat. Before tea and biscuits there is a chance to ask questions. These get going in a faltering way. The first one is, 'How long does it take to adopt a child?' Answer: 'It depends, but it can take a very, very long time.' Then, 'What are the chances of adopting one child?' Answer: 'We are not currently approving adopters who are looking for one child only as we have a shortage of adopters for sibling groups.' Another ripple of realisation across the room – the faint sound of hopes being dashed on the grey walls. Rob and I have luckily resolved that one between us already. We have agreed that we will go for broke and try for two children rather than go through the whole adoption process twice. Then comes a real shocker: 'Can you start on the adoption process whilst still having IVF treatment?' Adoption as an insurance policy. Margaret patiently explains that adoption is a very important decision and has to be embarked upon with full commitment. It is not in anyone's best interests that it is a half-hearted affair. I notice Margaret's assistant in the corner of the room writing something down. I wonder if she is noting the name of the IVF lady for future reference. Margaret goes on to talk about how important it is that any feelings of grief resulting from infertility have been dealt with, that the decision to adopt is a positive one, not merely a last-ditch attempt at forming a family. The atmosphere is lightened by the mention of tea and biscuits and the 'Registration of Interest' form.

'Let's skip the tea and go straight for the form,' says Rob. He doesn't like forced chit-chat but is quite at home with forms. Margaret is immediately swamped by couples – all wanting private questions answered. We wait, trying not to eavesdrop. Finally, it is our turn. We ask for the form, no questions. Margaret looks relieved. We have had enough aimless waiting so we fill in the form there and then and hand it to her. She will be in contact.

*****

Some weeks later I am lazing around at home, with a dizzying, seasickness of an ear infection. The world has taken on a dreamlike quality and has merged with Daytime Television – the primary weapon of torture for the unwillingly childless. The ten best children's party outfits, the ten 'must-have' toys for this Christmas, how to keep your very annoying children entertained this Christmas. Then another piece featuring a mother and her young daughter. The little girl has a medical problem and has been in and out of hospital for most of her life. The girl sits on the sofa, angelic, with discreet tubes poking out from underneath her clothes. Her mother is referred to as 'Mum' throughout, even when Doctor Daytime addresses her directly.

'How difficult has it been for you, Mum?' he asks.

But she is not *his* mum. She is a woman who used to have a name and an identity of her own. The presenter beams down on the mum. She's been so dedicated to her daughter, so selfless, they are going to give her a makeover. She looks fine to me, not like she needs a makeover. But she seems grateful and staggers down the catwalk sometime later in too-high shoes, a lampshade of a skirt, a bright jacket with sleeves that come up a bit too short and a scarf knotted around her neck, air-hostess style.

'And how does Mum like her new look?' the presenter asks, as if addressing no one in particular.

'Mum' is under pressure to gush over how wonderful she now looks, how she barely recognises herself. The Daytime style experts coo around her explaining how they achieved 'the look', how they completed the final obliteration of this woman's identity. I feel a little well of anger bubbling up – anger mixed with a fear that I will never be able to surrender myself like this. I could cause scenes in antenatal classes, scans, check-ups: 'I have a name, my name is Sally, I am not *your* mum, call me "Mum" again and I will…' I scream; the psychiatrist is called, before the 'unfit mother' form is signed. I am awoken from my mini-daymare by the adverts: 'Injury Lawyers for You,' the actor thunders in a threatening way. My head swims as my eyes struggle to focus on anything that isn't moving. I know that my ear infection is to blame for these dreamlike meanderings. Nevertheless, I also recognise in myself the fear of being sucked into the sausage machine of maternity, of my identity being patted and patronised into oblivion. I wonder if the adoption process is in some ways going to suit me better than the maternity process. I will have to work hard to show that I have an identity, that I have views and opinions and can make sensible choices. I will have to prove myself and I think I might be able to take on that challenge. The Daytime crew are on to a review of the soaps; they talk about them as though they are real life, as though the characters live and breathe, as though they are more alive than the mother of the sick child.

I return to work a few days later and the winter jobs are well underway – the clearing, the bonfires and the mulching, the endless mulching. We have 15 tonnes of compost to spread over the barren borders and two wheelbarrows between the three of us. I resist the temptation to work out how many loads there are in 15 tonnes, because then I would be able to work out how many days we will spend wheeling and emptying wheelbarrows and it will be a depressingly large number. Dean loves mulching and starts to get excited about the advent of mulching season just after the summer solstice. 'The nights are drawing in now and we will be mulching again before we know it,' he will say. Jon and I will catch each other's eye across the bothy and raise our eyebrows. We both prefer the summer months when the garden offers up something new to marvel at every day and the work is lighter. Dean hates having to work amongst the huge number of visitors who flock to the garden when it is in flower, feels as though he is on show. And in a way we are. The visitors like to ask us questions. 'How many gardeners work here?' is the number one question (answer: 'four'). 'What is that unusual tree?' is the number two question (answer: 'Clerodendron trichotomum'). I love the impromptu conversations that come my way, the interesting people that I wouldn't otherwise come across – the old man who remembers playing in the overgrown gardens as a child, the lady who wants to know how to prune her fig tree. But in the winter months there is little distraction from the mulching. Jon and I manage to string out a conversation about Charles Dickens for a good 30 minutes. We realise with a certain delight that we have never mined this rich source of conversation before. Jon says, 'How about Bruce Chatwyn after tea?'

'Yes,' I say, 'and Julian Barnes.' That will do us for a few more barrowloads. And will divert my mind away from adoption for another hour. Why hasn't Margaret got in touch yet?

*****

Clinging on to the inside of our letter box by a corner is a lovely white envelope, with a clear window and a red frank mark. It is addressed to Rob and me and I know immediately whom it is from. I should change out of my muddy clothes, shower and prepare dinner so that we can digest the contents of the letter properly, cleanly, together. But instead I do a little dance, scattering dried mud on the hallway carpet, and rip the envelope open. We are invited to a three-day training course, in February. We are into December now. Another long wait, but I am getting accustomed to long waits and there is a certainty to this one. By March, we will be trained and we will have passed through a square on the flow diagram of adoption. I ring Rob straightaway and tell him about the course.

'Fantastic. When? How many days is it?' Rarely has there been so much excitement over a training course.

I give Rob the dates – three days, each a fortnight apart. He immediately books in his annual leave. I'll have to start thinking up some excuses, a day out shopping maybe, a visit to relatives. At least I don't have to mislead Andy anymore, but there's still Dean and Jon to blatantly lie to.

*****

Mercifully the mulching comes to an end for another year. Jon and I are so pleased we buy cake from the teashop. Dean is in some kind of mourning. It is Christmas Eve so we are allowed to finish early. I share a lift home with Dean.

'Well, that's it for this year. We'll be mulching again next year before we know it,' he says to buoy himself up, 'and the troops will still be in Iraq.' He dreads Christmas even more than I do because it shines a light on what is missing – for me that's children but for him it is more than that. He cannot afford to buy a house on his salary so lives tensely with his parents. Christmas will be like a pressure cooker in his house. Christmas in ours will be relaxing but still a bit of an endurance event of politeness, being indoors too much, other people's too hot central heating and the group viewing of mediocre Christmas specials on the television. Rob used to get cross about my ambivalence towards Christmas but has now come to accept it. He accompanies me on the Christmas shopping expedition, planned and timed so that the whole thing is executed efficiently, avoiding crowds, avoiding Slade as far as possible. But we have to venture into Woolworths to buy a Thunderbird 2 for Luke, who is now five years old. We are accosted by a tidal wave of plastic that twinkles, chimes, beeps, flashes; it is overwhelmingly hot and crammed so tightly with shoppers that I have difficulty raising my arm to scratch my nose. Children are crying and parents are shouting, dragging and slapping. It is like highly sophisticated psychological warfare.

We pass Christmas pretty much as expected. Then we spend New Year with friends in London. All of us are childless and it is a relief to spend time with them, without being constantly reminded of children. We have a meal together and go into a comedy club and laugh and laugh. It strikes me that it is easier being childless in the city. Rob and I stay on in London for a few days and see a play and drink lots of coffee in grown-up cafes. Our conversations start to turn towards the year to come, what may be in wait. We calculate that it is five years since we started trying to have children and now we may finally be on the brink of making some progress. Our course starts in fewer than six weeks' time. If we get through the course then we will be allocated a social worker who will assess us.

'We should get approved as adopters this year,' Rob says. 'We could have a little family by next Christmas.'

'You mustn't say that,' I shush him.

'We'll get approved, no problem – there's no skeletons in our cupboards, not in mine anyway, unless there's something you're not telling me, Sal?' He laughs, sounding calm and confident.

'You'll jinx us.' I have held my breath over all this for so long that I dare not look forward to having a family.

'It's perfectly possible. We finish our training in March, we get assessed in say five months, we get approved. And then we are on the market for children.' He is definitely sounding calm. 'In fact, our children must be alive, right now.'

We have both been reading a lot about the children who end up in the care of social services and the sorts of early experiences they have had. The prospect that they are out there somewhere, not being cared for hangs in the air, unsaid.

'They are probably in foster care,' I offer, 'waiting for us.'

'Yes, good foster care, with lovely foster carers.' Rob tries to reassure us both.

We finish our coffees, wrap up in our coats and scarves and head out into the dark afternoon. The street and the shops are lit up. 'There is hope,' they seem to say. 'It is a new year.'

*****

There is something about spending a few nights in a sparse hotel room or staying with a tidy friend that makes me look at my own home through fresh eyes. We arrive home after spending New Year in London, open the door and are greeted by clutter and mess. Usually I am partially blind to the piles of paperwork that can't quite be filed yet, the collections of clean laundry that haven't quite managed to find their way into the drawers, but today I am not. And I am acutely aware that Rob and I may soon be inviting social workers into our home – they may not look upon the disorganisation as the sign of two creative minds who have better things to do with their time than to pair socks. They may just think that we live like pigs and that if we can't put our own washing away then we won't possibly rise to the challenge of bringing up children.

'This place is a mess,' I exclaim as though someone else is responsible for it.

'Yes, it does look untidy. And what's in that cup on the kitchen table? Is that mould?' Rob picks up the cup to look inside and disturbs the delicate balance; the spores slowly float up above the rim.

'We are disgusting and social services will think we are disgusting too. There's our new year's resolution – tidy the house. We have to become tidy people, like proper grown-ups.'

Rob agrees but in a resigned sort of way. He has seen this before, me suddenly having to embark on a marathon of tidying, without warning, and expecting him to do the same.

'I was hoping to sit down for a bit, watch a few things I've recorded on the telly,' Rob sort of pleads.

'Well, that's fine, you do that, but I need to get started, *right now*. You can join me later.' I try to avoid the hectoring tone and am not entirely successful.

We spend the next few weekends journeying to the loft, the dump and the charity shop. We sort through boxes of folders and books, bin bags of old clothes and curtains and collections of bizarre objects – a concrete Buddha, pots with dead cactuses in, broken aeroplane models and some stained rattan place mats. We argue over old tour t-shirts – Rob squeezes into a rather small Scritti Politti one, but won't consider throwing it out (it might be worth something); I decide to relegate my t-shirt to bed wear. We clean windows, dust skirting boards, hang pictures and wash paintwork. We buy new curtains, cushions and lampshades and invest in storage. I scan the bookshelf and decide that my shelves of literature and horticulture send a good, sound message about me as a person, whereas Rob's shelves of weaponry and destruction don't really hit the right note. Right-wing loner with lack of empathy for others is what the good people of social services will think. They'll be searching the wardrobes for his Nazi uniform before we know it. So most of the books go in the loft, a couple stay – An Encyclopaedia of Guns and Weaponry is only allowed to remain if its spine faces the back of the shelves, like a naughty child.

Two rooms are tidied but remain undecorated, despite their shabby 1980s decor of mint green, floral borders and dubious stencilling. Neither Rob nor I can face creating two little bedrooms yet, when our hopes are so brittle.

*****

The training takes place in a social services meeting room in a small, run-down provincial town. There is no direct road so it takes us an hour and a half to get there. The town has good architecture – a developer's dream if it were located just a little nearer to the wealthy parts of the county. But good architecture or not, it is shabby and sad. In a different town the Georgian shop fronts could easily be displaying well-designed German furniture or oil paintings and sculptures by renowned local artists. As it is, there is little work around, little disposable income and therefore a tired-looking Co-op, two banks, a pet shop and some charity shops have to service the people here. There is also a small library and a fair-sized social services block.

Mid-blue carpet tiles, white walls, white ceiling panels, no window, a flip chart with two black pens and a red pen, two urns of hot water, a basket of teabags (PG Tips and various herbal) and a semicircle of chairs – mid-blue to match the carpet tiles. I take in the familiarity of the surroundings. In past jobs I have sat in rooms just like this, to learn brainstorming, team-building, performance improvement, with the aid of flip charts and small group work. But I have no idea what to expect here. And the stakes are so high. This is much more than a training event. This is the first window that social services will get into Rob and me – into our beliefs, opinions, hopes. We walk over to the tea urns and a couple introduce themselves to us. They are Paul and Hayley. We pass around sugar and teaspoons and chat about what a long journey we've had, all to avoid the reason we are here. More people arrive quietly and head for the sanctuary of the urns. Yes, milk, please, with one. (Yes, two children, please.)

I see Margaret in the corner, taking papers out of a cardboard box on the floor. She holds them in one arm against her chest, like a teacher, and readies herself.

'OK, if you could make your way to a chair we will start. Can I just say that if anyone needs the toilet then the men's are down the corridor on the right, the ladies' I'm afraid are left out of here, out of the doors, across the courtyard and into the grey building. The fire exits are just beyond the men's toilets. We'll be working until 11 o'clock when we'll have a tea break and then we'll break at one for lunch. As you know, lunch is not provided so you can go into the town and get something there.'

She loosens her grip on the papers and gives us each a sheet with the day's itinerary on.

Adopters' Training – Day One

9.30–10.00	Introductions
10.00–11.00	Introduction to Adoption – video
11.00–11.15	Break
11.15–1.00	Reflections on Childhood
1.00–1.45	Lunch
1.45–2.30	Adoption Process
2.30–2.45	Break
2.45–4.00	Our Attachments

The introductions start. We are to say our names, where we live, what job we do and what has led us to consider adoption. Rob and I are about three-quarters of the way around the circle. I try hard to listen to everyone whilst composing my own introduction in my head. Paul and Hayley go first. Paul is a car mechanic, Hayley works in a pre-school. Hayley has had a transplant and has been warned against getting pregnant. They seem nice and not used to having to speak in a group like this. I feel sorry for them, having to go first, to share their pain with a room full of strangers. Next are an older couple. It is their second marriage. Ian has children from his first marriage but his wife Elaine doesn't. They would like children together. They are very smartly dressed. Ian runs an estate agency; Elaine works in a car showroom. Next is MJ. I try not to give into my preconceptions about MJ but fail. She is wearing a baggy jacket made out of a carpet, over an enormous quilted checked shirt, over dirty jeans. She has long, dark hair, which looks dirty, bad teeth and a smoker's laugh, which goes on a bit too long before turning into a cough. From the moment it is her turn she takes centre stage. She makes it clear from the outset that she has issues, which she will spare us the details of. I get the feeling that this isn't quite true, that she can't wait to share, but that she is building up our curiosity for dramatic purposes. Next it's Rob and me. Rob goes first. Ordinary childhood in Manchester, happy, only child but close to extended family, decent-ish office job, fertility problems so decided on adoption, here to find out more. I go next.

'Hello, I'm Sally, Rob's wife. I was born nearby. I work in a historic garden. We discovered we couldn't have children naturally about a year ago; I didn't want to have IVF. We did a bit of research and a lot of thinking and here we are, we'd like to adopt two children if we can.'

I feel on fire. Telling a group of strangers about our infertility was really quite easy and strangely liberating. Everyone looks at me with real understanding (apart from MJ who is puffing on an asthma inhaler in a 'look at me' kind of way).

Next to me is a slim, mousy woman. She shifts in her seat nervously. She starts to talk.

'I'm Debbie. I'm here with my husband John.' She glances at John and I notice he is holding her hand.

Margaret senses her unease.

'Hello, Debbie. If you could, and I know it's difficult, could you tell us why you are here?'

'Well, we would like to have children. We've been trying for over ten years now, unsuccessfully.'

She pauses and it is excruciating. I want to hold her hand too.

'We've had a lot of IVF treatment, unsuccessful treatment and we've come to the end of the road with that now, so we are thinking about adoption.'

Every word, every pause is filled with pain.

The room is quiet.

Margaret stands up.

'Many of you will have had difficult journeys, before you have even embarked upon this one. Many of you will have suffered loss and have gone through a grieving process. It is important that you have dealt with any feelings of grief before you go much further along this path. We are going to be talking about the sorts of children who social services place for adoption, children who have suffered chaotic and abusive lives and rejection and for whom adoption is their best hope of a new start. It is important for these children that they are not looked upon as second best. Now, some of you may not have talked even with close family about infertility and your journey here, but I encourage you to talk to each other and to seek support from each other.'

This is the first time that I have heard a professional, anyone, express any of what I've been feeling. I had thought that what I had been feeling was grief, but I didn't know I was allowed to call it that. I know that this feeling has diminished as I have got used to how it feels, how it colours my life. And I realise that actually I am ready to start thinking about the sort of family we might put together, the sort of children we might have. I don't feel fragile and teary like the poor lady on my left and I know I am lucky. I feel positive, excited.

The day is a revelation to me. We have to think of a precious item from our childhoods that we still own and then tell the group why it is precious and the memories it brings back. The stories that come out of our small group are full of little, marvellous details – so full of colour and humour. Then we draw spider diagrams of all the attachments we have to family and friends. Margaret makes us hold up lengths of string to represent each attachment. We hold each other's strings in turn whilst Margaret cuts through them with a big pair of scissors.

'This is to help you to understand that these children are being separated from people they are familiar with, even if these are adults who haven't cared for them properly. They may be separated from brothers and sisters, school friends, foster carers. And we need to understand this loss and to help them to keep their precious memories and things safe for them. To help them feel able to talk about them sometimes, without shame.'

The flip chart is opened to reveal a ready-prepared flow diagram. The flow diagram of adoption. It is full of blind alleys and dead ends but I am starting to see my way through it. This training, then our own social worker who will assess us, then we appear in front of a panel who will decide if we can adopt or not. We wait until we hear about potential children, or we can look for ourselves. Find children. Vetted by children's social worker. Another panel decides if we and the children are a good match. We meet children, we visit children, children move in, we adopt children.

'And how long might that all take?' asks Paul straightforwardly.

We are all pleased that he has asked it, although we know the answer already.

'Well, it all depends,' says Margaret and we collectively sigh.

'But the good news is that once you have been allocated your social worker, they have a maximum of 12 weeks to complete your assessment and to get you in front of the approval panel. There are strict targets now, which we are bound by, so the process can't drag on as it used to. Although we don't have any control over how long it would take to be matched with the children.'

'So how long does that take?' asks Paul. Thank you, Paul.

'Well, I've known couples to wait for a couple of years, whereas some have the details of children within days of their approval panel.'

I hope that is us.

'You may think that it would be good to be considered for particular children straightaway, but in reality it can be quite a shock.'

I would deal with it; it would be a good problem to deal with.

Rob and I drive the long, windy journey home, buzzing over our day. I have not seen Rob so enthusiastic over our adoption plans. He is impressed with Margaret, impressed with her handouts and quite liked most of the other couples. I secretly breathe a sigh of relief. Rob can be mortally offended by bad-quality handouts. If Margaret had littered her slides with bad grammar and spelling mistakes, it would have been a 'no deal' from Rob.

'I think I may tell my dad now,' says Rob, 'and Aunty Pam.'

After months, years even, of Rob not wanting to tell anyone about our infertility problems and our adoption hopes, it is like watching an enormous ocean-going tanker finally changing direction.

'I guess it would be better to give them some time to get used to it all. It might help them to feel included as well. How do you think your dad will take it?'

Rob takes a long pause. I know that things are a lot more complicated in his family than they are in mine. His dad, David, is a widower.

'I think Dad will be happy for me, happy to be a granddad, especially as Mum's not around anymore. And I think it's going to be important for him that I have a family.'

'Even if our children don't further the Donovan genes? What about all the big talk that goes on between you two – the Donovans are going to take on the world and all that, and your passing down your middle names through the generations?'

'That's just bravado, what me and Dad do. I really don't think he'll get hung up on genes. And maybe if I have a son, I can give him a new middle name.'

'So when do you want to tell him? When he comes to stay?' I venture.

'Yes, I think so. I don't want to do it on the phone. But I don't want to tell him with Pam. I want to tell him on my own.'

Pam is David's sister, Rob's aunt. Since Rob's mum died she has been there for David, sometimes a bit too much for David's liking. He is a quiet man and needs a bit of space around him sometimes. Pam cooks, launders, suggests outings that David might like to go on, with friends that David might like to see. She is a kind woman, doing the best she can. But sometimes I wonder if she takes care of David as a way of filling the empty space left behind when her husband walked out.

It is dark by the time we get home. We are both tired from the gears our brains have shifted through during the day. It is a good tired – a tired earned and indicative of movement and progress, rather than a stuck, sad, immobile tired.

CHAPTER 5

David and Pam arrive in a bluster of bags, wine, chocolates and flowers. They are pleased to see us and pleased to be released from their close confinement together in the car. David looks slightly dazed. We show them to the noticeably tidier spare bedrooms.

'Your place is looking just lovely,' says Aunty Pam, 'not that it hasn't always looked lovely.'

'We decided it was time for a tidy up,' I say, wondering if we've been rumbled in some way.

'I must say, you've worked incredibly hard; I've never seen it looking like this. You've done yourselves proud.'

Aunty Pam's eyes are in every corner of every alcove.

We have lunch together and then Rob and I execute our plan. I take Pam out shopping so that Rob can tell his dad about our adoption plans. I will then return to the house with Pam, so that Rob can tell her as well. I have had to get used to this level of planning in the Donovan family. Everything, everyone must be carefully managed so that the natural order of things is maintained and no one has reason to take offence at anything, which of course they do all the time.

Our shopping trip goes reasonably well. Pam can't help remarking that our small town shops are not a patch on those in big city Manchester. I remind her that we have three hours' parking for 20p, but that doesn't really cut it. I take her to our best cafe. She has to settle for a filter coffee and a sticky table but there's no getting away from the quality of the homemade cake. I sense in Aunty Pam an uninterest in anything I have to say, more than usual even. Then, from the moment we sit down, she launches into a monologue of unprecedented length.

'You know my father William, don't you?' (No pause for response.) 'Well, his mother was a Robertson and she was from Southport, she was one of nine children. Nine? Can you believe it?' (Again, no pause for response.) 'Well, there was Imogen, Florence, Archibald, Amelia and now what were the others called? Anyway her mother who was a Macintosh married Isaac and now he was one of six…'

It is a family history hijack. I am being led blindfolded, against my will, through a labyrinth of Victorian names. None of the names mean anything to me. Sometimes she tests me, to check I have been listening.

'And you remember, who was it Amelia married?'

I try to recover from my glazed expression. I struggle to remember. Amelia who? Did she marry Albert? Was Albert her son? Is there an Albert?

'She married Henry. Yes? Remember now? I know it's a lot to take on. I've been working on this for a while now and it's amazing how far it all goes back and how many relatives there are and I'm going to meet someone, who is related to Henry and he lives in Macclesfield, which is not all that far from me.'

As she motors on at full volume through her ancestors, I notice other people, on the tables nearby, starting to listen in and smirk. I have to muster all my focus to keep my eyes on Aunty Pam and to keep up my expression of interest. I make sure I interject the occasional 'wow' or 'ooh' for politeness. She explains that she has a whole pack of information at home that she wants to show me, made up of family trees and photographs. I wonder how Rob's news has gone down with his dad and whether Aunty Pam will manage to keep quiet long enough to take on the news herself.

When we arrive back, Rob and his dad are at the kitchen table looking at some papers – old air show brochures, some copies of Air International, yellowing photographs of a little boy next to a big aeroplane.

'You alright, Sal?' Rob asks me.

I think I may be wearing the same glazed expression that David was wearing after his long car journey with Aunty Pam. Aunty Pam disappears upstairs.

'Fine. Is that Farnborough Air show 1982? And is that you, Rob?'

'Me and a Spitfire. At my first ever air show.'

A dark-haired boy in oversized shorts and a stripy t-shirt stands to attention on the tarmac. A pair of enormous binoculars hangs from his neck. In the next photograph he holds up the programme to the camera.

'Great news,' says David. 'Rob has told me.'

He gets up and gives me a hug, just as Aunty Pam comes back into the room, laden down with paperwork.

'I've got something to show you all,' she clucks with self-importance.

'Rob and Sally have something to tell you first,' says David.

Pam stops in her tracks and looks at me. It is clear she thinks I am pregnant, with a little twig of family tree. Luckily Rob senses what could be an uncomfortable moment and leaps in.

'We are planning to adopt two children. We're having some training at the moment. We wanted to tell you before we got too far down the line.'

Pam rearranges her face and, to her credit, is over the moon.

'Oh my loves, fabulous news, fabulous.'

She doesn't know what else to say.

'The thing is, we've been trying for ages and well, I've got a problem with my,' (long pause while Rob contemplates talking about his sperm production with his aunt) 'waterworks,' (waterworks? You are a wonder of nature, Rob Donovan) 'so we decided to adopt and here we are.'

'Oh love, that's great. People still get pregnant you know even after years of trying, even when they've adopted children you know. I have a friend, Jennifer and her daughter has a friend and exactly that happened to her,' blunders Aunty Pam, trying her best.

The ancestral paperwork sits in the middle of the kitchen table, passing silent judgement on our genetic cul-de-sac.

'I'll put the kettle on,' I say, not knowing what else there is to say.

'Rob says that you'll get a social worker. Might it be intrusive?' says Rob's dad, trying not to wake the ancestral monster.

'I'm looking forward to it, getting on with things at last.'

I make the tea while we chit-chat about possible ages and numbers of children, imagine when they may arrive, what they will be like. Pam fidgets and can't engage with the conversation. Her insensitivity has gone beyond amusing now and is starting to annoy me. Finally, she cannot resist it.

'Rob love, I've brought along something to show you.'

Rob looks momentarily interested and the trap shuts on him. Out come the black and white photographs full of strangers bearing Rob's forehead or hairline. Out come the fuzzy photocopies of census pages. I catch David's eye and mouth, 'Do you want to come and look at the garden?' For a man who has no interest in gardening, he is remarkably keen to inspect ours.

*****

The last two training sessions are like meetings with old friends. We greet each other and swap stories about our hopes for the future. We sit in the same seats to avoid upsetting the balance. The nervous lady and her husband do not attend any more sessions and Margaret says that perhaps they are not ready to continue right now. She says that it is important for us all to put the brakes on at any time in the process if it is getting too much.

The subjects get more and more challenging. We move from our own childhoods, to those of our potential children. On our second training day, Margaret opens the flip chart to reveal two circles – one is complete with arrows around it and one is broken.

'When a baby has a need, it communicates its need to its carer by crying,' she says, pointing to words around the circle that say 'Need' and 'Cry'. 'The carer will respond to the crying by satisfying the need and comforting the baby.' The words 'Satisfy' and 'Soothe' appear further around the circle. 'The baby will usually then have a period of happiness, perhaps interaction with the carer, until it has another need.'

'And around the circle the baby travels, learning to trust its carer, learning to bring its emotions down through soothing and comforting and then enjoying and learning further from its interaction with the carer.'

It all looks so simple. I think about my nephews and my sister. This chart encompasses exactly what she does with them all day. We move on to the broken circle.

'Now in a neglectful home, the baby will experience a need and cry and maybe their carer will not come and satisfy their need. The baby will continue to cry and maybe its need is satisfied eventually, maybe not. Over time the baby will learn that no one else will satisfy its needs consistently, so it no longer cries.'

I remember the television footage of Romanian orphanages, the silence.

'The baby will become self-contained but will still be experiencing hunger, discomfort from a dirty nappy, but they have learnt that to cry either brings no or insufficient reaction from a carer or indeed even shouting and maybe even violence. These babies are living in a highly uncertain world; they will experience fear and may often be left alone for long periods of time. As a result they may have delayed speech, delayed walking and not surprisingly will often have difficulties at school, such as problems focusing on work, forming friendships and conforming to rules. You see, they have learnt that the only way to survive is to be self-sufficient, to be on high alert all the time as a way of avoiding being hurt and to trust no one else.'

We all sit in complete silence, embarrassment even.

'To a greater or lesser degree, these are the sorts of children who you will be considering for adoption. Some will have had the added difficulties of drug or alcohol dependent parents.'

There is a long pause. No one has any questions.

'Shall we take a short break?'

We all jump at the chance of talking about the inconsequentialities of tea making. I catch Margaret's eye. I wonder how difficult it is for her to have to deliver this message to a room of hopeful parents.

Having barely recovered our composure, we are to talk in groups about the sorts of behaviours that our children might have, the reasons why and what could be done to help improve the behaviours. Margaret explains that we are not to be in the same group as our partners and looks around the room trying to put us together. As long as I'm not with MJ I don't mind.

'Sally, you can go with Paul…and…MJ.' I wonder what her thought process has been, why Paul and I have to put up with MJ.

We are given three scenarios, each on a different card. The first says: 'Star is four years old. She spent two years with her birth mother Kerry who neglected her. During that time Kerry had several boyfriends, one of whom was violent towards her. She socialised with lots of friends at home and was known by her neighbours as “a bit of a party animal”. Star was adopted at the age of three. Her adoptive parents have noticed that Star will go to strangers and often wanders off when they are out together.’

We huddle in our group. Paul is keen to get things started.

‘She might be used to lots of strangers being around. Maybe she didn’t have a lot of consistency,’ he says.

‘She could have been left with the friends or the boyfriends a lot, especially if Kerry was out partying,’ I agree.

We both look at MJ.

‘My mother had loads of friends around when I was growing up and I was left in front of the telly with a can of Coke while all the adults were talking.’ MJ goes on. And on.

‘And I do have problems with trust now, especially with men, and I’ve had to spend years in therapy to resolve my issues.’ She maintains just a little too much eye contact.

‘So what could Star’s parents do?’ I say, hoping to get back to the reason we are here. I look at Paul. MJ starts up again.

‘And my mother was not capable of showing me affection, never took me out, never bought me nice stuff.’

‘They should keep close to her, at the park, in situations like that,’ says Paul, his voice giving away his frustration with Planet MJ.

‘You are entirely on the right lines there,’ interrupts Margaret, ‘well done.’ I know she is trying to derail MJ, but it doesn’t work. MJ can relate personally and dramatically to every scenario. We somehow manage to keep on track, by giving her the occasional sympathetic facial expression and then by ignoring her and then talking over her. Eventually she disengages.

The last hour of the session is hard work. We are all full up with information and emotionally weary. My mind starts to wander about. What sort of child would I be best suited to? A quiet, withdrawn one that needs drawing out? Or a noisy, boisterous one? I would be better at quiet and withdrawn. Maybe it's not as straightforward as that. What will I do if they won't do anything I say, if I have no control? What if they scream in the supermarket aisle, smash up the Corn Flake display? What if they will only eat crisps and processed cheese? Perhaps I'm not going to be a strong enough character? I concentrate on Margaret again as she rounds up the training. We will be allocated social workers who will be contacting us soon. ('How soon?' says Paul.) She will be staying for a while to answer any questions.

We all ready ourselves to leave and wish each other luck. MJ heads across the room to me, holding a small piece of paper.

'Sally, I thought we might, like, get together sometime, share experiences, you know. I've written down my phone number for you.'

'Over my dead body,' I think.

'That would be great,' I say. 'I'll give you a call.'

*****

Work is a lovely diversion from the constant streams of thought that dominate my headspace. It is coming into spring, proper spring. Not the brittle spring heralded by the first snowdrop, borne more out of longing than reality, but the warm, green, floral spring. A single coach load of visitors does not a spring make, but the car park is half full and the visitors start to come back, albeit fleeced and cagouled. Dean goes into his spring grumps and keeps away from everyone. Jon and I feel cheery now that the winter drudgery has come to an end and we can chat to the visitors, answer their questions and generally bask in the warmer weather. Andy has asked me to take responsibility for showing small groups around the garden, explaining the history and the design. I love it. I love my job and I think I will miss it when, if, we ever have children. I have planned to stop work for a time and then to return maybe part time, once the children are at school.

I come home to another envelope. I can spot them now, the envelopes from social services; bright white, with smudged red frank marks. I don't even entertain waiting until Rob gets home from work. I open it as carefully as an excited person can.

> Dear Robert and Sally,
>
> I am writing to introduce myself as your social worker. My name is Mel Matthews and I work in the Adoption Team at Social Services. I will be assessing your suitability as adopters.
>
> I wish to arrange a series of meetings with you at your home. Please could you call me on the number above to arrange our first meeting.
>
> Yours sincerely,
> Mel Matthews

This is it. We are on our way. We are on the next leg of the journey. I feel an almost uncontrollable need to ring Mel Matthews right this moment, but it is ten past six, well outside office hours. I try anyway and the phone rings and rings to an empty office.

The next morning I wake up and immediately feel the anticipation of the phone call. I get dressed and make my sandwiches to the inner soundtrack of what I will say, how I will introduce myself, the questions I will ask. I decide that I will ring at ten o'clock, a time which says 'keen' but not 'desperate'. At half past nine I speed walk across the garden, ignoring the imploring looks of the early visitors, eager to lure me into a long conversation about the pruning of winter jasmine or the climbing habits of the forsythia. The office is empty. Great. I have the phone number written on my hand. I dial the number and wait. I can hear my heart beating in my head and wonder if this is the first thing Mel Matthews will hear of me.

When she answers she sounds friendly, warm and I have no need for my over-prepared opener.

'Let me explain a bit about what will happen. Basically I need to come and visit you and Rob together, on maybe a weekly basis. We will probably need about six sessions. I'll prepare a Form F, which will contain all the information about you. This will go to the panel who will then consider your approval as adopters.'

She sounds chirpy, positive and businesslike. We arrange the first meeting, not at some distant time in the future, but next week, barely enough time to bring the house up to full Social Worker Acceptability Standard.

I am filled with an energetic happiness, which rocket fuels me through the rest of the day. The sun shines and my eyes struggle to adjust to the new greens of the shoots and the leaves. Soon we will be planting out the summer bedding and bringing the orange trees into the open after their winter holiday under glass. We have everything to look forward to.

I get home and ring Rob, then Alice, then my mum. Alice and my mum are glad to share some good news at last. We talk about the sorts of questions that might be asked, how long the process might take and how intrusive it might be. Alice and Mum are under the impression that this stage could take months and months, years even. I hope that they are wrong. Mel seemed confident that it would be a matter of a small number of months. So far our contact with social services has not lived up to the prejudices I have soaked up from the newspaper headlines.

We spend the weekend deep cleaning. Rob does not see the need, doesn't think that Mel will look in our cupboards and drawers and draw conclusions from the detritus hidden away within them. I like to plan for the worst-case scenario and I don't want to be told I cannot adopt children because my tea towel drawer is clogged with old serviettes and birthday candles or because the wardrobe doors in the spare room hardly shut because of the jumbled boxes of college notes trying to escape. On Sunday evening, pleased with our toils, we have takeaway curry to celebrate and to avoid messing up the kitchen.

'I'm not living in a show home,' says Rob.

'Rob, we don't live in a show home and we never will. This is how most people live and how we are going to have to pretend we live, at least until we have some confidence that social services think we are reasonable, normal people.'

I struggle to get the lid off the plastic box containing my chickpea curry and orange sauce splats on to the work surface. I know that there will be a forever stain unless I remove it immediately so I spray on some kitchen bleach.

'What happened to the eco products and the laissez-faire approach to housework?' he says as the lid on his plastic box suddenly comes free and chicken tikka masala splashes across the work surface and on to the tiles.

Within moments of the evil orange dye making contact with the kitchen surfaces I have wiped it away, like a grown-up woman in a television advert.

'I'm not comfortable living like this,' Rob moans on.

'It won't be for too long. Don't forget to tidy your side of the bedroom tomorrow.'

'What's wrong with my side of the bedroom?' He is indignant.

'The leaning tower of clothes? The massive pile of books?' I could go on but stop myself. I sense that easygoing Rob is about to be pushed too far and I picture mules being dragged along dusty roads in old cowboy films. If he crosses the line now then all progress will stop, completely.

*****

On the agreed day (Tuesday) at ten minutes before the allotted time (four o'clock) Rob and I, respectably dressed, with a notebook, a pen and a diary on the coffee table, wait in our clean house for our social worker to arrive. Going against stereotype again, at five minutes to four a navy blue Nissan Micra pulls into our drive. We resist the temptation to run to the window like excited children but instead wait for the knock on the door. We also resist the temptation to answer the door immediately but leave enough time to make it look as though we have been busy doing something else and have lost track of the time.

'I hope I've got the right house.'

Mel is all warmth and confidence and loveliness. She has dark, neatly bobbed hair and a naturally upturned mouth. She is tall and, I think, kind of motherly – the sort of woman you could imagine being a midwife. We all sit down and I perform the tea ritual to ease us into this rather unusual situation. Mel takes her tea black and with no sugar. She does not want a biscuit. This woman means business.

She talks us through the form she will gradually have to fill with our lives – the Form F. It seems straightforward enough. We start on the basics – our full names, our dates of birth, where we grew up, the jobs we do and our extended family members. Mel then wants to know why we want to adopt children and how many we would like. And we talk sperm counts and doctors' appointments and grief. She searches our answers for signs that we might not be committed to adoption, asks us if we have considered IVF treatment, makes sure we are not secretly undergoing it now. Despite Mel being a stranger to us, it feels comfortable and normal to share this with her. Perhaps because she has a professional relationship with us, she doesn't feel obliged to make all the usual noises ('I'm sure if you relax it will happen for you soon', etc). She listens so kindly and carefully.

Talking to her, I realise that I really do want to do this and that I'm no longer weighed down by grief. It feels like free therapy. Having to explain our motivations really does help to sort them out. It is wonderful to be looking to the future, to be planning.

During the next few sessions we talk about our attitudes to all sorts of things – religion, race, money, work, food. I have never talked so intensely with anyone other than Rob and although his views aren't new to me, it is interesting to hear him expressing himself to someone else, from scratch. It feels like our courtship is happening all over again and I am reminded of all the things I love Rob for – his common sense, his unswerving belief in equality, his dry humour. Mel is particularly interested in how we operate as a couple and in particular, how we resolve disagreements. There isn't much that we really disagree on. Rob is less sociable than me and isn't that enamoured of the great outdoors and of course we have the carnivore/veggie divide that seems to so fascinate everyone else. We talk about my tendency to sulk and Rob's stubbornness – both of which can go on for days. Mel gently suggests that we might work on a more adult way of resolving differences.

*****

As Mel gets to know us better, she starts to talk more about the children.

'Because they've missed so much, most of the children we place are operating at a level that is significantly below their biological age,' she drops in, putting her tea down. 'It's important that they are parented as a younger child would be, that they get a lot of close attention, interactive play – you would need to get down on the floor and play with them, at their level, be silly with them, playful.'

Sounds great, I think.

'These children may resist close contact,' she picks up her tea and looks away.

There is a pause.

'We have an adopted daughter, from Romania. She was left in an orphanage. She's 12.'

Rob and I both show our interest.

'She has always resisted cuddles and close contact. If I knew then what I know now, I would have tried much harder to initiate contact. The research is so strong now, but when she was younger we had no support, no advice. Everyone thought she should be OK because we adopted her when she was so young.'

'How are things now?' I ask.

'It's tough. She finds friendships difficult because she always needs to be in control. And she can make bad choices and can get into a lot of trouble as a consequence. But we are getting better support now. And I've done a lot of research into attachment disorder. I've got a couple of books for you to read.' She lifts some weighty books out of her bag. 'These books will be the best insight you ever get into your children.'

I realise that we are talking children, real children. There are no 'mights', 'maybes' or 'potentials' in the sentences now. Mel is coaching us and she knows what she is doing. I take the books from her. They are about hurt and broken children, about accepting and healing. I offer a plate of biscuits around and for the first time Mel takes one, a Hobnob. Maybe by the time this process is finished we'll be scoffing bourbons together. She readies her pen again and then a complete change of gear.

'Does it cause any problems with you, Rob, being a meat eater and Sally, you being a vegetarian?'

I decide to turn this to our advantage.

'I cook a meat version and a veggie version of say a curry or a pasta sauce or sometimes we eat different things. We're very flexible. In fact perhaps our children would have choice and variety as a result.'

Lots of writing. I wonder if Mel is trying to find some major schism between us, to make us somehow more real. Then, 'We are nearly done. I've applied for your approval panel date and so I will finish typing up your Form Fs next week. I'll get you a draft so you can see what I've written about you, to make sure it's accurate and fair.'

Neither Rob nor I can hide our delight. We are nearing the end of another box on our flow diagram to parenthood.

'I don't anticipate any problems with the panel. I wouldn't put you forward if I didn't think you'd be approved.' Mel smiles broadly.

*****

That evening Rob and I go to the pub to celebrate the occasion of us being recognised by social services, or at least one employee of social services, as decent citizens. We indulge ourselves with beer batter fish and chips and chocolate profiteroles. We huddle together and swap excitements.

'Told you we'd get through the assessment,' says Rob.

'It's best to play safe and assume the worst,' I say, 'and we could have come a cropper on the veggie thing.'

'Lentils are not going to be obstacles, Sal.'

I drink my lovely, soothing beer and feel a little bit of worry relaxing out of me.

'We should book a holiday,' says Rob out of the blue, which is unlike him. 'Our last holiday without children, a big one. Where do you want to go?'

I know exactly where I want to go.

'Canada. Big, wide-open, mountainous, lakes, moose, pancakes, the whole lot.'

'You book something as soon as we've got the date of the panel.'

'There's one condition,' I say.

Rob raises his eyebrows.

'We can't call it our last holiday without children.'

'Why?'

'It will be a jinx.'

I take another sip of beer and some more tension melts away. A plan is forming at last.

*****

Rob collects our Form F from Mel's office on his way home from work. I have made spaghetti bolognese (one meat, one veggie) and we eat and read at the same time, trying not to splatter the paperwork with sauce. We search for the doubts, the uncertainties, the potential problems and there are none. Mel thinks we are bona fide good people and suitable adopters. Rob is 'shy' and I am 'a bit of a leftie', which I'm not sure is entirely true. The veggie/meat thing is mentioned of course. We turn to the section on the children we would like. It is a tick box list of ages and sexes. Then underneath, a denser list of boxes, which summarise a long session we had with Mel, when we essentially had to specify the children we would adopt. It shows that we will not consider children with physical disabilities, genetic diseases or who have suffered sexual abuse. On paper it looks brutal. We won't have you, you or you, but we'll take you and you. Our initial reaction was to tick many more boxes but Mel insisted that we think about what we could cope with far more deeply. I know she was right, but it still feels callous, cowardly and choosy. In a month from now, on 25 August, we will sit in front of the panel who will decide upon our future. We have the option not to attend if we are 'too scared', Mel says. But there is no way that I am going to spend the day deadheading bedding plants whilst a room of professionals make decisions about my life.

I head up the stairs to bed. The doors to the two spare bedrooms are ajar. I pause in the hallway and try to imagine little children, asleep in their beds, cosy under brightly covered duvets, teddies and toy tractors around the place. I slowly open the door of one of the rooms and look inside. I can almost imagine what it should look like. The little shard in my heart shifts. Last weekend we had spent an evening with friends, at their house. Their children were asleep upstairs. They know of our plans and were interviewed by our social worker. Nevertheless the talk was of nothing but babies and children. Rob and I both left feeling sad and it hit home again that we will never have our own babies. I am certain that we will feel differently when we finally adopt our children but it is disconcerting to get another glimpse of those old feelings of loss. It has not been a neat process, the grief process. I was disappointed that our friends could be as insensitive as they were, but I suppose it's impossible to understand if you haven't been there, haven't felt and tasted the grief, felt it poisoning your blood, clouding over a sunny day. When I try to imagine getting pregnant, growing in size, giving birth, I can't. Most of me has digested the reality that this will never happen, like a path not taken. But occasionally the black hole gapes open, just for a short while. It is there all the time but being buried deeper and deeper. I wonder if it will ever heal over completely.

*****

August in the garden is a restful time – a pause before the autumn jobs start. I spend the morning on the ride-on mower, listening to music, in shades, shorts and a sun hat. It is blissful. In the afternoon we deadhead in the borders; it is easy, light work and we all chat. At half past three, Andy appears with a tray of teas and cake. We sit together on the stone steps overlooking the garden and laugh and tease each other. The warmth of the stone soaks through me, a deep warmth that soaks my body and could send me to sleep. The occasional visitor makes a comment, 'That's the life,' or 'Nice work if you can get it.' We all smile back.

The following day I am dressed up in skirt, boots and shirt. It is a cooler day, which means I can wear my lucky boots. I am not a superstitious person but I like to guard against bad luck all the same and whenever I wear my lucky boots, good things seem to happen. I don't think I ever mentioned that side of myself to Mel.

We are in some kind of holding room, waiting to be called. Mel bustles in a bit late, all files and paperwork and hair pushed behind ears. She seems a bit flustered, maybe nervous. Rob says he isn't nervous. I know I am and it is a deep, fluttery nervousness, which makes my voice breathy. Mel is called in. And we wait. A lady who we don't know comes into the room – a short lady with neat red hair. She introduces herself as the social worker who organises the panels. She seems to know who we are and reassures us that we will be fine. Then she tells us that it's time.

We follow her down a corridor, through a door and then I am faced by the thin end of a very long table. Each place of the table is occupied by faces that lean in towards us. We are asked to sit down and not to feel nervous. The faces introduce themselves. There is a paediatrician, some social workers, a lady who was adopted as a child, an adopter and a man who is something to do with the council. We smile at each one in turn as their names flow over us. They want to confirm some information on our form. Yes we want to be approved to adopt two children, preferably one of pre-school age and one a bit older, we don't mind which sex (although unofficially Rob is desperate for a boy and a girl). There is lots of nodding and smiling. Then the questions.

'What would your approach to challenging behaviour be?' says a lady from somewhere in the distance.

My mind momentarily panic freezes and then I recall something I've read about not making threats that can't be carried through and not setting children up to fail. The faces nod, not quite all together, like a Mexican wave of nods. Rob adds something about not isolating and excluding. That gets more enthusiastic nodding and some writing. Then there is one final question. And I have to stop myself from smirking.

'We understand that Rob, you eat meat and that Sally, you are a vegetarian. Do you intend to bring up your children as vegetarians?'

'My children will be deprived of meat, bacon crisps and jelly – they will be raised on a bowl of brown rice and chickpeas a day,' is what I am tempted to say. But I give a nice smiley answer about choice and variety, which everyone is relieved about.

Rob and I are asked to leave the room. We are led back to the holding room where we are given coffee by the short, neat social worker.

'You've done well. You might not be waiting long,' she says just as Mel re-enters the room.

Mel is red-cheeked and high-voiced. She puts her papers down and lets out a giant sigh.

'That was my first panel.'

'You've never done one before?' exclaims Rob.

'I completed my training earlier this year. You two are my first couple.'

'I'm glad we didn't know that any earlier,' I say.

'The panel are going to recommend that you are approved. They were very strongly in support. The Director of Children's Services has to sign the form and that should happen this week. Congratulations. You will make fantastic adopters.'

I stand up and I give Mel the biggest, hardest hug that I can.

'I'd never have guessed you were a rookie,' and tears of utter relief roll down my cheeks.

CHAPTER 6

Half past four in the morning and we pull into our drive after the long journey from Gatwick Airport. Rob switches off the engine and we sit for a brief moment soaking up the silence. Then we drag our suitcases into the house, which looks unfamiliar after a fortnight away. Two empty wine glasses and a wine bottle sit on the draining board. Bathed in relief we had toasted our approval as adopters. Our trip to the mountains has cleansed us of the nervousness and anticipation and marked the transition from hopeful to expectant. 'I'm not looking forward to going back to work on Monday,' says Rob with a yawn.

'No, nor me,' I yawn in sympathy.

A huge pile of mail obstructs the front door. I dump it on the kitchen table, then play the answer phone messages. The first is Rob's dad wishing us a happy holiday. The second is my mum wishing us the same. Then the third. It is Mel.

'Rob, quick.'

We huddle around the answer machine.

'Hi Rob and Sally, I wasn't sure when you were due back. Give me a call, would you? I've got some news.' She sounds happy, excited almost.

'Oh my god,' says Rob, 'do you think it's about children?'

'It can't be – it's too soon and we can't ring her until Monday! I don't know how I'm going to contain myself.'

'A boy and a girl,' says Rob, sounding sure again.

'Don't get your hopes up. Two girls or two boys would be brilliant as well.'

'It would, but I want a boy and a girl.' All of a sudden Rob is sounding a bit more particular than he ever had with Mel.

The uncertainty unleashed by Mel's message and the jetlag throw us both into a horrible, unsettled state. Neither of us can sleep, read or even sit still. So we keep busy, we go shopping, eat a huge breakfast, go for a walk and then generally get on each other's nerves. Now we are both desperate to get back to work, just so that the phone call can happen. Neither of us would feel comfortable making this call from work so we agree that I will go in a bit later than usual and ring Mel from home.

My hands are shaking as I dial the number. Please be in, please be in. Someone picks up the phone; it is her assistant. Mel is soon found and she asks after our holidays. I hurry through the pleasantries and then she drops the bombshell.

'There are two children who could be a potential match for you and Rob. Have you got a pen?' I can hear excitement bubbling up through her professionalism.

'They are four-year-old Jaymey and one-year-old Harlee. Currently placed with foster carers within the county. They've had a very chaotic time. I have their Form Es here and if you and Rob are interested you could come and collect them and read them through. If you're still interested we can go from there.'

'Mel, you said it would take ages!'

'I said it *could* take ages but in truth your information went out to a few interested social workers even before you were approved.'

'I've got to ring Rob.' I am jabbering, pacing around the kitchen. I'd often imagined taking a positive pregnancy test. I wonder, is this my blue-line moment?

'Just remember, Jaymey and Harlee may not work out. The matching process is complicated. We are waiting for a court date for the Freeing Order. The Freeing Order means that the children are legally freed from their birth parents and can be placed for adoption by social services. I'm told that there shouldn't be a problem with this.' She pauses. 'I am so pleased for you. I couldn't wait to tell you.'

I ring Rob and he answers after the first ring.

'Tell me. Tell me. It's a boy and a girl?' says Rob.

'*It's a boy and a girl!*' I shout down the phone.

'*You are kidding me!*' Rob shouts back. 'How old?'

I tell him all I know and after agreeing to pick up the forms Rob laughs and says, 'See you later, Mummy!'

I get to work in time for tea break and hear all the news from the past fortnight. An elderly visitor tripped over on the steps and an ambulance was called and the teashop has changed its plastic chairs for metal ones. It feels comforting to be with everyone again. They ask if I want to mow the big lawn with the ride-on – a prized job. I note this small act of kindness. I've been away on a holiday and yet I get to be eased into work on my return. As I wash up the mugs in the grimy sink, Andy asks how things are. I had told him about our successful approval panel and he was as excited as a puppy.

'We've had a phone call, about a possible match with two children.'

'You're going to be a mammy. Congratulations,' he smiles.

'We've got a lot to go through before that happens.'

'Don't leave too soon, pet. You're the only one who gets my jokes.'

I scoop the pile of used teabags into the bin, which needs emptying, and scrub away at the sink for a bit with a dirty, threadbare scourer. The sink is stained with dirt and tea. Then I scrape at the tannin on the inside of Andy's mug.

'My tea won't taste as nice now,' he laments.

'And you won't be getting your daily inoculation of germs.'

'We won't miss you in the garden, might miss you in the kitchen though.'

'You're a funny man, Andy.'

Rob gets home from work before me. He sits watching the television with a thick A4 envelope by the side of him.

We take a form each; I have Jaymey's and Rob has Harlee's. From the outset I am thrown into another world. In stark black type the form unemotionally describes a tangled little life. I have to read some sections over and over to understand the mess of relations, half-relations, siblings and half-siblings, boyfriends that appear and reappear. Then the sections, with extended attachments that cover the injuries, the abuse, the excuses that were given, the hospital admittances. It goes on and on. Burns, missing teeth, cuts, scars, bruises upon bruises. Then a section on neglect: left alone for long periods, not fed adequately, left in the care of friends and strangers. There isn't much about the birth mother, just that she probably wasn't parented well herself. She is attracted to unsuitable, violent men, who abuse her children and who she can't leave, even if her children are removed as a consequence.

We swap forms without speaking. Harlee is Jaymey's half-sister; her father is unknown. She seems to have been accepted though, unlike Jaymey. There is no evidence of physical abuse – perhaps she got out before it was her turn. But she has been restrained for hours in a car seat and is extremely anxious about food. She will happily go to strangers and shows no attachment to her birth mother. These little lives are almost unbearable to read about. But this is not the time to look away. We read the forms several times over and each time we take in a bit more.

'Well,' says Rob, 'I'm in.'

'Yes, so am I.'

The following day I wait in the social services reception area for Mel. She breezes in holding a small brown envelope.

I tell her how hard it had been to read the papers and that we would like to proceed.

We sit down on grey plastic chairs and Mel opens the envelope. She pulls out two photographs. One is of Jaymey and Harlee together, sitting on a brown patterned carpet. Jaymey has his arm around Harlee's shoulders. She is propped up with cushions around her. The other is of the two of them either side of their birth mother on a worn, yellow sofa. None of them are touching each other. The first thing that strikes me is the children's auburn, wavy hair, golden skin and brown eyes. Jaymey's hair is shaved around his ears and left long on the top and at the back. He wears corduroy trousers and a jumper with a tractor sewn on to the front. He clutches a small car in his toddler's hands. Harlee has the chubby cheeks of a one-year-old and is dressed in a pink pinafore dress and pink tights. She is holding something to her mouth. They are both beautiful.

I hadn't thought beforehand about whether their physical appearances would be important to me. If I'd been asked then I'd have answered an emphatic 'no', because we are taught that it is wrong to judge a person by their looks, a book by its cover. But my unchecked and honest reactions are raw and unreconstructed; these little faces appeal to me, attract me.

There is something disturbing about the images. The children's faces are blank. Their eyes, their mouths, their postures even, are completely without expression. They have been told to look into the camera and this is what they have done. There is no fun attached, no meaning, only bewilderment. I have tried to avoid looking into the eyes of their mother, the woman whose children I want to have, because I feel like a voyeur – an intruder. But her image is compelling. She is small and wiry, with long brown hair pulled into a tight ponytail. She is wearing navy blue tracksuit bottoms and a grey polo t-shirt and is sitting, knees apart, like an adolescent boy. The insides of her arms carry several homemade, smudged tattoos. Her face has a look of total defiance. She looks like a fighter. No clues to the connections between this woman and these two children are evident from the photograph. They could be three strangers.

'Aren't they lovely?' says Mel, breaking the spell.

'I can't believe how beautiful they look.' I can't take my eyes off the pictures.

'They don't look unlike you and Rob. They could pass as yours.'

'Can I show them to Rob?'

'You can have them for now. If you are both interested then I need to set up a meeting with the children's social worker, Lorna. She'll meet you to make sure she's happy with you. It shouldn't be a problem. She'll be able to give us a bit more information on the status of the Freeing Order as well,' says Mel.

I leave the social services offices and head straight for my parents' house. I can't go home right now and pace around on my own. I show them the pictures. My mum has tears in her eyes and my dad goes into the kitchen to boil the kettle.

'They look like they belong with you and Rob,' my mum says.

*****

I make a long 'To Do' list, which involves filling, sanding, painting and carpeting the two spare rooms. Due to a ridiculous, unresolved belief in fate, which doesn't encumber any other part of my rational life, I decide to refer to them as spare rooms and not as Jaymey's and Harlee's bedrooms. To do otherwise would tempt the worst kind of luck, endangering the fragile connection that the children have with Rob and me and these two empty, echoey rooms. Worst-case scenarios and barely formed hopes float randomly in and out of my mind. I indulge in hopeful daydreams of the future like a guilty pleasure and then talk myself down to break the spell. The cold blast of dread will pass across unexpectedly: 'what if?', 'what if not?' That familiar state of unknowing – of not being in control – has come to stay again, blowing hot and cold, like a cranky, unpredictable old aunt.

*****

I leave work early in order to meet Mel and Lorna. Rob is already home when I get back and has plumped the cushions and filled the toilet with pungent blue toilet gel. We put the kettle on and arrange some chocolate digestives on a plate. Mel arrives and we talk formalities. She recommends that we find out as much about the children as we can from Lorna – that this shouldn't just be about her testing us out. After all the assessments so far it feels like hard work having to summon up the energy to impress someone else. Rob checks his watch and fidgets. Lorna eventually arrives and I meet her at the door and introduce myself. She is hard to make out through her long layers of clothes and her many bags. She wears black snagged tights and collapsing high-heeled shoes, which carry great globs of mud across the hallway and into the sitting room. She accepts a drink (coffee with two sugars) and biscuits (three). She immediately launches into the dates and processes of the various court orders that must be granted before the children can be placed with us. I try to follow her logic but she jumps around and back and as I nod I realise that I am confused. Rob clearly is too and we both start to ask questions to clarify the order of things and the dates. She starts to communicate with us as though it is all terribly straightforward really and we should have been listening more carefully. Rob is bristling. His expression, his posture and his tone of voice are all conveying his intense annoyance with this woman. I do my best to smooth things over. She is getting to me too but we have no choice; we have to win her over if we want to have any chance of adopting Jaymey and Harlee. I suggest more coffee. Lorna stands up.

'Yes, coffee would be great and I need to look around your house,' she says directly.

'Rob, why don't you make some more drinks and I'll show Lorna around,' I suggest.

Rob is on his way to the kitchen before I've finished my sentence and Mel offers to help him. I hope she is going to calm him down.

Lorna invites herself into every room, even our bedroom, which sports Rob's leaning tower of clothes and an overflowing laundry basket. Her shoes continue to shed blobs of mud across the carpets, which she doesn't seem to notice.

We reconvene and Lorna starts to question us. It feels like a grilling. What hobbies do we have? Do we have things we do separately and together? How active are we? Are we able to set boundaries? How assertive are we? It goes on for an hour but by the end it seems as though we have won her over. Rob has just about managed to keep a lid on his frustration. Mel does her best to support us and to point out that much of this was covered in our assessment. But Lorna is clearly a lady who likes to be in control and so we roll over and give into her questioning whilst at the same time explaining just how assertive we can be.

That evening we resort to the freezer for emergency pizza. We have undergone the job interview of our lives and are both emotionally wrung out, again. It was an important step – meeting Lorna and hearing more about the children – but it was difficult having to perform, especially for Rob.

'That bloody woman,' says Rob, sliding the pizzas into the oven, 'so loud and domineering. I had to bite my tongue.'

'I suppose she has to be a bit like that to work with the sorts of families she does,' I venture.

'I'm not one of those. She had a nerve asking me whether I would be able to be assertive with a schoolteacher.

I have difficult situations every day at work. She spoke to me like I was a child. Bloody cheek. And she trod mud everywhere.'

I speak to Mel the following afternoon. Lorna liked us and is going to proceed with us as adopters for Jaymey and Harlee. The Care Order has been heard but the judge has not yet issued his written ruling. She thinks that the birth mother has the opportunity to appeal the decision, but would have little chance of success if she did so. Mel talks me through all the chances that the birth mother has been given – chances to turn things around, to prove herself capable of parenting her children. Each chance is missed, squandered. I don't know if she couldn't believe her children would ever really be removed or whether she didn't want to play along with the system. She has two older children in the care system so she must know what the consequences are. And when she has decided to put up a fight during a social services meeting or a court hearing, she has been fighting to keep Harlee and not Jaymey. Maybe Jaymey came along when there were just too many children in the house and then by the time she got her head above water he was past the cute baby stage. Maybe Harlee is wanted because she is still at the age of immobility, she can be dressed up in pink and left in her cot when she is being too demanding. And how has it felt for Jaymey, being raised by a mother who doesn't want him? Does that explain the injuries and the neglect? What about the neglect of Harlee? Maybe this is what we do to our children when we have no sense of ourselves, no place in the world, when we feel worthless? And this is visited on the next generation.

*****

Before the malformed sperm reared their misshapen bodies, I had assumed, like most young women, that I would get to play a part in choosing my children's names, or at the very minimum hold a veto. In the middle drawer of my bedside table is a list, made years ago, of my favourite names – Rachel, Anna, Betty for a girl; Jack and James for a boy. Rob was stuck on Enid for a girl. I argued it is a horn-rimmed spectacle of a name, which I would veto. He wouldn't budge. All that is irrelevant now because our ready-made children will arrive in our family with their own ready-made names. Perhaps we could adjust 'Jaymey' to 'Jamie', but 'Harlee' is surely a made-up name, maybe something to do with motorbikes. Despite knowing that changing an adopted child's name is a selfish act I can clearly imagine a wisp of embarrassment on introducing her. 'Yes, Harlee, H-a-r-l-e-e, no, not as in Davidson.' I like a safe, solid name, with a small dash of colour, not attention-seeking names taken from soap operas or Greek tragedies, which come with a side-order of cultural baggage, or bizarre names that say 'look how creative and out there I am'. But my safe choices probably pinpoint me as accurately as anyone else's.

*****

The old, flaky paint comes away easily. The wooden window frames in the larger spare room haven't been painted since we moved into the house and well before that. They are a sickly caramel colour and blend in beautifully with the beige and candy pink floral border, which has taken me hours to scrape away. The physical work is not quite enough to take my mind off the children – when we might be matched with them, when we might meet them, whether a distant relative is going to come forward and take them in. So I listen to a very dull history programme and then Woman's Hour ('if you haven't made your Christmas cake yet then it isn't too late'). I keep scraping and settle into the old cardigan of Woman's Hour. I can't believe that even Jenni Murray is talking about Christmas and it is still November. Nevertheless, if I had to come up with my top five ambitions, then one of them would be to appear on Woman's Hour. I don't know if Jenni would be much interested in what I would have to say – 'Mulch and Mulching, for and against' or 'Why is it so difficult to buy attractive workwear for women?'

I daydream about being interviewed by her, 'So. Sally, what inspired you to design your own range of waterproof combat trousers?'

'Well, Jenni, I think it's important to feel good at all times *and* to have somewhere to keep your secateurs, so my collection is all about practicality *and* fashion.'

The phone breaks my daydream and I hurriedly knock the paint scrapings off my clothes and hands before running downstairs to answer it. It's Mel. I take a deep breath.

'We've got a date for the Matching Panel – 8 December. And we've arranged your first meeting with Jaymey and Harlee for a week after that.'

'Before Christmas...'

'You could meet the children several times before and then they would be placed with you after Christmas.'

'What will the Matching Panel involve?'

'I represent you and Rob, and Lorna represents the children. The panel will ask any questions they have but it should be a formality. All the paperwork is in place. So, happy Christmas. I bet you've never had a present like this before.'

'I can't believe in three weeks we'll be matched.'

'You need to prepare a scrapbook that can be given to the children before they meet you. With pictures of the two of you, your house, perhaps the children's bedrooms and extended family. Anything you can think of really to introduce yourselves. And make them colourful.'

I ring Rob straightaway and he is as excited and nervous as I am. There doesn't seem to be anything that could go wrong now, but I still can't feel unbridled happiness, just in case. I get back to the scraping. These bedrooms might have little occupants very soon.

Lorna rings and we have a strange, stilted conversation. She is chattier than she was during her visit here and it takes me a while to adjust. She wants to give me lots more information about the children, information that doesn't fit into any forms. I am immediately aware that soon after the children are placed with us, Lorna will be out of our lives and this information will go with her. There is so much that I have to find a pen and scribble some notes. Some situations frighten Jaymey: he is not comfortable with noisy groups of children and he can be scared of men. Both children have spent a significant amount of time restrained in cars and cots. The two older siblings are very damaged and now in specialised care. Then an incident that she rattles through but that catches me in the pit of my stomach. During a supervised contact session with Jaymey, Harlee and the older children at a family centre, one of the social workers asked the birth mother, Trudy, to supervise her children more and not leave it to the social workers. Despite the older children being out of control, Trudy singled out Jaymey for strong discipline. Lorna says that Jaymey stood still in the middle of the mayhem and silent tears rolled down his expressionless face. He was not comforted by his mother. I picture his face from the photograph we have of him. I think of other children I know who cry big, loud, open-mouthed tears. What has happened to this child that has taught him to cry in silence?

*****

'Been shopping? I hope you got yourself something lovely.'

'I got *us* something lovely; two scrapbooks, two rolls of wrapping paper, one with cars on and one with lollipops on, some glue, some stickers and a Bob the Builder comic. I thought we could make up the books for Jaymey and Harlee.'

It had felt strange looking for these things in the newsagents and the bookshop. I hadn't been quite sure where to find stickers and had had to ask and I dithered over paper suitable for a one-year-old and a four-year-old. It had struck me that I don't know what Jaymey and Harlee like – that I don't know them at all. It has made me more nervous about meeting them, worried that I won't be able to make a connection with them, won't know what to say to them.

The books that will introduce us to our children come together: photographs of us on holiday, at work, our house, a family party, some pictures from the Bob the Builder comic and the wrapping paper. I write in black felt-tip pen 'Mummy', 'Daddy', 'your new cousins', 'Granddad David', 'Granny and Granddad on holiday', 'your new house', 'your new bedroom'. Our future.

*****

On the day of the Matching Panel I am at work pruning the apple trees in the orchard and making a bonfire with the prunings. It is a job we all enjoy – light work and a bonfire always brings us together. After work we are going to the pub for our Christmas meal and I am hoping that I will be able to celebrate being matched with the children. Mel is going to ring Rob as soon as the panel has finished and Rob will then leave a message on the garden office phone for me to ring him. I am relieved to be working with Andy, Jon and Dean today; we chat and joke about arrangements for the evening. We work through the trees in pairs and I am paired with Andy. We have to acquaint ourselves with each tree, its shape and how it fruits. Each presents like a puzzle to be worked through with patience, and with each unwanted branch that is pruned the beauty of the tree reveals itself. Jon and Dean don't like the look of the pruned trees, find them too severe, but I love the clean, blunt shapes and the promise of spring blossom and autumn fruit. After a while we are all subsumed by the trees we are working on and continue silently. Before long it is break time and we stock up the fire with prunings and head back to the bothy for a cup of tea. I drop behind and manage to look into the office, no message from Rob. It is probably too early to hear anything. I do the same at lunchtime and again there is no message. Despite doing my best to keep my mind on work in the afternoon I cannot stop worrying about the matching. By three o'clock I decide I have to ring Rob. He says he hasn't heard from Mel. He sounds concerned but tries to hide it: 'Don't worry, it'll be fine.'

The rest of the afternoon is torture. I can't think about anything else and cold feelings of dread wash over me. I replay Mel's reassurances over and over and I know everything ought to be fine but if it is, why hasn't she rung?

We pack up and Andy and Dean head off to put the vehicles back in the sheds. I walk across the lawns and up the path with Jon and make an excuse to go into the office. My hands are shaking as I ring Rob's number.

'Just tell me, before I have a mental breakdown.'

'It wasn't a problem with us, or the children. Bloody Lorna hadn't updated Jaymey or Harlee's paperwork so the panel refused to hear the matching. They've given her a week to do the updates and another panel has been arranged for two weeks' time.'

I know I shouldn't feel devastated because this is a delay and not a 'no' but I am shattered; I can't think of anything to say to Rob. I hunch over the desk and rest my head in my hands.

'Look, it'll be fine, we just have to wait a bit longer.'

'I can't believe it.'

'That *bloody* Lorna. The paperwork was out of date when we read it and that was weeks ago.'

'We won't be meeting Jaymey and Harlee before Christmas now.'

Rob rings off and I can't move. I close my eyes and listen to the tone of the empty telephone. Out of control is how I am – reliant on forms and gatherings of people I don't know and phone calls. And now Christmas is in the fucking way. Everything will stop and I'm going to have to endure another claustrophobic forced festivity without having met our children.

*****

Mum and my nephew Harry both have December birthdays and so Rob and I invite my family over for tea. I have shopped for a cake and a big number three candle, and made jellies and bought ice cream. Alice rang beforehand to check that I was in a fit mental state to have them all over. I told her that I need distracting, and a birthday party with a three-year-old and a six-year-old would probably do the job very well. Jaymey and Harlee's bedrooms are finished now and I am keen to show them off with their new carpets and checked curtains, Jaymey's wild animal duvet set and Harlee's rabbit cot covers. I am proud of these rooms but I can hardly bear to look into them now for fearing that they will never be occupied – that they will become little memorials to children never known. The birthday party is fun and Luke and Harry utterly wear me out. I am left wondering if the special kind of energy that my sister has – the sort that has to keep coming all day to deal with toilet visits, spilt drinks, wiping, playing, crying – will ever come to me.

*****

The second Matching Panel is successful. This time I make sure I am working at home that day and Mel rings me in the middle of the morning.

'The panel were unanimous and think that you and the children are a great match for each other.'

I feel relieved but still raw.

'And what about the Freeing Order? Has that been heard yet?' There's a pause. 'I didn't think the children could be placed with us without it?'

Mel explains, 'It appears they can and the legal people and the social workers think there is such a small probability the Freeing Order won't go through that they want to go ahead with the placement. They think it's in the interests of the children to be placed as soon as possible. But you and Rob need to agree and understand that if a relative decides to take them, then you will have to give them back.'

'And how come this has only come to light now?' I am angry, but I know it's not Mel's fault.

'Take some time to think about whether you want to take the children now, or whether you want to wait until the Freeing Order is in place.'

It doesn't sound like much of a choice.

Rob and I talk well into the night; going over and over the options and occasionally letting our frustrations spill out. Despite pretending to really consider not taking the children now and waiting until all the legalities have been tidied up, we both know what we need to do.

'You know my feelings about Lorna,' says Rob, yawning, 'and there's a whole other bureaucratic machine out there that we have no control over.'

'What do you want to do, have the children now, or wait?' We have thrown this around for long enough and we need to reach a conclusion.

'Take them now,' says Rob.

'So do I.'

The next morning I ring Mel and she sounds pleased and relieved. She asks me to get my diary out.

'We've got a firm date for the introductions, the first working day back after New Year, which is,' she pauses and I can hear her turning pages, 'the fourth of January. We'll start with a short meeting that you and the foster carers attend, plus me and Lorna and our managers. We have to do some paperwork, agree which days you will see the children and then the date that they will move in with you. The meeting will take place at Jaymey's foster carers' so you will meet him straight after the formalities are done. Then you can drive over to Harlee's foster carers' home and meet her.'

I write the meeting in my diary and then flick back to today. Two weeks lie between the dates and in the middle of them is Christmas.

'When do you think the children might move in with us permanently?'

'If the introductions go well, a fortnight after you meet them. We don't like to drag it out – children get very unsettled by the uncertainty.'

I can't take on the information, the actuality. I glance into the near future and it seems distant and unreal, like someone else's future.

'If during the introductions you feel that you're not going to bond with the children, you must tell me. It is in everyone's interests that you tell me.'

We say our goodbyes and wish each other a happy Christmas.

*****

Rob comes home from work on Christmas Eve with a carrier bag from a toyshop. He puts it on the kitchen table.

'Christmas presents. A green tractor for Jaymey and a yellow rabbit for Harlee.'

He looks proud and I know that this is his way of marking the little bit of a bond that is forming between a new father and his children. We take the toys upstairs and put the soft, yellow rabbit in the corner of Harlee's cot and the green tractor on Jaymey's bookshelf. They are the only toys in each of the silent bedrooms. It feels like we have performed some kind of ritual.

PART 4

In the Family Way

Early Days

CHAPTER 7

Monday

The church bells ring out two o'clock, three o'clock, then I give in to the insomnia and read for a while, hoping the change of mental scenery will unstick my anxious mind. When a fitful sleep eventually washes over, I have panic-filled dreams about turning up late at the wrong exam hall, having forgotten to revise calculus, and opening an exam paper full of calculus questions. When the clock radio comes on, the familiar sound of confrontation on the Today programme pushes aside the dreams and I realise I have a sore throat. I take a shower but the hot water fails to soothe the shivering and jittering. This is it: the day when our children's paths finally converge with ours and start to bind together, when we set eyes upon each other – unfamiliar faces that will become so deeply familiar in time. This day has stood out in the distance, like a finishing post, but now that we are in sight of it, a whole other landscape stretches out ahead. At every step the social workers have made it clear that if we feel the connection with the children isn't there, then we must be honest – tell them that things aren't working. Better that the children are let down early on, rather than once they have moved in, settled in, started bonding. We must try not to add to their already long list of broken attachments. No matter how hard things get, we are not letting go of these children now. I am nevertheless dragged down by a feeling of dread that they won't take to us, that they will hide behind a sofa and refuse to come out when they see us, that they will cry when we come near them. Maybe they will refuse to do anything we say and we will have no control. I try to imagine what they are both doing right now, eating breakfast out of plastic bowls, getting a wash, cleaning teeth and I wonder whether they have any understanding at all that they are about to come face to face with new parents and that in just two weeks' time they will be moving to a new home with these strangers. I am terrified for myself and terrified for them. I don't know how to care for two small children, full time. I don't know what they eat, what they like to play; I don't know how to get them ready for bed; I'm not sure that I even know how to talk to small children. They are going to be left in the hands of an amateur.

The drive to Jaymey's foster carers' home goes horribly quickly and as we find the house, in the quiet cul-de-sac, and park in the street, my heart beats hard and adrenaline unsteadies my hands. A small, blue scooter rests against a garage door. Rob rings the bell and we stand on the doorstep, shivery and scared. Mel opens the door, smiling and welcoming, and breezes us into the sitting room, which is jammed with people sitting in a circle on all manner of different chairs, sofas, stools and garden furniture. A small middle-aged man with grey hair and glasses comes towards us and offers me his hand.

'You must be Sally and Rob. I'm Bill, Jaymey's foster carer, and this is Thelma, my wife.' He ushers me to the tall, dark-haired lady sitting next to him, who also comes forward and we shake hands.

We are standing in the centre of the room. All eyes are upon us. Mel indicates a small space on the sofa. Rob sits at the end and I wedge myself between him and Mel. A small, dark, mousey-looking woman holding a clipboard and a chewed biro sits opposite. She smiles benignly at us, like a vicar to his flock.

'Rob and Sally,' she says, 'welcome to this Practical Arrangements Meeting. This will take about half an hour, after which Bill will collect Jaymey from his pre-school and you will meet him. Then you will go to Harlee's foster home and meet her there. Now, this meeting is a legal requirement and we have certain forms that we have to complete. First I will introduce you to everyone here.'

She goes around the circle. There is Mel, who of course we already know and we all share a little collective laugh at that, which dissolves a bit of the awkwardness. Next to her is her boss, a slight man in a purple polyester shirt with a darker purple polyester tie. Then there is Lorna and the woman speaking is Lorna's boss. Last we are introduced to Harlee's foster carers, who smile.

'Right, now that is done,' says the mousey lady with the clipboard, 'could I have your full names and address, please?'

Rob's body tenses up and he lets out an audible sigh of disbelief. I know exactly what he is thinking – could they not have copied this information out from the myriad of other documents that have our names and address on? But we have to continue to play the game, like good people, for a while longer, so I answer in my best smiley, polite way. Then we are given badly photocopied forms to sign.

We get our diaries out and arrange visits with the children plus two nights when they will stay over with us. We plan to see them at mealtimes, at bedtimes, for toddler groups and trips to the park. We are asked to try to think of places we can take them and then are given a long list of locations that will now be out of bounds to us because of the proximity of one member of the birth family or another. Finally we calculate the date when the children will be permanently placed with us. It is two weeks and one day from today. In that time we have one free day. Rob has two weeks of paternity leave and we have decided to try to reserve this for when the children move in with us. So during this fortnight of introductions he is still meant to be at work. We are both lucky that he has a sympathetic boss.

The meeting ends and the social workers leave in a bustle of paperwork and folders. We are left in the house with the four foster carers. Thelma and Bill offer us tea and sympathise with how overwhelming this all is, then Bill leaves to collect Jaymey. Harlee's foster carers are Philip and Kim. They hold back initially and then once we are left alone, approach us and shake hands and congratulate us. They give us directions to their home, another half an hour from here, and offer to give us lunch there.

'It's annoying having to sit and go through the paperwork when all I expect you want to do is meet the children,' says Philip.

'We're used to all that now,' says Rob, sensing he has met a man after his own heart.

'Well, you're going to love Harlee. She's such a sweet thing, full of energy, into everything,' he says.

'Into *absolutely* everything,' laughs Kim.

We shake hands again and joke that we are going to be seeing a lot of each other over the next fortnight. They leave and Thelma appears with two cups of tea.

'You'll be needing these, I expect. Such a big day for you. Jaymey has been looking at the scrapbook you made him and is so excited to meet you.'

She has a gentle, quiet manner. A nice lady. She has looked after Jaymey for a year and a half – has been the most consistent presence in his life.

'It must be difficult to open up your house like this,' I venture.

'We don't normally have to host quite so many people,' she laughs, 'but we're glad that Jaymey will be getting a permanent home. We're so fond of him. He's a lovely, lovely boy.'

She looks down into her tea and blinks back tears. Wrapped so tightly in our own drama, I hadn't given her situation a thought. She has taken this child into her home, cared for him, grown close to him and now has to hand him over to someone else.

'I'm sorry,' she says, getting a tissue from her sleeve. 'I'm happy for Jaymey, I really am and you both seem really nice.'

'Have you fostered many children?' asks Rob.

'Yes, we've been fostering for about 15 years now. There are some photographs of some of the children over there on the bookcase.'

By the window, squeezed on to three shelves are lots of happy faces – older children, younger ones, some smiling carefully for the school photographer, one on a swing, a few holiday snaps taken at the seaside. All these lives have passed through this house.

A car pulls up.

'That will be Bill and Jaymey,' says Thelma, throwing me a smile.

She goes out to meet them. My hands start to shake again and my heart thumps in my throat. I hear little footsteps, running on the concrete drive.

'Jaymey, let's just take your shoes off.'

Quiet, then, 'Where they? Where they?' and a small face appears around the door and then a little hand clutching a small tractor and then a little boy stands at the threshold. His eyes flick between us. He looks so much smaller than I was expecting, rounder, more gorgeous. His dimpled cheeks are carried up by a slight smile.

We remain seated, not wanting to overwhelm him with our height.

'Hello, Jaymey,' I say.

'You Mumally?' he asks.

'Yes I…yes I am, I'm Mum Sally.'

'And you Daddy Football?' he says to Rob.

Rob looks blank.

'He's been calling you Daddy Football,' says Thelma, 'he's seen a picture of you in a football strip in his scrapbook.'

'Yes, I'm Daddy Football,' says Rob, 'what have you got there?'

Jaymey says a few words, which neither of us can make out, and then passes Rob the tractor.

'That's great. I bet it can lift lots of heavy things.'

Jaymey runs over to the corner of the room to where a wooden castle has been set up. It has battlements, a drawbridge and a trebuchet that can lob plastic boulders over the castle walls. He picks up one of the boulders, runs back to Rob and gives it to him. He issues instructions and then turns to me.

'You ee dat? You ee dat?' he says, pointing at his castle.

'Do you want to show me your castle?' I ask.

His small, soft hand takes mine and leads me. Our first touch. He indicates that I should get down on the floor and then he shows me how to fire the trebuchet, pulling it back against the elastic band and firing the boulder. Each time he fires it he laughs and glances at me to check if I laugh too. When I do, it makes him laugh more, as though he is allowed. Then he jumps up, runs back to Rob, grabs the boulder back from him, runs back to me, gives me the boulder and says, 'You go.'

I set the boulder in the trebuchet and let it go. I do it cack-handedly and it fires in the wrong direction. Jaymey laughs, looking at me.

'Again, again?' he says.

I fire it and again it goes off in the wrong direction. He giggles, shakes his head in mock disbelief at my incompetence and collects up the boulders. Despite his young age, his humour shines out of him.

'I owe you,' he says and repeats it again and again when he sees my look of puzzlement.

Bill, who has quietly come into the room, rescues me, 'That's it, you show Mum Sally how to do it.'

Later Bill suggests that we all go into the garden so that Jaymey can show us his football. We kick the ball around and Jaymey suddenly gallops off shouting something. He picks up a plastic spade and starts digging in the cold, wet soil. I watch him. His hair seems darker than it was in the photographs and has grown around his ears and been cut into a little boy's haircut. His brown, deeply set eyes are fringed by long, elegant eyelashes. He smiles at me and I notice his bottom front teeth are gappy and misaligned, where one is missing. Under his right eye is a long, silvery scar.

'You dig, Mumally.' He offers me his yellow spade.

I bend down next to him, take the spade and dig away making a small hole.

'Where's that Daddy Football gone?' I ask him.

Jaymey looks around, sees Rob playing keepy-uppy and runs to join in. I see Thelma through the kitchen window, washing up the mugs, and go inside and join her.

'He has a lovely sense of fun.'

'Oh he does, he has such a good sense of humour and a twinkle in his eyes,' she smiles. 'And he's sociable, he likes to be around people.'

As I dry the mugs, we get to know each other a little, chat about ourselves.

'There's quite a lot of information that Bill and I need to give you over the next fortnight, not the things that are recorded in the documentation, but the small things – what Jaymey likes to eat, his favourite television programmes and then there's his speech therapy and so on. Have you found him difficult to understand?'

'Well yes, but I'm sure I'll tune in.'

'He's had a few speech therapy sessions, but we've waited months for an appointment. I'll give you the reports.'

I thank her and we carry on washing and drying cups silently for a while. Thelma seems to be preparing to tell me something.

'We think he's spent an awful lot of time either on his own or with his older siblings, so his language hasn't been able to develop normally. He doesn't seem to have any relationship with Mum, he never talks about her and she often doesn't turn up to their contact sessions.'

'And does that upset him?'

'He has never talked about anything that has happened to him, but he is always upset before and after a contact with Mum. He's not upset in that he cries; he gets very angry and a bit aggressive.'

'And what about the siblings, how does he feel about them?'

'Again, he doesn't seem to have a strong connection; in fact he appears to be quite scared of them. They've been allowed to run wild and play rough.'

I make a bland, inadequate statement about how awful this is and then feel guilty.

'We've kept photographs and taken some video of Jaymey's time here, which we can give you. But he came here with very little – a few clothes and that was all. There are no baby photographs that I know of, no mementos. Sometimes the birth family will put together a book or a memory box for the child, but Jaymey hasn't got anything like that.'

At that moment the door flings open and Jaymey is standing there crying, holding out his thumb.

'Hurt, hurt,' he says urgently.

Thelma is straight to him, bends down and calmly comforts him. 'That must have hurt, young man, let's have a look, would you like a plaster?' Jaymey is immediately soothed by the mention of the word 'plaster'.

'Bob, Bob,' he says through little sobby gulps.

'Shall I put on a Bob the Builder plaster?'

This little tradition has clearly been played out many times over the past 18 months. I wonder what will happen the first time Jaymey hurts himself at our house. Will he wish for Thelma and will I ever be able to fill her shoes?

*****

An hour later we pull up outside Philip and Kim's stone cottage and sit quietly for a moment. The house is in a small, sparse village and set back from the road and into the hillside. Water drips off the trees and runs across the tarmac. Further down the hill is a river bridge. The sound of water racing over stones and through bowed branches gives this place a faraway feel. It is not in a part of the county we have ever visited and it is not on the way anywhere.

'Are you ready for the next one?' says Rob.

'Come on then.'

Philip and Kim are at the door as we walk up the steep slope. They seem much more relaxed than they were at the meeting and happy to see us. We are welcomed in and offered more tea.

'What a big day for you. You must be exhausted already. Let me get Harlee, she's in the room next door playing with the cat.'

We sit awkwardly like Victorian parents waiting for the nanny to present the child. I look around the room. The furniture has been moved around to block access to a wood basket, a video player and CD cabinet with a fireguard. Eventually Harlee is coaxed into the room, on unsteady legs in lilac tights. She takes a look at us and stops, open-eyed, and then her bottom hits the ground as her legs give way with the surprise of seeing two strangers in her sitting room.

'This is your new Mummy and Daddy,' says Kim.

'Hello, Harlee,' we both say.

I hold out my hand to her but she looks away.

'Are you feeling shy?' says Kim to Harlee. 'She used to go straight to anyone when she first came to us, so this is a big improvement,' she says.

Harlee crawls over to the other sofa and pulls herself up, takes a small toy that Philip holds out to her and puts it in her mouth. She looks at Rob and me warily and then staggers over to the fireguard, slots her little fingers through the holes and shakes the guard vigorously so it rattles.

'Harlee, no, come and see what I've got here,' says Kim.

Harlee is not to be so easily diverted and gives the guard another shake. The guard tips and she falls backwards, hitting her head on the carpet. I expect her to cry but she pushes herself up on to her feet and walks to Kim to investigate the toy she is holding out. Her hair is thicker and longer than in the photographs and less curly. She has paler skin than Jaymey and she is rounder and chubbier.

Rob asks Harlee what she has. She holds up some plastic keys. He gets his car keys from his pocket and holds them out, letting them jangle. Harlee looks interested for a moment and then turns back to Kim.

I move from the sofa to the floor and put my mug down next to me on the carpet. Harlee spots the mug, drops her plastic keys and is over to me so quickly I barely have time to remove it. Philip and Kim are both amused.

'You can't put anything down, or leave anything out when Harlee is around. She started walking from the first day she came here and she hasn't stopped since,' says Philip.

'We've had lots of toddlers here and we've never had to barricade the video and the stereo in before,' adds Kim.

I do a mental circuit around our sitting room, the tower of CDs, the open television cabinet, the framed photographs on the low shelves.

Kim goes into the kitchen to make lunch for us all and I reach for a stack of plastic cups and take them apart. I reconstruct half the stack as Harlee watches every move that I make. I give her the next cup in the sequence. She looks at me suspiciously, but comes closer and takes it, drops it on the stack and it collapses. We all make a big fun noise out of the toppling and I start rebuilding. Again, I give her a cup and this time she takes it and I help her put it on the tower. After it wobbles but stays up, we all clap and say, 'Well done, Harlee,' and she smiles. Rob joins us on the floor and Harlee hands him a cup and then another and another. She knocks over the tower again and we cheer.

Kim calls us all into the dining room. Harlee is there first, reaching up her arms and trying to climb into her high chair. I lift her in and as soon as she sees her plate of finger food on the table she reaches out her arms and starts to shout. She can barely wait to be strapped in. Kim puts a few pieces of breadstick and some half grapes into a bowl. Harlee, arms outstretched, continues to shout.

'OK, Harlee, it's coming, it's coming.'

The bowl is placed on the tray of the high chair. Harlee is into it straightaway. She picks up a half grape in each hand and puts them both into her mouth at the same time. Then she pushes in a piece of breadstick and another. Her mouth is full and yet she hurriedly puts in another grape. She barely chews and then swallows great lumps of food down, just before more goes in. As her bowl becomes empty she shouts again and Kim replenishes it. The same hurried, anxious eating continues. Kim fills the bowl with grated cheese and gives Harlee a small plastic spoon to eat it with. The spoon gets dropped on the floor and Harlee puts great fistfuls of the cheese into her mouth. Eventually she is down to the last few strands and her little fingers struggle to pick each one up individually. We chat around the table and eat our cheese rolls. I see her eyeing up my plate, watching every mouthful that I take, so I break off a piece of bread and give it to her. She puts it in her mouth and instantly reaches out for another piece.

'This is just like feeding the ducks,' I laugh.

'Wack, wack,' she replies.

*****

At home we ring our family and friends and share the details of our new children: the funny things they did and said, how sweet they looked, how adorable they are and how busy we are going to be over the next fortnight. No one can quite believe how soon they will be moving in with us. We receive free parenting advice from some: don't spoil the children, all they will need from you is love and they will soon settle in, show them who's in charge right from the start. We make bland noises of non-committal agreement and remember all the professional advice we've been given, which sounds nothing like this. Then Rob and I sit together, collapsed on the sofa. The day washes into me and over me. I feel like a dreamy version of myself, in a strange parallel world. If I woke up to find I had dreamt about the room full of social workers on their ill-matching furniture, about meeting children in strangers' homes, then I wouldn't be at all surprised. There is so little normality to anchor to, no points of reference.

'Go to bed Sally, you look awful. I'll bring you up a hot lemon,' says Rob.

I give in and lie in bed, unable to read, unable to sleep. My mind goes over and over the day. When I think about the coming fortnight, sudden shocks go through my stomach.

Tuesday

The following morning my mum rings.

'Did you sleep alright?' she asks.

'Yes, on and off.'

'I was just wondering and I know it's not at the top of your priority list, but when do you think your dad and I might get to meet the children? I realise that they need to settle in with you first.'

'As soon as the introductions are over, I would think.'

'See how it goes, but that would be lovely. I'm looking forward to meeting them so much, my new grandchildren.'

*****

At Bill and Thelma's house lunch is laid out on the table in the conservatory. I cast my eyes across the selection and wonder if Jaymey's food is coming out separately. He hurries us all up and shows us where he wants us to sit. He puts himself between Thelma and me and opposite Rob. Straightaway he is pointing at things and helping himself. His plate fills up with cherry tomatoes, pickled beetroot and onions, quiche and coleslaw.

'I like beetroot,' he says with gusto, stabbing a piece with a Bob the Builder fork.

I watch with wonderment as he eats everything and then helps himself to more. I think of excruciating mealtimes I have shared with friends' children who pick away at crisps and little cubes of cheese whilst their mothers forgo their own food to beg them to eat a carrot stick or a sliver of cucumber ('but you love cucumber, show Sally how you can eat cucumber'). If your four-year-old will eat a whole cherry tomato washed down with coleslaw and topped with a pickled onion, then I imagine that is really something to brag about.

'You like beetroot?' Jaymey asks me.

'I love beetroot – it's one of my favourites.'

'Me too. I love beetroot.'

He smiles and nods approvingly, as though I have passed another test. Next he eats an apricot yoghurt with noticeable bits in and then Thelma asks him to go to the toilet before we go to the park.

'*No!*' he stamps.

'Come on, we're going to the park in a minute.'

'*No!*'

Thelma grabs his hand and hurries him away complaining.

A jagged, cold wind cuts through everything and the sky is a dead grey. The park is bleak and muddy. Jaymey runs from swings to slide to swings to climbing frame and demands that I follow him around. Then he watches some older boys skateboarding on a ramp. Once they've gone, Rob and Jaymey roll the football from one end of the ramp to the other. When it is time to go I introduce the idea in an upbeat, sing-song voice. 'Come on, Jaymey, time to go now.'

'*No!*'

'Maybe we could have a drink when we get back.'

'*No.*'

He runs off. Thelma goes after him, takes his hand and brings him back, and we walk home.

Wednesday

We arrive at Kim and Philip's house in time to put Harlee to bed for her afternoon sleep. I worry that Kim will expect me to know far more than I do about nappies, wipes and bedtimes and that I will finally be revealed as a fraud. But she is patient, explains everything from how to undress Harlee, to how to deal with a dirty nappy, and the best nappies, wipes, nappy sacks to buy. Throughout this lesson, Harlee lies on her mat with both her fists in her mouth. Her eyes flit around, sometimes fixing on me, sometimes not.

'Do you want to carry her upstairs?' says Kim.

I would love to. I have not wanted to come into this situation and upset the balance between Kim and Harlee – not wanted to appear pushy – but also not wanted to seem distant and unwilling. I lift her off the mat and sit her in the crook of my arm. Her body rests against mine and she puts her hand on my shoulder. I put my other hand on her waist and jiggle her a bit. She looks worried and reaches out for Kim, keeping her gaze firmly on her. Kim walks next to us, up the stairs, reassuring Harlee. We go into the tiny bedroom, which Harlee shares with one of Kim and Philip's daughters. I put her awkwardly into the cot, dropping her the last few centimetres. Kim says, 'night night,' confidently and without fuss, and we leave the bedroom. I hear a bit of movement and some snuffling and then silence.

'Well, that seemed quite easy,' I venture.

'Yes, she sleeps well now, but it's taken some sleep training to get to this point.'

I want to sound knowledgeable about sleep training, but I'm not. I've sat in on endless conversations between friends – obsessing almost about their child's sleep, boasting about how much or moaning about how little – and I've heard enough to know that sleep training appears to be one of the most contentious child-rearing issues that there is. If you sleep train your child you are either looked upon, at the one extreme, as a mother-dictator and at the other extreme as a no-fuss, no-nonsense parent who understands the value of sleep. If you don't sleep train then maybe you are a relaxed mother-earth type or maybe you are indulgent and out of control and will be sharing your bed with your teenage children if you do not get a grip. I wonder where I will find myself on this spectrum of opinion.

'When Harlee first arrived here, she screamed and went rigid every time she saw the cot. She was frightened of it. She had been left alone in a cot for such long periods, that for her it was a place of fear and loneliness.'

I don't know what to say.

'She screamed for hours through the night, kept us all awake,' she laughed.

'So how did you get her to sleep through, in such a short time?'

'I kept going in to her, holding her hand, stroking her forehead, talking a bit. And she shares a room with my daughter, so she comforted her through the night as well. As Harlee settled in more, we let her cry for longer and longer periods and after maybe a week, she was sleeping through the night.'

'Isn't there lots of debate about sleep training though?' I ask.

'Not in this house. If I don't sleep, if my family don't, then we can't be good foster carers – Philip can't function at work, it's as simple as that. And you saw how easily Harlee went to sleep just now – no tears, no upset. I'm then free to do the laundry, the cleaning, to speak to our social worker, to start preparing our evening meal. I can't do any of that when she's awake.'

I feel as though Kim might be someone I can anchor to.

Friday

Rob goes to work and I go with Jaymey and Thelma to their local toddler group. The three of us get into Thelma's battered, white Peugeot. Jaymey wants me to sit in the back with him and he chatters about how much he likes watching the bin men empty the bins into their lorry. We park outside an old, red-brick church hall. It is raining and cold, and mothers hurry their children inside, heads down. Some push prams with plastic rain covers on, little feet poking out from underneath. The hall is huge and peeling, and smells of damp, dust and old books. Women – they are all women, most of them much younger than me – sit around the outside of the hall on plastic chairs, chatting in small groups. The children – maybe 40 of them – race around on scooters, trikes and plastic tractors. Jaymey immediately spots a free tractor and claims it. An older lady, who looks like the playgroup leader, approaches Thelma and me. We are introduced and the lady shakes my hand and says how pleased she is for Jaymey. I feel some of the chatting around the room subsiding and the attention switching to us. Thelma, Jaymey and I don't fit the standard family model that most of the mums are part of, by some way. The lady leaves us and we stand awkwardly for a while. Then it is time to find our children and take them to the painting table. I look across the sea of heads, all darting around, changing direction, running, pedalling, chasing. Magically, from out of the crowd one little head, crowned with auburn curls, as though a spotlight were on him, stands out. He is mine. I am like an emperor penguin, hearing the call of my chick, over the calls of all the other chicks. I glance to Thelma and she indicates that I should take Jaymey. I walk through the crowd of children.

'Jaymey, shall we do some painting?'

He stops what he is doing. Takes my hand and leads me to the painting table.

That afternoon I arrive back home, go to the fridge and my To Do list, stuck to the door with an 'I Love Vancouver' fridge magnet, meets my eyes accusingly. I slouch in front of the television, eat a peanut butter sandwich and drink tea from my big, comfort mug. I feel paralysed, emotional, hormonal, but with a growing feeling of warm satisfaction. I think I may be bonding.

Monday

We met our children a week ago and in a week's time they will be in our care, not legally ours but one step closer to it. Essentially, I become a mother next Tuesday. When I walk to the post office or put the bins out my neighbours would not see any outward indication of this. If they looked closely into my eyes, maybe they would see something in my expression – a manic bewilderment, with a dash of exhaustion and a splash of happiness. Nothing that would indicate what was coming though. There is a certain convenience to looking like a mother-to-be, sporting a pregnant body. People will stop and say 'How lovely,' and ask, 'When is the baby due?' It spreads the news organically and prepares everyone for the arrival of the new baby. I resolve that starting with our next-door neighbour, Jean, I will have to tour the neighbourhood and phone the outermost circle of our friends and colleagues, to spread our news before the children arrive. Rob squeezes in a morning's work and then we head off to collect Jaymey and Harlee for their first overnight stay. We are both looking forward to seeing them in our own home but worried that the children will be scared of spending a night in a strange house, with two relative strangers.

Jaymey is nowhere to be seen when we arrive. By the front door is a small overnight bag with some cars on the top. Then he runs down the stairs holding a large, stuffed Bob the Builder, who sports a Velcro tool belt. He tries to pick up his bag, 'We go now?'

We laugh. I am relieved.

Harlee is dressed up in her best pink corduroy pinafore dress. She walks straight to me and holds out a toy. She smells luscious and sweet as I carry her to the car. She seems pleased to see Jaymey. He is less so, gathering his toys around him, out of her reach.

The journey is tense and long. After about 20 minutes our passengers get restless. Harlee is far more attracted by Jaymey's toys than her own and he whisks them away from her, while she squawks her disapproval. Harlee has shared toys with another foster child, a few months older, who was adopted recently. Since being in care, Jaymey has not had to share with anyone.

The first sight of their new home is less important to them than a tussle over a plastic horse. We prise the horse out of a tight fist and Rob carries Harlee into the house. I take Jaymey. He holds my hand tight. I relish the touch. He looks up to the top of the house.

'See that window there?' I point. 'That's your new bedroom.'

He opens his eyes wide.

'Shall we go and see it?'

He picks up speed, racing up the steps. Once inside he points to his shoes and looks at me pleadingly.

'You don't need to take them off yet.'

I open the stair gate and he races up the stairs on hands and feet. He stops on the landing and waits for me to show him the way.

'This is Harlee's room and this is yours.'

I open the door to reveal the crisp, matching blue bed linen, the new teddy sitting against the pillow, the blue checked curtains, the bookshelf with two or three new books on and the green tractor that Rob had bought him for Christmas. To one side of the bookshelf is a large, wooden toy box with a hinged lid.

'Granny and Granddad made you this, to put all your toys in.'

He opens the lid and looks inside.

'Is empty,' he says.

'Well we need to fill it up then. When you come here next week, it will be forever. You can bring all your toys with you.'

'And Thelma come too.'

That night Rob and I sleep a strange half sleep, as though semi-conscious, half listening out for sounds, feeling the weight of responsibility for these two children heavily. I wake with a shock. My eyes open and Jaymey is standing over me, his face inches from mine.

'Good morning,' I manage.

'Me, drink, now, peas.'

It is a quarter to six.

Tuesday

After we take the children back, we phone my parents, Rob's dad and some friends and report back on the overnight stay.

'Well? How did it go?' says my mum.

'Better than we thought. They both slept all night, they ate well, we all played together. It was great.'

'I can't wait to meet them.'

'I know. It won't be long now.'

Wednesday

The snowdrops flower amongst great, green bunches of leaves, and daffodils barely show through the thin grass in the lane outside Kim and Philip's cottage. The wet, cold winter has smothered the spring in grey. We take Harlee for a walk in her pushchair. She happily burbles and plays with a toy. I chat to her – look at the stream; see the birds, up in that tall tree; let's go through the puddle. She is quiet but looking everywhere. She spots a dog in a garden, points, strains against the straps of the pushchair and woofs at the dog. It is a strange gruff noise, which makes us laugh. Rob stops the pushchair and I bend down to her.

'Do you like dogs?'

'Wu wu wu wu wu wu.'

Saturday

The second sleepover goes smoothly. Both children make themselves at home immediately in a way that would appear rude if they were adults, but is so heartening. Harlee is happy and easygoing. There are a few battles over toys. Jaymey arranges his cars in neat rows, which she walks through and over, squashing and scattering. We take them to the park and follow them around lifting them on and off swings, standing at the bottom of the slide, pretending we can't see Jaymey when he hides. When it is time to go, Jaymey protests and refuses to move. He looks tired.

'Would you like me to carry you for a little bit?'

He slowly walks over to me, puts up his arms and then jumps up and wraps his legs around me. He clings to me and it feels delicious – to be needed, to be first in line. As we walk back to the car park the clouds come in a dark black grey and it starts to hail. Within seconds the hail is blowing into our faces and stinging our cheeks. Harlee and Jaymey both scream. Rob wrestles the plastic hood of the pushchair down and Harlee settles. Jaymey nestles into my neck but the hail still lashes at his ears and neck. I undo my coat and pull it from around my body, so I can cocoon Jaymey in part of it. He hangs on to me so tightly it hurts. The hailstorm ends as quickly as it had begun, just as we reach the car. Both children marvel at the layer of hailstones on the ground, the size of petit pois. They pad their feet up and down.

'Hurting no,' says Jamey.

I take a second to work out what he has said.

'Yes, hurting snow. Naughty snow.'

Sunday

Jaymey pretends not to see Kim and Philip's car outside our house and carries on playing. They stay for a while and we return a little bit of the hospitality that they have shown us over the past fortnight. Harlee goes straight to Kim and takes her to show off her new bedroom. Jaymey barely looks at anyone. Then when it is time to go, Rob carries the overnight bags into the car.

'We'll see you on Tuesday, when you come here again, forever. Do you want to leave a toy here?'

'Not Bob. Cars.'

'I'll put them in your new toy box for you and they will be here waiting for you to come back.'

'Me stay here with you now,' he says, with a note of hope in his voice.

'You're going to go to Bill and Thelma's now, with Kim. And we'll see you in two sleeps.'

I lead him to the car and he starts to cry. As I lift him in he clings on to me and won't let go. He starts to scream and the sound grabs me. He looks pleadingly at me through red, streaming eyes and it is all I can do not to cry too. I have to force him into the car seat, his body rigid, his arms reaching out to me. He doesn't understand what is happening. I remember some chocolate snowmen in the cupboard, left over from Christmas.

'Jaymey, would you like a sweetie for the journey?'

'Yeess,' he wails.

I run back into the house to the sound of screaming and grab three foil-wrapped chocolates. I give two to Jaymey and then break one up for Harlee, who seems unmoved by the situation. I help Jaymey to unwrap his sweet and he sobs quietly. Then everyone is in the car and we wave them off. Tears break out as I watch the car disappear and Rob puts his arm around my shoulders. He looks teary too. Back inside, the house seems empty and quiet as though something is missing. I can't settle into anything useful so I watch an hour of people wanting to move to the country, looking critically at old vicarages and cottages, calculating how far the commute to civilisation would be. Spots of rain hit the window. The garden is bare and, beyond that, the fields are muddy.

That evening, my mum makes us a meal. Rob and I are both wrung out, almost unable to speak. It is soothing to have some home-cooked food. Then Alice comes in with the two boys who rush in and hug us both. Aunty Sally and Uncle Rob. They know that the two children in the photographs will soon be moving into our home and that Rob and I will be their parents. But Luke and Harry don't understand any more than this. Our relationship with them is going to be different, but I hope that doesn't mean it is less close. Everyone agrees that at least the children must be ready to move in with us and how quickly this has happened. It hasn't felt quick to us. It has been the most intense two weeks of our lives. We have a strange lingering feeling of dislocation, as though we have been released from bed rest after a long illness.

Tuesday

On the big day – placement day – we both wake up with a kernel of excitement in our stomachs. Rob declares he has a cold, and looks ill. Despite all our best intentions of bouncing energetically into parenthood, we are already run down.

'You can't be ill today,' I say.

'I know – I'll be alright.'

It is definitely a lucky boots day. I change and make Rob a cocoa. He drinks it in bed and watches the weather forecast on the television.

'I'm not in the mood for political debates on the radio today,' he says.

The weatherman is talking of more cutting easterly winds and snow in the north.

'Will it be naughty no, do you think?' says Rob, imitating Jaymey's new term for hail.

He must be ill because he lets me drive his car, but nevertheless there is still a small amount of sighing and foot tapping as I neglect to overtake something or drive too comfortably within the speed limit. We pull up outside Bill and Thelma's house and once again the blue scooter is resting against the garage door. I spot a little face at the window next to the front door, just poking up above the window frame – so familiar – straining to look out. I feel such pleasure at the sight of him. The door opens and he is standing there, a bulging bin bag in each hand, trying to drag them out. Bill appears at the door and talks to Jaymey, taking the bin bags off him. We get out of the car and Bill approaches us, Jaymey at his side.

'Hello, as you can see Jaymey is very excited to see you. He's been ready for hours, waiting at the window.'

Rob starts to pack the bags into the boot of the car. Jaymey helps him.

'I'm afraid Thelma isn't taking it too well. She's really pleased for you all, but you know, she's a bit upset,' says Bill to me quietly.

He indicates that I can go into the house to see her. I find her standing up in the kitchen.

'Thanks so much for everything, Thelma. You've been great. We'll keep in touch. Maybe you would like to come and see us soon?'

She nods, unable to speak, and I say goodbye.

Back outside, Jaymey clambers into the car.

'Hey,' says Bill, 'aren't you going to say goodbye to us?'

He climbs back down and receives a hug from Bill.

'Where Thelma?' he asks.

'In the kitchen – see if you can find her.'

He runs into the house shouting for her. A minute later he comes back out and gets into his car seat. He is ready to go.

Bill waves us off and then we lose sight of him as we turn the corner.

Jaymey is keen to get out of the car when we get to Kim and Philip's house. He marches in and heads straight for Harlee.

'We going now,' he says and starts to pick up her toys.

She stands up and smiles when she sees Rob and me. She runs to us and I pick her up. She is warm and she looks into my face and touches her nose against my cheek. There is no fear.

'Come on, let's go home.'

CHAPTER 8

'What size are they wearing now?' barks the shop assistant, avoiding eye contact.

'I don't know.'

'Well, roughly then, so I know roughly what size they might be now.'

There is a measuring board several feet away from us.

'I'm sorry. I don't know.'

She sighs, rolls her eyes high up into their sockets and slopes off to get the measuring board. She cannot comprehend that I don't know the size of my children's feet, when it is in fact worse than that: I don't understand children's foot sizes at all. She kneels down in front of the children with great effort and rolls their trousers up. Harlee stands on the board and the tape measure is tightened around her foot.

'Wide feet,' says the assistant as though this is something bad, as though only imbeciles have wide feet.

She disappears through a door and reappears exhausted, with several boxes. Harlee tries a few pairs of shoes on and we choose a purple leather pair with a t-bar, decorated with appliqué flowers. She looks pleased with her first pair of shoes, holding up her feet, pointing at them and looking from Rob to me.

Jaymey is fitted with a pair of trainers, which he calls 'football shoes'. Then the assistant takes an instamatic photograph of the two of them. They sit on a padded bench, their legs dangling above the ground. Both of them look bemused. Neither is smiling.

Still wearing their new shoes, we go to the bookshop next door and to the children's section at the back of the shop. The selection we have at home is pitiful and needs supplementing. It is difficult to know where to start – what would be suitable and enjoyable – and I feel as unconfident as I did in the shoe shop. Jaymey is drawn to My First Book of Tractors. For Harlee we choose a large alphabet book with tabs to pull and flaps to open. From a display stand I choose a book based purely on its cover and its title – a kindly looking mother fox holds a little fox in her arms. Both are comfortably bound together under the starlight. We pick a book of nursery rhymes as a family present (and so Rob and I can brush up) and a book of fairytales. We head back to the car park and realise it is only a quarter to ten. We have been awake for four hours.

'Crane,' says Jaymey, pointing into the sky. Above the small shopping centre is an enormous crane, with an operator in a metal box right at the top.

'How man get there?'

'That box travels down to the ground and the man gets in and then the box moves up.'

'Why?'

'Well, so the man can get in?'

'Why?'

'So he can drive the crane.'

'Why?'

'Anyway, we're going back to the car now.'

'Why?'

'Because we're going home.'

'*No!*' he shouts and runs off.

I run after him and grab him by the arm, then bend down to him. He struggles and shouts louder and louder. People start to slow down and stare as he tries to get away from me. I worry that it looks to the bystanders as though I am being too rough so I let him go, hoping he will calm down. He runs nearer to the road, so I grab him again and lift him up. He kicks and struggles.

'Come on, back to the car,' I say, trying to sound chirpy and in control.

Rob is by my side with the pushchair and we walk as quickly as we can, me holding this writhing, red, shouting child, looking like a child abductor, feeling a bit like one. I can almost sense the CCTV cameras following us and the operators remarking on how unskilled a parent I am. Back at the car and despite his efforts to stay rigid, Rob folds Jaymey into his car seat. I put Harlee into her seat. She is contented and looks at her brother with a puzzled expression. I struggle to fold up the pushchair and then chuck it and the carrier bags into the boot. Rob and I exchange 'what do we do?' looks and then a few minutes into the car journey there is silence. I glance back. Harlee is chewing a plastic nurse and Jaymey is asleep.

We arrive home and sit in the car for a moment, soaking up the peace, until Harlee throws the nurse at her brother and wakes him up. There is angry consternation. Everyone is noisily herded up the steps to the front door, shoes are removed whilst avoiding falling down the steps and we are back in our stair-gated home. I take the new books and the children into the sitting room. Rob is in the hallway. Harlee has learnt that the hall can lead into the kitchen, where there is food, so she squawks the food squawk, which is becoming a familiar call.

After a drink and a biscuit everyone is calm. Harlee sits on my knee and we look through her new alphabet book, lifting the flaps and sliding the tabs. She returns over and over to B for banana and C for chocolate and rubs her tummy and licks her lips. Then we play clapping and tickling games. Rob lies on the floor rolling up bits of a newspaper that we haven't had the time to read and Jaymey picks them up in the bucket of his tractor and deposits them in a pile.

Later Mel rings to check on how we are doing. I recount the incident in the shopping centre.

'Remember,' she says, 'he is functioning at a younger age than his actual age, so always try to imagine what you would do with a younger child.'

'OK, but does that mean grab and walk, because people stare at me when I do that.'

'Yes it does – you can talk to him soothingly at the same time, but make it clear that you are in control. And you are going to have to get used to being stared at.'

'And Harlee's food issues. She screams for literally the entire time that I am preparing the food. I feed her breadsticks but she eats them so quickly, I'm not sure that's the right thing.'

'I think you need to gradually stop placating her with breadsticks. Maybe cut down on the frequency and the quantity over the next week, but keep reassuring her that her food is coming and remember to keep the mealtimes at roughly the same time each day, then she should start to realise that she can trust you not to leave her hungry.'

I make lunch to the background music of squawking and wailing and hear Rob doing his best to distract her. I quickly butter bread and cut up apples. The squawking pings my adrenal glands, makes me do everything at speed. I shout that lunch is ready and Harlee is off the starting blocks before anyone else, rattling the door and then appearing at the stair gate. Her food disappears in an urgent gorging almost before I sit down with mine. Then Rob spoons a yoghurt into her mouth. She hurries and presses him for each spoonful to come quicker and she swallows them down in forceful gulps. He takes her up to bed for her afternoon sleep and I sit and chat to Jaymey for a while.

'You've done well eating all that,' I say.

'I like yoghurt.'

He puts the empty pot and the spoon down. His face is smeared.

'Shall I get the magic flannel?'

He looks puzzled. I'm not sure where I've got that from either. Maybe something from my own childhood that has suddenly risen to the surface of my memory.

'The magic flannel wipes away all the crumbs and yoghurt from little faces.'

He dutifully tips up his head so that I can clean him. I take my time and look properly, wiping over his mouth, cheeks and nose. I run my fingers through his hair, then put the flannel down and sit him on my lap.

'You are my best boy, do you know that?'

He avoids my gaze and fidgets away my words uncomfortably.

'Aunty Alice and Uncle Mark are coming to visit us this afternoon.'

'Who them?'

'Alice is my sister and Mark is her husband and they have two children called Luke and Harry.'

He looks at me as though I am saying the most bizarre thing.

'You know how Harlee is your sister? Well, Alice is my sister.'

'Children are coming?' he asks.

'Yes, two boys.'

'Coming to play?'

'Yes, coming to play. You can show them your new room and your toys.'

'Children, coming to play.' His face is lit up by a great big smile.

'They come now?'

'Soon.'

He climbs down from my lap.

'I tell Daddy Football.' He runs to the stair gate and shouts up the stairs, 'Daddy Football, children are coming, to play.'

He looks back at me. 'Today?' he asks.

'Yes, today.'

'Daddy Football, children coming *today.'*

We hear Harlee moaning from her cot. I show Jaymey how to creep like a mouse along the hallway.

Rob and Jaymey play various themes on vehicles collecting rubbish, dumping rubbish and driving over rubbish. Whenever Rob tries to lie flat on the carpet to steal a moment of horizontal rest Jaymey is on top of him, shaking him and trying to open his eyelids with jabby little fingers. Harlee has made noise in her cot for long enough now that I don't think she is going to go back to sleep so I get up from the sofa.

'Where you go?' asks Jaymey.

'I'm going to get Harlee – she's awake.'

'No she asleep, you leave her, you play with me and Daddy Football. Here is tractor for you. Here is rubbish for you.' He presents it like a question, like pleading.

'But Harlee is awake and she wants to come and play too.'

'OK I get Harlee, Daddy Football you stay here and play tractors.'

Before I realise what is happening I am in the control of a four-year-old. I continue to debate the issues for far too long, then leave the room to the sound of Jaymey shouting his displeasure and throwing cars at Rob. Meanwhile, Harlee's shouts have become loud and frequent. What about me? Don't forget about me.

The shouts cease as soon as she hears me open her bedroom door. She stands in her cot, holding on to the rails. She smiles a lovely, chubby smile and jumps up and down. Dressed in an all-in-one, short-sleeved white cotton suit, her wobbly legs, bowing out slightly, her toes curled as though hanging on to the mattress. Her legs have folds of chubbiness on the insides, which melt me. As I approach the cot she holds up her arms to be picked up. I lift her out and hold her close.

'Hello, baby girl,' I say into her warm neck.

She grabs my glasses and a few strands of hair in one hand and pulls.

I put them back on and shift Harlee so that she is directly facing me. She goes for the glasses again so I take them off and shake my hair against her, to tickle her. I try to look at her face but she is chin to chest, going for my buttons now.

'OK, let's change your nappy and get you dressed. You're going to meet your cousins this afternoon.'

As soon as she is on the changing mat she casts around for something to grab, but I have already learnt to keep all nappy paraphernalia out of her reach and give her a plastic dog, which she chews. I chat aimlessly to her as I get her a clean nappy and dress her, folding her arms and legs into the clothes. Then I clap her hands together and her feet together, crossing them over her body and singing some nonsense. A sudden moment. A baby, in my house, a baby who smells like a baby, who has a cot and a pushchair, who wears little clothes. She is my baby. Despite broadcasting to everyone that I wasn't that fussed about babies, that I would be happy with older children, school-age children, I think I was lying, protecting myself, trying not to say the unsayable – that I really wanted a baby and I couldn't have one and it hurt. And although I am now tired beyond any tiredness I've ever felt before and overwhelmed and anxious about the future, I find myself in our house with a baby and a toddler and they are the sweetest things and we are a family.

As I hear my sister's car pulling into our drive it hits me how important it is that Alice likes Jaymey and Harlee.

It is not like introducing your newborn to your family – a little piece of genetic Plasticine, innocent and lovable with no sharp edges yet. And we can't pull the conversation off the shelf marked 'Meeting Your Sister's New Baby – What to Say', which is full of references to various family resemblances – chins, mouths, foreheads, eyes – during which it is polite and customary to share the resemblances out equally between father and mother. We are all going to have to be a little bit less lazy without a script to follow.

The introduction goes well. Jaymey shows everyone his new bedroom and Alice stays in there to play with him. Harlee takes a liking to Luke who, at six, is young enough to play interesting games with and yet old enough not to mind being led by her. Only Harry, now four, is put out by the arrival of our children. He refuses to join in and won't look at them. It is clearly a big shock, suddenly having two, ready-formed cousins.

Once they have left we show Jaymey and Harlee the scrapbooks we made, with our family pictures in. I show them the photographs of Alice, Mark, Luke and Harry and they point to them. They both want to look through their books. On the last page is a photograph of Rob and me, standing together on our front doorstep. It was taken last autumn, in the sunshine. Harlee leans into the page and kisses our picture.

*****

Rob wakes up with another sore throat and runny nose and so he wins the lie-in for that morning. He just about makes it downstairs looking dishevelled, as my parents arrive, bearing teddy bears and storybooks. I introduce them to Jaymey and Harlee as 'Granny' and 'Granddad' and they both stare at them open mouthed.

'Granny and Granddad are my Mummy and Daddy.'

Jaymey looks flummoxed that I should have such a thing as parents. My mum sits alongside Harlee and reads her a book and my dad is quickly recruited as a carpet-level refuse collection operative, taking his orders directly from Jaymey. When it is time for them to leave my mum says, 'I expect it'll be just like with a newborn, the first six weeks will be difficult and then you'll be coping fine.'

It is said with common sense and love so I don't tell her that that is not what the books say.

Rob looks ill and exhausted and not capable of playing one more moment of 'move the rubbish'. I put Harlee to bed for her afternoon sleep and get Jaymey dressed up in his anorak, hat, gloves and wellies. It is cold, damp and dank outside. We walk along the road for a while and cut off down a lane and then over a stile on to a footpath. I have done this walk many times, striding across the fields, looking up at the buzzards and the rooks' nests, treading down nettles and brambles, avoiding the boggy bits, dodging excitable dogs. But with Jaymey, the nettles and brambles become enormous, the boggy bits come up over his wellies, most of the dogs are taller than he is. I watch every step for him, lift him up over branches and across deep puddles. He doesn't seem bothered though and chats, mainly questions, 'What's that?' and the endless 'Why?' We stop frequently to examine tiny things that I have never noticed before; a knothole in the wooden bridge over the stream, which Jaymey pushes a stick through, some tiny dirty coloured fish that dart about, disturbing the silt. Occasionally I point out a bird or something in the distance, but his focus is down and small. I spot a laurel bush near the water.

'Shall we make a boat?'

'Why?'

I pick off a leaf and curl it back, pushing the stem through the centre of the leaf. A simple boat, which always floats, as long as the curl is right and which even has somewhere for the boatman to shelter. I drop it into the water, just ahead of the bridge and we watch it disappear underneath. When it reappears, Jaymey claps.

'Me go?'

I make him a leaf boat. We watch it float under the bridge and celebrate its reappearance. I remember playing laurel leaf boats with my dad, racing them across the weir in the woods near our house. We walk back home along the road and Jaymey holds a stick in one hand and my hand in the other.

*****

Lorna visits. She wants to 'see how we are getting on' and drop off some things from the birth family. Nothing to worry about. We carry out a cursory tidy, just good enough. She parks outside the house and I see her open the boot of her car and pull out two, maybe three bin bags. They are full. I go out to meet her and am given another two bin bags to carry. Then on the back seat is a cardboard box. We take them into the house and fill the hallway.

'The bin bags are full of toys that Trudy has sent for the children and in the cardboard box is a memory box for Harlee.'

I had heard about memory boxes before – a collection of special things put together by the birth family to remind the child of them.

'Is there a box for Jaymey?' I ask.

'No. There isn't one for him.'

I show her into the sitting room, offer to make drinks for everyone and then grab the cardboard box, run upstairs and hide it on the top of our wardrobe. I know that Jaymey would spot the box and want to know what was in it and I am not ready for the conversation.

Jaymey is visibly unnerved by Lorna's presence in our house. He sits on my feet, leaning back against my legs and maintains a clinging physical contact with me throughout her visit. When I am talking to her he tries to bring my attention back to him. He talks over me, taps my leg repeatedly and then finally turns his cup upside down, spilling a small amount of juice on to the carpet. He does it purposefully and then watches for my reaction. Lorna also watches. I feel on parade. Rob goes to get a cloth. I wonder what I should say.

'Jaymey, don't spill your drink.'

He pretends to do something with his sock and then tips up his cup again, looking at me out of the corner of his eye. I decide that I don't want an assessed confrontation so I ignore him.

'He should have a consequence for that,' Lorna says.

Rob returns with the cloth and the situation unsticks.

'Their lifestory books are almost ready. A trainee social worker has been preparing them as part of her project. She'll deliver them to you.'

She is watching Harlee who, for the entire visit has been on the move, picking up toys, bashing them against other toys, climbing on Rob, trying to reach for things that have been put out of reach. She is never still.

'Very busy isn't she?' declares Lorna.

And I guess she is 'busy', but Lorna says the word as though it is a euphemism for something else. She doesn't elaborate.

Once Lorna has gone, Jaymey casts around for an argument. Whatever Harlee reaches for, he takes. He pushes her over, stands in her way and will not be distracted. She seems mildly cross but continues moving around, picking up this and that. Rob suggests another game of 'rubbish collection' with Jaymey and I sit Harlee on my knee with the picture dictionary. Whilst we look at the pictures and talk, Jaymey shouts for me and when this doesn't work walks over and thrusts a tractor in my face.

'*You play too!*'

'Jaymey, I'm reading with Harlee, you're playing with Daddy.'

'*No!* I read too.'

'I'll read with you later.'

Harlee quietly gets down from my knee. Jaymey doesn't wait for her to be clear of me before he climbs up.

'Mmmm for man,' he says and turns the page.

Once the children are in bed, I get the cardboard box down from the top of the wardrobe. Inside is another pink box. On the front is a pencil-drawn picture of two teddies, arms around each other, against a creamy heart-shaped background. 'Love Forever' it says underneath. The box is packed with a silver half a heart pendant, a plastic silver coloured key in a see-through box that says 'You Have the Key to My Heart' on it, a key ring with a guardian angel on it, a tiny pair of high-heeled shoes and a smaller box with 'For Baby's First Tooth' written on in pale grey. At the bottom of the box is a big envelope, open, with a card inside. The same smiling teddies hold out a banner that says 'We Miss You'. Inside the card, in rounded teenage handwriting is written, 'We are not meant to be apart but we will be thinking of you every day until we are back together as we should be with lots and lots and lots of love from Mummy.'

I am caught between feeling that I am a sham parent who has usurped another woman and a sickness at the schmaltzy tat, the fake, pink love and care, bought off the shelf from a gift shop, not making up for anything. Maybe she thinks that Harlee is too young to remember, that she can be anaesthetised by this pink crap – brainwashed into thinking that her removal from them was just part of some great conspiracy. Maybe she thinks that her baby's fear of hunger can be soothed away by the teddies, that they will make it alright that her brother was left in his own shit for hours and beaten and burnt. Buy enough love from a shop and the months of neglect will painlessly melt away – it won't hurt at all. It has nothing to do with memory. It has been purchased and constructed. Sugar coating on a dog shit of a life.

And there is nothing for Jaymey. Why is there nothing for Jaymey? Because she feels nothing for him or is the pink not pink enough – the sentiment not sickly enough – to hide the hypocrisy of giving the battered child a box for his first tooth? I repack the box and take it to show Rob. He looks through it quickly and silently.

'I'm going to put this in the loft.'

'But don't you think we should leave it out for Harlee?' I ask.

'Look, Harlee is going to wreck this in five minutes, she won't understand what it is and I don't want to see it every day.'

The bin bags contain an overwhelming amount of toys. I feel guilty even acknowledging my own reactions but the toys are rubbish – some of them are broken, they are not appropriate for small children, the sound buttons on some of them don't work, they have strange things written on them badly translated from Chinese or Korean. There is one book: a Disney version of Peter Pan. I want to get rid of the lot but we agree to keep the best and put the rest in the loft. We have been told over and over that we must acknowledge and accept that the children have a past, that to deny their past is to deny them. The toys cover half the floor space of our sitting room. I can't quite pin down the root of my unease.

Harlee wakes up five times during the night. Each time I go into her, talk to her and hold her hand. Her cheeks are flushed and I know that she is coming down with Rob's cold. At six am when I wake up sensing Jaymey's silent presence standing over me, I feel like my eyelids are glued together. I try my best at a chirpy start to the day.

'Morning, Jaymey,' I whisper, 'did you sleep well?'

'Drink now.'

We negotiate the stair gates between us and the kitchen and I make him a drink in his new spill-proof beaker. Just as we settle down in the sitting room, I hear Harlee stirring upstairs. I wonder if she will go back to sleep but within a few moments she is screeching.

'Jaymey, I'm just going to get Harlee.'

'Me too.'

So he follows me upstairs, through the stair gates into Harlee's bedroom. She stands in her cot red-faced and snot-smeared. Jaymey stays close by me as I change her nappy and wipe her face – so close I can hardly move my arms. We all go back down the stairs, Jaymey walking right beside me. I switch on the television thinking that this will keep them amused for the few minutes it will take me to make a drink of milk for Harlee and a strong cup of tea for me. As I fill up the kettle I hear the sound of chaos coming from the sitting room. I rush in and Harlee is sitting amongst a mass of CDs, the wooden shelves pulled down beside her. She is unfazed by the near miss and continues to try to open the CD cases. I move her out of the way, push the shelves back up against the wall and put the CDs back. 'No,' I say as firmly as I can without shouting. Jaymey gives her a long lecture, which she ignores. I move some toys within her reach and head towards the door. As I glance back she is shuffling along the carpet on her bottom back towards the CDs. I pick her up and carry her to the kitchen; Jaymey comes too. The moment Harlee is in her high chair the food squawk starts, which I silence with a beaker of milk. She drinks it so quickly there is barely time for the kettle to re-boil, before the squawking starts again. I hurriedly make my tea and then lift her out of her high chair as she grabs for the hot drink. It is still only quarter past six when I sit down; Jaymey playing tractors at my feet and Harlee climbing on me with a book to read to her. I have never felt so desperate for the first caffeine fix of the day. Neither child is even vaguely interested in the television; they want me, both of them. When Rob comes down at eight o'clock I feel as though I've done a full shift.

'Hello, my family,' he says, yawning. ('You have no right to yawn,' I think poisonously.) 'Have you looked outside?' ('Of course I haven't looked outside – I can't even go to the toilet without it being a major logistics operation.')

He lifts Harlee off me and takes her to the window. Jaymey climbs up on me and I carry him. It is barely light outside, but the snow lights up the trees and the ground. Harlee looks nonplussed; Jaymey is beside himself.

'No, no, it no, it no.'

Harlee runs her finger down the window, collecting the condensation, and then puts her finger in her mouth. Jaymey complains when I want to get changed on my own and shouts when he hears me boiling the kettle again. I intend to have a blissful five minutes, getting changed, slowly, in our bedroom with the television on. I lie out on the bed, Michelangelo-style. Wired and tired. From downstairs I hear 'Mummy, Mummy, Mummy, Mummy.' Then, 'Where Mummy? Where Mummy?' Then, 'Mummy now? Mummy come now?' I could always ignore other people's children, but I can't tune out the bleating of my own little lamb. Finding it impossible to relax, I get dressed in a rush, pulling on what I was wearing yesterday and the day before yesterday, rushing, like I do everything now.

It is barely half past eight in the morning and we are all in the garden. The snow has silenced everything. Harlee bends down and tentatively touches the snow, puts some on the end of her tongue. Jaymey crouches down and gathers some in his mittens. Rob helps him to roll a bigger snowball, then adds a head, then stones for eyes and sticks for arms. We take photographs – the first of us all, at home. We look happy. We look like a proper family.

'Back to work tomorrow,' says Rob.

And that will be it – the end of his two-week paternity leave. Some of the dread that I feel leaks into my expression. I also feel a little pathetic. I am not the first woman ever to have to care for two children for a few hours on my own. But every little part of the day has to be thought through, managed, so that the right food reaches the right mouth at the right time, the right socks reach the right feet, the right teeth are cleaned at the right time with the right toothbrush and the right toothpaste. I have to make sure that no one smells, no one's nose runs too freely, no one falls down the stairs, no one reaches for the knife I have just used or the razor left within reach. I also have to police the pushing, the snatching and the slapping that disturb and curtail everything. And all this is even before we think about going out anywhere.

'You'll be fine,' says Rob.

CHAPTER 9

The first few weeks I spend with the children on my own pass in a foggy oblivion of adrenaline and exhaustion. Each process, each manoeuvre, has to be thought out from first principles. I quickly work out that if I get the children and myself almost ready, then I can strap them in the car whilst I search for the stray sock, restock the nappy bag or brush my teeth. I shop in the only supermarket that has side-by-side child seats in the trolleys. I now use an old 'hands free' handbag, which I can wear over one shoulder and across my body. I have to shower in the evenings after Rob gets home but before the children go to bed because the sound of the shower wakes them up. I put Harlee into her cot if I need the toilet and then listen to her screeching until I fetch her again. There are locks on every single cupboard and drawer and every pen is out of reach. I have learnt that Harlee's preferred sense is touch. Whatever she sees isn't real to her until she has touched it, whether that is part of a dead bird lying by the side of the road or some black grease in the door mechanism of the car. Anything left within reach is to be examined, squeezed, pressed and often tasted. A container of used teabags and partly decomposed cucumber and cabbage, destined for the compost heap, which I leave on the side in the kitchen, is dragged on to the floor and the contents squooshed between tiny fingers in the time I turn my back to dry my hands on a tea towel. I stand her on the bath mat, turn around for a nappy and she is climbing on the water pipes, reaching up for Rob's razor. She is never, ever still. It is as though she is attracted not only to things that are new and interesting and out of her experience, but also to things that cut, smash, indelibly stain. I have heard parents say of their children that they have no sense of danger, but Harlee literally seeks it out, senses the slightest weakness in security and heads straight for it.

Jaymey needs me every moment he is awake. It is as though he is not a person on his own – that he fears for his existence if he is not witnessing me reacting to him in some way. Some days he seems happy and easy with himself and me and we have fun and grow closer. Other days, everything I suggest is met with 'no'. He screams when I am with him and he screams when I leave the room. He can't bear me giving any attention to Harlee so he does anything he can to draw my attention away from her. He might talk constantly, maybe call out, 'Mummy, Mummy, Mummy, Mummy, Mummy…' until I never want to hear the word again or just fill his unease with meaningless sounds. He won't let me read to her, feed her or change her without trying to take the leading role. He drags out every last bit of energy I have. One afternoon, at about half past three I am so tired and overwhelmed that emotion constricts my throat and I know that if I can't keep myself under control I am going to disintegrate, here, in front of the children, when I haven't yet completed the most challenging time of the day – tea, bath and bed. I ring Rob at work. I can hardly speak.

'Rob, I need you to come home.'

'It's only four o'clock. Can't you hang on for an hour?'

I can only communicate the minimum.

'Come home, now.'

'Are you OK?'

'No.' My voice wobbles.

Rob senses that I am on the edge and I hear him packing up his desk as he puts the phone down. Throughout the phone call, the children observed me closely. When I put the phone down and sit on the floor, Jaymey moves a few of his cars to my feet and plays leaning against me. Harlee brings me an armful of books. I open one and struggle to see the pictures through watery eyes. She points at the page and then looks from the picture to me. I try not to meet her eyes. I can't stare at the watery picture any longer so I look at her and try to smile reassuringly. The rising of my cheeks pushes the water out of my eyes and tears leak out. They move in closer. They are rattled. Jaymey drives his car into my leg.

'Mummy? Mummy? Mummy?'

He gets cross when I don't answer and the words starts to come out as an angry, 'Mummeeeyah, Mummeeyah…' each syllable fired at me.

I notice that he doesn't once look at my face, but keeps his gaze on his cars. When more tears come, Harlee nestles into me and head-butts me a kiss. I mouth 'thank you' to her and she looks puzzled.

When Rob gets home and opens the sitting room door the relief I feel comes out in swallowed sobs.

'Go upstairs,' he says squeezing my arm and handing me a big bar of chocolate. As I run up the stairs I hear him.

'Hello, you two. What have you been up to today?'

'Where Mummy gone? Where Mummy gone? Daddy, where Mummy?'

I need to cry loudly and properly so I put myself under the duvet to muffle the sound. I cry for an astonishingly long period of time. Then I sleep. When I wake up it is dark. My glasses are jammed into the side of my nose and the tears are crispy dry on my face. I hear muffled sounds from downstairs. I lie still, staring into the gloom, not sure if I can contemplate returning to the day. Then I get up, rearrange myself, take a deep breath and walk downstairs.

'Hello, family.'

Rob is sitting with Jaymey and Harlee either side of him. Both of them are in their pyjamas.

'Hello,' says Rob, looking concerned, 'I was just telling Jaymey and Harlee that you were feeling poorly, poor Mummy.'

Harlee puts both her arms out and I sit next to her and give her a cuddle. Jaymey continues to look at his book. When I get up and kneel down in front of him he does all he can not to look at me and cuddles closer into Rob.

'Right, it's bedtime now,' says Rob.

Jaymey gets down and walks past me. Harlee puts her hands around my neck and kisses my cheek. Jaymey turns away when I try to kiss him.

The following day I take Jaymey and Harlee swimming, partly to get us out of the house and removed from the scene of my meltdown and partly because it is what normal mothers do with their normal children and I need to feel normal. I have already thought through the changing room logistics. We bag a large cubicle so that I can keep Harlee in her pushchair whilst I get myself and Jaymey changed. I change Harlee on a pull-out changing table. Then I load up the pushchair with our bags, make Jaymey hold on to the handle of the pushchair whilst I carry Harlee in one arm and manoeuvre the pushchair with the other. Jaymey is very excited about swimming and it is something he was used to doing with Thelma. As far as I know, Harlee has never been swimming before. I negotiate the locker with my one free hand and we make our way to the small pool. I fit Jaymey's armbands and he is down the steps and away smiling and laughing and kicking his legs. I sit on the steps on the edge of the pool and sit Harlee on my knee so that she can't escape. With my one free hand I blow up the sit-in rubber ring that Alice has given me. Harlee looks puzzled by the whole experience. I try to imagine how strange this must be for her, when the bath is the only experience she has of being in water. There are other small children floating around in similar inflatable devices, which Harlee points to. I position her feet over the holes and lower her in. She reaches her arms over the side and flicks her hands through the water, sending up little splashes. She looks at me, to check my reaction. I reassure her and run my own hands across the surface. Encouraged by my action, she does the same again, this time making more of a splash and smiling. We continue this process together until she is laughing and kicking her legs. I swim behind her, pushing her along. She is suddenly anxious that she can't see me, so I propel her along from the side.

'Shall we swim over to Jaymey?'

She laughs and so we dodge between other children and reach Jaymey.

'I didn't know you were such a good swimmer.'

He turns on to his back and shows me some big kicks.

'Backstroke as well. That's fantastic.'

He points to a small, plastic football that is floating in the water. I reach for it, push it under the water and then let it go so that it fires up into the air. He swims to it and does the same. It reappears close to Harlee and she reaches out a hand. I give it to her. Jaymey shouts, '*My ball!*' and then splashes water in her face. Other mothers look, other children look. Harlee screams. I give Jaymey the ball and take Harlee back to the steps, get her out of the rubber ring and sit her on my knee where she happily kicks her legs in the shallows. I reach for another ball and throw it across the pool to Jaymey ('here's another ball, I haven't forgotten you'). He swims with it for a while and throws it back to me. We seem to be so much louder, to take up so much more space than the other children and mothers in the pool – our splashes are splashier, our ball throwing higher. There is some tutting and obvious movement away from us. In another life, I might be the tutting mother protecting the delicate children, so I feel self-conscious, but at the same time both my children are happy, I can see them, there are no sharp edges or sudden drops anywhere or hot drinks or muddy puddles within reach. I put my head back, breathe in, hold my breath and then close my eyes and let out a huge sigh. I remain still for a few moments; the warm water laps around my legs.

We exit the warmth of the pool, with wet hair, into the cold February wind. I ignore the voice lecturing inside my head on the perils of wet hair and a cold wind and head for the bakery. It is only a short walk and something I must do, something from my tick list. We stop outside the bakery window and marvel at the display of iced donuts, Danish pastries and fairy cakes.

'You can choose whatever you like,' I say to Jaymey. He is so happy he skips a little dance. Harlee points at everything, her eyes wide open.

Jaymey chooses a gingerbread man. I buy Harlee a chocolate fairy cake, an enormous Chelsea bun for myself and an iced bun for Rob. We eat them at home. I watch Jaymey bite off all the Smartie eyes and buttons first. Harlee is going for the world cake speed-eating record.

We pass a peaceful afternoon. Rob gets home, anxious about what he might have to encounter.

'How is everyone? Did you have a lovely day?'

'Daddy, Daddy, we went wimmin, we went wimmin. We had cake. I chosed a dinderded man.'

*****

Mel rings before her planned visit that afternoon.

'I'm going to give you a package and I need to explain what is in it over the phone, so that we don't have to discuss it in front of the children. First, there are two videos for you. They are of the final contact meetings that each child had with the birth mother. Jaymey's birth father chose not to attend. I haven't seen them myself yet but I'm going to before I come over to you this afternoon. Second, I have a letter for you and Rob from Trudy, the birth mother. It is…well…it is her version of events and she doesn't acknowledge her part in losing the children, but it is quite sweet in places. I would read it and then put it away if I were you. Don't let it put you off course.'

Mel hands me the package when she arrives and I put it on top of a kitchen cupboard before the children see it. We go into the sitting room and chat, the children at my feet, bashing toys into my legs. She asks how we are getting on, now that Rob has gone back to work. I explain that there are generally good days and bad days, without much in between and that I can't work out what it is that sets the scene for either. She suggests that we focus on playing on the floor with the children and on having fun.

'And I need to make mealtimes easier. I have to cook to the soundtrack of Harlee wailing and with Jaymey hanging on to my legs. It's driving me crazy.'

'I've been thinking about that one. How about you buy Jaymey a special toy, something he really likes, which only comes out when you cook tea and which he plays with in the sitting room? It might make him feel special and free you up a bit.'

I like the idea and I can think of exactly what to buy him.

'Have you got Jaymey into a pre-school yet?'

'I've visited our nearest and they are very full, but they've offered me a Wednesday afternoon and a Monday morning. We start next week. I'm going to stay for the first few sessions.'

'Maybe you could build up to a few more sessions before he starts school in September. You've missed the deadline for the applications for primary school now. It doesn't mean that Jaymey won't get a place for September but you will need to contact your local school first and have a look around. See what you think and ask if they have spaces for this coming year. If they have, then you won't have a problem getting in.'

I decide that I will get the pre-school start over with first before I cold-call the primary school.

'And the Freeing Order? Any news on a date?'

'We should hear within the next fortnight. We are still not anticipating any problems there.'

As a reward for surviving each day I eat chocolate in the evening, every evening. I have never eaten so much before. It has become like a drug. I collapse into the sofa after the final nappy change, the teeth cleaning, the bedtime stories then the washing up and the laundry and I feel that some of the exhaustion will be melted away by a big slab of cheap, sweet, milk chocolate. I don't have the mental fortitude for the dark 80 per cent stuff, just like I can no longer watch films with subtitles or wear 100 per cent wool jumpers. I need comfort and ease. I am going to read Trudy's letter and watch the videos, in one hit – in a double whammy. I am not going to ruin my chocolate fix, so I am saving that for afterwards.

First I lie on our bed and open the letter. The writing is in the same, teen, rounded script, which I have seen before in the schmaltzy cards.

To Jaymey and Harlee's carers,

> I did the best I could for my children and it was not good enough and so they were taken away by social workers. The social workers have always had it in for me and I had no chance. I don't blame you and I hope that you look after them well. We will miss them very much, especially their two older brothers.
>
> It is important not to keep secrets from my children. Secrets are dangerous things which can get out of control and do lots of damage.
>
> We have done lots of lovely things together which the children will always remember and I can't wait until

> we see each other again and are reunited as a family, forever. Nothing personal against you, maybe we will meet up one day.
>
> From Jaymey and Harlee's mummy
>
> Xxxxxxxxxx

Also in the envelope is a photograph of Trudy and Mike. They are side by side on a sofa. She is holding a cigarette between the fingers of one hand. Her legs are crossed, she is slouched into the sofa and is leaning back looking at Mike and half-smiling, looking for approval. She is wearing the same tracksuit as she was in the earlier pictures I had seen of her and this time the top layer of hair is scraped back into a tight ponytail. She is a wisp of a woman, pale and bony. Mike is leaning forward, his elbows resting on his knees, his chin resting on his knuckles. He is a big hulk of a man, shaved head, tattoos on his neck and arms. His clothes are tight. He stares into the camera. His look is terrifying. The threat comes out of the picture. The image reminds me of a police photograph. Members of the public are advised not to approach this man. There is not a drop of warmth. This is how he chose to be remembered.

The letter leaves me mixed up. The message is clear – Rob and I are temporary carers, plugging the gap before this temporarily interrupted family are back on course. It has been written by Trudy. She clearly feels that the bureaucracy is against her. Her tone is defensive and doesn't indicate that any lessons have been learnt. Fleetingly I wonder if there is some truth in what she writes, that she has done her best and that she has been branded as an unfit mother by an inflexible system. Then I recall all the second, third and fourth chances squandered, the pages of neglect in the children's files, and the two don't marry up.

Still reeling from the letter and the photograph I watch the videos. First Jaymey's. Some muffled conversation between a social worker off-camera and Trudy. She is sitting on a spongy sofa in a bleak room. Jaymey is playing on his own.

'Jaymey, come over here. See Mummy.'

Jaymey continues to play, avidly, as though he hasn't heard her, as though if he plays hard enough he can pretend he is somewhere else. Trudy tries again, half-heartedly and then sits looking absently around the room. Jaymey continues to play. They look for all the world like two strangers who have inexplicably and unwillingly found themselves in a room together. After many minutes a social worker's voice is heard. She says something about engaging with Jaymey. Trudy sighs, waits a while and then walks over to Jaymey, picking up a random toy on the way.

'Look what Mummy's got.'

She stands over him, holding out the toy. He looks up, takes it and puts it down next to him and then continues to play.

'What do you say then?'

He looks puzzled.

'Ta Mummy, that's what you say.'

He looks scared and lost.

'Ta.'

A social worker pulls up a small plastic chair next to Jaymey, for Trudy to sit on. She duly sits there, legs outstretched and crossed, looking at her feet, arms folded against her chest. Occasionally she holds out something for Jaymey, which he takes without looking at her. Then she gets up and walks out of the room and out of Jaymey's life.

For her final contact meeting with Harlee, Trudy wears a different t-shirt and has a carrier bag with her. She walks into the room and rattles the bag. At the sound Harlee is immediately up and staggering towards the sofa. Trudy lets her look inside the bag and take out the large, supermarket-sized packet of chocolates. Trudy pulls the packet apart and gives one to Harlee. Harlee puts it in her mouth and immediately holds out her hand for another. She does the same with that too and the next until her mouth is full. Trudy jokingly attempts to hide the sweets behind her back. Harlee climbs on to the sofa and slides her hand behind Trudy to reach the sweets. She laughs as she holds on to them but Harlee is persistent and is then rewarded with more chocolates. This goes on until the packet is empty at which point Harlee walks off and sits down next to some toys. Trudy rustles the sweet packet again and Harlee gets up, travels far enough to see that she is being tricked and then returns to her toys. Trudy watches her play for a while, trying to talk to her. Eventually she gives up and leaves the room.

I switch off the television, slide the video back into its case and sit in silence.

The name of the condition given to the damaged children of the neglectful and chaotic is 'attachment disorder'. I have worked my way through enough of Mel's reading list to know that these children have, at one extreme, experienced no real attachment to a primary carer or, at the other, unsatisfactory, perfunctory attachments to many carers. From the privileged position of my own attachment-filled life, I'd not thought much about the concept of attachment – considered it to be a bit nebulous perhaps. Don't we all form attachments all the time; aren't we programmed to do so? It seems that we are not. We learn how to form attachments to other people from our primary carers, who are usually our parents. I had just watched a mother saying goodbye to her two children, whom she may never see again, and she could have been bidding farewell to her neighbour's rabbits. There were no tearful farewells, no sobbing desperate hugs, no begging, no 'I'll love you forever, don't forget me.' Maybe Trudy wasn't going to play along with the farce; maybe this was her way of retaining control. But it didn't look as though she was making a choice; she didn't know how to be with her children. More disturbing though was the behaviour of Jaymey and Harlee. Their fear and self-containment was staggering, at their young ages, already hard-wired not to trust, not to let their guard down. Their aloneness was cruel. I was left wondering in whose best interests this meeting had been.

*****

The next day the health visitor comes. She asks a few basic questions – the children's names and dates of birth, their immunisations (which I know), whether they've had chicken pox or not (which I don't know). Then she tells me how important it is to clean their teeth twice daily and how they should eat lots of fruit and vegetables and not too much sugar. She says that children need routine and stability and that she is sure things will soon settle down just fine. She says I can come and see her if I need to ask anything about things like toilet training or diet. I act out polite and grateful. I can't begin to tell her how things really are.

*****

Another day, another visit, this time a trainee social worker, Bethany, is coming to drop off the lifestory books – the books that will explain to the children their lives so far in simple words and photographs. She insists that she must sit down with Jaymey and go through his book with him, page by page. I place myself across the table from them. She starts with a photograph of the hospital he was born in, then a picture of the house he lived in and then some pictures of his birth parents and his two older brothers. I watch Jaymey do everything he possibly can not to look at the book. He lies across the table, reaches for a tin of pencils, then shakes and bashes it. He pretends to fall off his chair, claims to need a plaster and then produces some fake sneezes. Bethany is patient but eventually begins to get jarred off, starts to say things like 'sit up' and 'keep still'. She looks very young. I wonder if she has had any particular training in this. She leaves with some advice – 'show the book to him every so often, leave it in a place where he has access to it.'

Once we have waved her off, the full force of Jaymey's discomfort is unleashed. He throws everything he can lay his hands on – most of it at me and Harlee – he rolls around on the floor kicking the furniture. When I pick him up he goes floppy so that I can't sit him on a chair. Finally I sit him on my knee and hold him. He starts to pretend cry, like a baby, then looks at me, his face bright red, and tries to hit me. I'm aware that I am no longer trying to cuddle him but am now restraining him and I'm not sure that this is what I should be doing. Will he think that I am being abusive? If anyone looked through the kitchen window, would they think the same? So I let him go and he runs around and around, bumping into things, kicking the walls. Harlee is also screeching. I cannot deal with them both like this so I negotiate the cupboard lock and get her four long breadsticks. This should buy me a few minutes of quiet from her.

'I want breadsticks!' shouts Jaymey.

'You can have yours when you calm down and sit at the table,' I say.

'*No. No.* I not sit at the table.'

'Well, you can't have breadsticks then.'

'*I hate you!*'

Later I put them both in the bath. Jaymey cries and cries and is inconsolable.

When peace finally comes and the children are in bed I sit down and stare at the wall. I stare for so long that my brain powers down. The silence is a lovely painkiller, suspending me in a state of semi-consciousness. But underneath the numbness is a background jangle of nerves. When Rob comes into the room, I can barely turn my head and speak to him.

'What happened today? Jaymey was horrendous at bedtime.'

'The trainee social worker visited with their lifestory books. Jaymey was completely thrown by her, the book, everything.'

Rob pushes for more detail. My memory has powered down too. I can't remember the order of things, exactly what I said and did, at what point. I can barely find the energy to sound out the words I use.

'Do you want me to get your chocolate?' says Rob.

I look up at him and muster up enough energy to raise my eyes pleadingly and murmur, 'yeesss'.

Although I go to bed exhausted, I sleep badly, waking in the night, mulling over the events of the afternoon. My mind plays out the same thoughts over and over again, without conclusion or perspective.

The following day the three of us go to my parents' house, partly so that I can have a break from the house and from my thoughts for a while. I need to go shopping for food. Mum and Dad offer to look after Jaymey while I go to the supermarket. I sit Harlee in the trolley and we sweep in through the big open doors. I feel as though I am on holiday. I get up a bit of speed and let my feet leave the ground momentarily. Ahead of us is the clothes department. It is full of children's clothes, nice children's clothes – corduroy trousers and fleeces for boys, embroidered jeans and striped t-shirts for girls. This is my moment, I decide, the moment when I break away, when I stop dressing my children in the clothes I don't like, the clothes that have the stamp of Trudy all over them – the shiny, stained polyester t-shirts, always full of static, the 'Watch Out! Princess in Training' sleep suits. I choose khaki and navy, sky blue and purple, stripes and camouflage. I buy a roll of bin bags. I will clear out the broken toys that are strewn across the house, get rid of the clothes that I am ashamed to see my children in. It feels right that Rob and I at least start to assert ourselves, our values, our tastes, our beliefs.

*****

We arrive, all gorgeous in our new clothes, at the pre-school and have to crowd into a lobby area before we can be let into the hall. I needn't have worried about how to fend off questions from the other mothers about our newcomer status, because no one speaks to me. We are glanced at suspiciously. We stand and look at our feet. The doors open and everyone else knows what to do. There is some sort of peg and coat system and somewhere for lunchboxes. Then the children each choose a table to go to where there are various activities set up. I spot the pre-school leader, Helen, making her way over to us before she is waylaid by several of the mothers. We stand self-consciously. Harlee struggles to get out of her pushchair, Jaymey clings on to me.

'You stay, here, with me?' he asks.

'Yes, I'll be here for the whole morning with you.'

Eventually Helen comes over. She kneels down and greets Jaymey first and tells him how pleased she is that he is going to be coming to pre-school. Then she asks Jaymey to introduce her to Harlee. She leads us to a table where a laminated label has been made up with Jaymey's name on underneath a picture of a tractor. In the morning he is to find his label amongst the others, hang it on a peg and then hang his coat on the same peg. Helen shows Jaymey the activities on each table and he chooses to play in a big box of sand. Helen invites Harlee and me to join in. Harlee can barely contain her excitement. She digs with a small spade, then drags a rake across the surface. I show Jaymey how to make shapes with the moulds and don't spot Harlee moving to the adjacent table, grabbing a handful of beads from under the noses of an astonished group of girls making necklaces and dropping the beads into the sand, mixing them in for good measure. As I pick the beads out and brush the grit off them, she is off again, this time to the salt dough table. To the consternation of the children there, she pushes a few sandy beads into the salt dough. Then I watch her look intensely at one of her fingers, which has a lump of the dough on the end. I can almost see the idea coming into her head. She puts the dough in her mouth and as she moves it around with her tongue the slow realisation that the taste is disgusting shows in her expression. She opens her mouth over the table and in slo-mo bionic woman style, I get a tissue out of my pocket and dive at the salty dribble, just catching it before it soaks the remaining dough. The other children stare at us disconcertingly. Our mummies have warned us about people like you. One of the pre-school helpers says not to worry, that it's OK. But I sense that it isn't OK for us to wreck their carefully laid out activity tables. I sit Harlee down with a drink and we read some books together. Every few minutes Jaymey looks across to me and waves.

When we get home there are two messages on the phone. I wonder if they are from friends wanting to come and visit our new family. One is from Rob asking how Jaymey's first day at pre-school has gone; the other is Mel sounding concerned. Can I ring her as soon as possible?

'Sally, are you going to be around this afternoon? I need to come and see you. Nothing to worry about.'

There clearly is.

We sit around the kitchen table. Mel produces a badly photocopied form.

'I'm afraid to tell you that the solicitor acting for the family court, where the Freeing Order will be heard, has accidentally sent this to the birth family.'

She shows me a sheet on which some of the details have been redacted, except one of the redacted words is just about readable through the black pen. The word is 'DONOVAN'.

'This sheet shouldn't have gone to the family at all. The paperwork was photocopied and sent out by a trainee at the solicitor's firm.'

I look at the paper, then close my eyes and shake my head.

'Fucking hell,' I mouth.

'I know. It's very poor.'

'The consequences of this could be huge. And of all the ways in which our details could leak, it's a bloody solicitor.'

'We're going to make an official complaint. The authority's solicitor recommends that you get some legal advice.'

'And what good would that do?'

'Well, in the worst case, if the family tracked you down, you may incur costs such as moving costs.'

'Do you think they would try to track us down?'

'Certain threats have been made, which are probably idle ones.'

I rest my head on the table, imagine tying the solicitor to a chair, swinging big bags of shopping at his head. A flying Müller Corner pot would slice his cheek open. It would be like Pulp Fiction, but with anger.

I need strong tea. I stand up, fill the kettle and switch it on. Mel explains how I am to keep us all safe. First, if I see Trudy or Mike in the street I am to head into the nearest shop, head for the most senior looking member of staff, stand by them and phone the police and then social services. Second, if they knock on our front door (our front door for god's sake) then I am not to open it but to ask them politely (politely?) to leave and then to call the police and social services. Third, I am to be careful about calling for my children in public as Harlee has such an unusual name.

I take a long, slow mouthful of tea and feel the warmth of it spreading down my throat into my stomach where it sits uneasily. I feel utterly gutted.

PART 5

Extreme Times

Life and Loss

CHAPTER 10

The moment when the clocks went forward, such a minor adjustment, has been life changing. It was as though simultaneously the sun came out and the wind stopped blowing, the rain clouds gave up and the Donovan family pressure cooker relieved itself of some steam. We now spend most of our time outdoors, unburdened by ill-fitting hats, missing mittens and wellies that fall off. Oh the joy of dressing everyone in a pair of trainers, trousers and a t-shirt! Oh the joy of one sandpit, two buckets and a football! I don't get to sit down anymore, ever, during daylight hours, so I'm weighed down with exhaustion and bore everyone about how tired I am. Rob and I have an ongoing 'tired' competition. I'm more tired than you are. No, I'm exhausted. Well I'm wrung out. I trump your wrung out with, I've got absolutely nothing left in the tank. But the upside to exhaustion and unbridled worry is that despite my nightly chocaholism, I have lost a whole stone in weight, something that I am ashamed to say has made me very happy indeed. So thank goodness for small things, and smaller bottoms, because everything does look better when the sun shines. My paranoia over being hunted down has eased. There were a few miserable weeks after the 'lapse in security' when I was in a spin. Is that tracksuited stranger following me? Why is that white Micra tailing me? Surely it must turn off soon? What will I do if it follows me into our street and stops outside our house? Did that person just take a photograph of me? I was a half-crazed insomniac imagining I was Jason Bourne.

Our entire family have now met Jaymey and Harlee. Rob's father, David, and Aunty Pam came to stay for a weekend and quietly got to know them. They brought thoughtful and well-chosen presents. David seemed thrilled to be a granddad, but as always at times of new beginnings, there was a sadness for those missed – a sadness that he was not able to share his pleasure with his wife, Rob's mother. Jaymey asked David, 'Granddad? Do you have a granny?' None of us knew what to say.

I can look back over the past three months and see that we have made progress. We have all settled into a routine of sorts. I know more or less what meals everyone will eat. I know when the conditions allow for a proper meal to be prepared and when meltdown is likely to occur in the time it takes to heat up a pan of baked beans. When food is being prepared, Harlee screeches just a little bit less whilst Jaymey plays quietly with his new Playmobil bin lorry. He happily goes to three sessions at the pre-school, on his own, and one of those sessions takes place on a Wednesday afternoon during which Harlee sleeps for an hour and a half. Wednesday afternoons have become a shining beacon in the week. I sit or often lie on the sofa, sometimes I even read a newspaper, consuming the news as though I've been in a remote country, cut off from all communication with the outside world. Bedtime is akin to a military operation. It requires a deal of stamina, but we have learnt that no time invested in a smooth bedtime is wasted time. And when we sit together singing the CBBC bedtime song, it heartens me that we have survived another day and that with each day we are more strongly connected to each other – we have more shared jokes to laugh at and more joint experiences to reminisce about. 'Oh the time has come, to say goodnight, at the end of a lovely day…' But no amount of shared family experience will count for anything without the Freeing Order, following which the path will be clear for the

Adoption Order. Four weeks to wait and it won't go through on a nod – the birth family have decided to contest it. I am told confidently by Mel and Lorna that the case is clear, that social services has all the evidence it need, and more, to show that Jaymey and Harlee can never be cared for by their birth family. But, they warn, there is always the small chance that a vital piece of evidence will be found to be lacking, a signature will be missing, the judge will wake up with the flu, a motorway accident will prevent the right people from being present, delaying the proceedings. It puzzles me that the birth family choose to fight now at this late stage, at what must surely be the last chance saloon for any parent – the point at which all legal ties with your flesh and blood are severed forever. They have refused to play by the rules up to this point, refused to bow to authority and now rush to arm themselves for the final battle. I sense that Lorna is worried about facing Trudy and Mike at the family court. She must provide the evidence that shows the children are not safe with them. They have clearly scared Jaymey and they have scared me from afar. I need my children to be free of them and I cannot think about what the ultimate outcome would be for us all if the Freeing Order doesn't go through. I am thankful that the children know nothing of this battle for their futures being played out in the court and hope that they don't soak up any of my anxiety.

I can never quite shake off the feeling that Trudy and Mike are not only part of our children's lives, but part of Rob's and mine too. They are like silent partners – infiltrating, influencing, blocking. Our home contains not only things that they have chosen, such as toys and clothes, but photographs of them and letters from them. I knew we would have someone else's personal items in our home and it hadn't crossed my mind that I would be anything other than comfortable with that, but what I hadn't expected was to feel threatened and a bit violated by them. Each image and each sentence is shot through with meaning, sometimes clear and sometimes more hidden. Some of the images say, 'See what a close family we were, see what you've ruined.' Others grab me by the throat and shout in my face, 'I'm going to fucking kill you and no one will care.' Trudy and I have exchanged another letter. Mine was bland. Hers was defensive and proprietorial with a flavour of menace. Sometimes I see this clearly and sometimes I wonder if it is a product of my paranoia. I am now to write four letters, four times a year – one to Trudy, one to Mike and one to each of the two older siblings. I have been given instructions by social services not to write anything that would identify where we live, go to school, work or holiday. So I am to write about an idyllic family life, leaving out any of the glitches that often drive our day such as 'If I raise my hand too suddenly to rub the sleep from my eyes, Jaymey winces then rolls up into a ball,' or 'Harlee seems highly anxious and is unable to sit still and relax, ever.' I must write to my new penfriends because it is in the best interests of the children; everyone knows that for a fact and there is supposed to be plenty of research to prove it. All the same, I have decided not to tell Jaymey that I am writing to the people whose photographs he refuses to look at and whom he refuses ever to talk about, because I'm not altogether sure that it is in his best interests.

Now that we have established a structure to our days and everyone is getting used to the order of things and what happens at certain times, it feels like a whole other level of challenge has risen to the surface. Maybe we are getting towards the end of the 'honeymoon period', which I have heard so much about (some honeymoon), or perhaps I am just noticing things that I was too tired to notice before. In any case, things feel bigger, louder, more frequent and more intense than they do in other people's families. When Jaymey loses his cool with me, or his sister, he seems as though he really wants to do some damage and if he was big enough then he would. If he shouts an insult at me, then it might be, 'I'm going to punch your…eyes, kill you…eyes', which doesn't make sense but leaves me horribly unsettled, wondering if he has heard something like it before. If he regresses into baby-like behaviour then it will be full-on role-play, which will take place over an entire afternoon. And it has become clear now that we are raising two only children, children who both expect our full attention, at all times. Their day is one long competition for attention. I can scream louder than you. I can push you over into Mummy's flowers and make her cross with you. I can tip over your drink and Mummy will think it was you. I can lean over in the car and undo your seatbelt and Mummy will be cross with you again. Mostly it is Jaymey inflicting his jealousy on Harlee, but she will cross a room to walk through his carefully arranged cars and then watch him explode like a firework. They are like baby birds in a nest – wired with the knowledge that he who cheeps the loudest and reaches the highest gets the worm. It is as though survival is not possible for them both, as though it must come at a cost because there is not enough love to go around. When I exchange experiences with friends or family I hear over and over, 'Well, all children do that.' Which is sort of cruel and kind at the same time. Kind because people who care about you want everything to be alright for you and to provide comfort; cruel because it indicates that there is an over-reaction in there somewhere, an over-dramatisation. Mel gets it. She listens properly, sympathises and then offers advice. Her most uttered words to us are 'structure' and 'supervision'. And those two words describe my life now.

*****

Rob and I went out for the first time last week. My parents babysat. It was our wedding anniversary. We dressed up and went for a meal and talked about the children. Lacking in opportunities for meaningful adult conversation, I found myself floundering for other topics. My usual hunting ground for source material – interesting documentaries on the radio, newspaper articles revealing the latest research into something – are now well off my radar and so, like a vacuous shell, I couldn't think of anything else to talk about. I also found myself unaccustomed to and unpractised at eating for leisurely enjoyment and we were all done and ordering coffees by nine o'clock.

'I think we should book a holiday,' said Rob, just like that, out of nowhere.

'I'm not sure we are supposed to, so early on,' I replied, like a head girl.

'We should book a holiday cottage in Cornwall, near the sea. It would be fun. It would be normal. Make it so,' he laughed.

And then I imagined us building sandcastles and paddling in the sea and watching ice cream melting down the arms of our children, mixing with the sand and the suncream.

*****

After several phone calls, we have finally got a speech therapy appointment for Jaymey. I have been told that because he now lives in a different area, albeit in the same county, he has plummeted to the bottom of the waiting list. His assessment, previously carried out in the south of the county, is not recognised by the speech therapists in the west of the county, barely 50 miles away. So I have had to be on the case, ringing every few days, politely complaining, making a nuisance of myself. I am not a natural complainer and on my own behalf would rather put up with bad service than complain, but I am fast learning the skills I need to make sure that it is my chick who gets the worm. My mum looks after Harlee, and Jaymey and I drive the short distance to the Speech and Language Therapy Unit, which is situated in a shabby, Victorian building in town. Jaymey worries about where we are going.

'We are going to see a lady who is going to help you to say some new words.'

He looks perplexed and worried. This could be someone else becoming involved in his life, who may strap him in a car seat, put his belongings in the boot of their car and take him, full of fear, to another strange house.

'Don't worry, I'll stay with you. And afterwards we'll have a play at Granny and Granddad's.'

The waiting room is deserted and very quiet. There are some broken toys in a box, some books with pages missing and a puzzle with frayed pieces. We slump into a collapsing foam chair; Jaymey sits close and we flick through his tractor book together, remarking on bucket sizes, cabs, lights and drivers. Eventually a door opens and Michelle, the speech therapist, invites us in. She is about my age and casually dressed in Birkenstock sandals and linen trousers. She looks creased and worn down. She explains that she will do an assessment of Jaymey's speech today and then we will receive notification of our first proper appointment in the post.

'How long will it be before the next appointment?'

'I can't say.'

'Well, roughly then?'

She looks tired.

'It could be another six months. We have a long waiting list.'

'You know Jaymey's background, do you?' I enquire. 'Yes, I've had a quick look through his file. There are many worse off than him, so he's not a priority case.'

And that puts me in my place, for now.

The assessment takes ages. Jaymey sits at a low table by the window with Michelle and she shows him lots of pictures, which he has to describe. Each set of pictures encourages a different sound or blend of sounds. The pictures are black and white line drawings, badly photocopied and badly drawn. I look over their shoulders and know that I would struggle to work out what some of the drawings are of. There is a dismembered torso, with a tight belt on. It looks like an egg timer, but the word she looks for is 'pinch'. To a four-year-old boy, the car looks much more like a van, so he is corrected. The ice cream is not ice cream but 'lick' and the sweets could be anything – rabbit droppings, buttons, stones. Jaymey becomes bored and gazes out of the window, which looks out on a small patch of land on which some building work is underway. There are signs of digging and some cones and hazard tape marking out an area. A man pushes a wheelbarrow of soil and then disappears out of sight. Then two more men appear, in hard hats. Jaymey gets excited.

'Look, Mummy, builder, nother builder.'

'Oh yes, I wonder what they are doing?'

Michelle's face makes something like a smile and she says Jaymey should get back to the sheet of drawings. He tries but the temptation is too much and he keeps looking up to watch the builders. Her frustration becomes more evident and her voice takes on a nagging tone.

'Come on, Jaymey, concentrate on this.'

Then, 'Jaymey. Jaymey. Concentrate.'

I want to grab her by her crumpled collar and shout, 'Give him a break, he's four years old, he's scared, he wants to talk about the builders.' But I don't.

Once the ordeal is over and she has written a long list of sounds that Jaymey cannot make and that he substitutes for sounds he can make, she turns to me.

'Can Jaymey make himself understood to people outside his immediate family?'

'No, not very easily. I translate almost everything. And he is isolated at pre-school because the other children can't understand him.'

'He definitely has concentration problems.'

She lays this out like an accusation. And I am cross that she has said this in front of him, as though he isn't there. His eyes are downcast and he fiddles with his t-shirt. ('Of course he's got fucking concentration problems – what do you expect?')

'When does he start school?'

'This September.'

There is a long pause while she writes something down. I anticipate a little of the expertise and inspiration that we have waited all this time for. I give up and ask, 'Are there any exercises we can do with him before our next appointment?'

'Well, I'll photocopy this sheet for you and you can point to the pictures and encourage him to say the words. It's also important not to correct him but to echo words back to him, emphasising the correct sounds.' She offers this as though it has taken a momentous effort and we should be grateful. I spare a thought for her – she is tired and probably overworked and has no money to buy nice materials with. But a little bit of warmth – some understanding – would have helped.

We leave the crappy building with the crappy photocopy of the crappy pictures. It feels as though we are at the bottom of the heap and I doubt that Jaymey feels any differently.

'You did really well,' I say to Jaymey.

He doesn't look at me.

'Let's go back to Granny and Granddad's and have a drink and a biscuit.'

'Yeh, din an bihi.'

*****

Every spring our local school strings a banner up across the gates advertising its spring fair. Somehow the crisp tombola, the guess-how-many-marbles-in-the-bottle game, the bouncy castle and the ride-the-impossible-bike game have never attracted me. This year, all of a sudden it looks like a great afternoon out. The school playing field is crowded. Children are milling around in little gangs burdened by giant tubes of sweets, candyfloss, hot dogs and inflatable hammers. Helpers walk purposefully across the field, carrying bags of change, raffle tickets and messages for the vicar, who is compèring the event over a very loud tannoy. Between his announcements, 1980s music is piped over the event. I tune into Thriller by Michael Jackson and watch the children on the bouncy castle ('no one's gonna save you, from the beast about to strike'). I wonder if the vicar is trying some subliminal messaging. Rob has stayed at home to clear out the garage, that being preferable to attending any event involving a raffle. So I trail around with Harlee in the pushchair and Jaymey running alongside. They are both taken with the candyfloss and point at children carrying it. Jaymey is struck that this other-worldly stuff is something that children are eating – that it must be food.

'What that fluff that boy eating?'

'That's candyfloss. It's pink sugar, all spun together.'

'I have some?'

Harlee's food squawk is sparked with added enthusiasm.

We queue up at the candyfloss van and they are each handed a pink cloud on a stick. Jaymey stares at his, his eyes popping out. The breeze catches it and it moves slightly, not like a cloud but as a whole, like a head of hair covered with hairspray. He tries to lick it but it moves around the stick away from his tongue.

'Try and take a little bite.'

He tastes some and after a short moment of uncertainty decides it is delicious. I look across to Harlee. She has pushed her whole hand into the centre of the candyfloss. Her whole hand then is pushed into her mouth. Her hands and face are covered in dissolving, disintegrating pink sugar.

The music on the tannoy fades out ('I know not everybody, has a body like you…') and the majorettes are introduced – a troupe of about 15 ribbon-swishing girls wrapped in inadvisable Lycra all-in-one costumes. They swish their ribbons to 'Reach for the Stars' and little children in the audience jig and bob to the music. A hand touches my arm. It is Andrea, the lady we bought our house from. Next to her is a tall woman, about my age, with two small children.

'Hi Sally, I just wanted to introduce you to Anna. She lives along the road from you.'

I shake Anna's hand, 'Hello, nice to meet you.'

'You live next to Jean, don't you? I'm further down from you, nearer the school, the house with the motorbike outside it.'

'I know the one. Have you lived there long?'

'About five years, how about you?'

'About the same.'

Andrea says she is due to do her stint on the cake stall and leaves.

Then Anna says, 'Would you like to come over for coffee sometime? My two boys are always looking for playmates.'

'We would love to.'

We agree to meet up next Thursday morning. As Anna walks away and the majorettes swap their ribbons for batons, I smile. We have our first play-date. I am going to spend time with another grown-up, whom I'm not related to. And she seems nice. Oh happy days. Later on, as we queue for tea and cake I spot Andrea. 'Thank you,' I mouth to her.

'It's OK. I know how difficult it can be, being at home and everything.'

And I have been treated to a small kindness. Before having Jaymey and Harlee I had listened from afar to mothers of young children and wondered what they were moaning about. Many of them didn't have to go out to work every day and stayed at home with their children. What could be so difficult about that? Now I know differently. Since giving up nine to five work in exchange for something much more gruelling I don't seem to have a single friend. I feel like a tragic case. My friends all live some distance away, or are friends from work, or friends who I hiked with or went to concerts with. I have seen mothers together, in cafes, going in and out of each others' houses and I have felt jealous, an outsider. The pre-school mothers have kept their distance; most of them seem to have longer attachments with each other, established during pregnancy classes.

I look forward to meeting up with Anna a ridiculous amount. We arrive at ten o'clock on the dot. Jaymey is very excited to be invited to someone's house. I just hope that everyone behaves. Anna greets us with a 'hello everyone' and a 'come inside' and a 'let's see what there is to play with'. Her two children, boys, are sitting in the middle of the large kitchen, playing with a wooden train set. Jaymey is shy but one of the boys – the older one – gives him a train. Jaymey puts it on the track and pushes it up and over a bridge, letting it run down the other side. Harlee sits down next to the box of track and I show her how to interlink the pieces. I tentatively turn away from them and Anna and I discuss tea and milk and sugar and then juice and biscuits. We talk, a little awkwardly, about what we used to do – Anna was a caterer; and our hobbies – Anna is a keen artist. I talk about my gardening, which seems like a distant memory, and remark that her garden is lovely. Every few minutes we are interrupted by Harlee who tries to reach for the biscuit packet or is trying to undo the boys' track or play with a train that someone else was playing with. I sit her on my knee and Anna gives her a wooden board with removable pieces shaped as different vehicles. Each piece has a peg on the top. Harlee is kept busy for a few more moments, trying to ram the digger into the tractor slot and then the racing car into the saloon car slot.

Just as Harlee starts to empty a large toy box of its contents all over the train track, I gather everything up and we say our thank yous and leave. I invite Anna and her boys to our house the following week.

That weekend Rob's dad visits. He arrives on Friday afternoon before Rob is back from work. We sit in the garden and watch the children. They roll a ball in and out of a play tent and tunnel that a neighbour has given us. He coughs and struggles to breathe and I notice that his skin is looking grey. He is not a man who is comfortable talking about himself or sharing his worries so I try to enquire casually, 'So is everything alright with you then?'

'Oh, fine thank you. Jaymey is enjoying that tent.'

We pass the afternoon exchanging pleasantries – which car Rob is going to buy next, the holiday house we have booked – and then we walk slowly around the garden, occasionally rolling the ball back to the children. I hear Rob's car pull up and then see him at the back door. David turns to say hello and then we walk slowly back to the bench under the kitchen window. As David sits down, Rob mouths to me 'Everything alright?' and I mouth back 'Don't know.' David coughs again.

'That's a nasty cough. Are you alright?' asks Rob.

'Oh yes, you know?'

'You want to go to the doctor's with that.'

'No, I'll be fine.' He says it in such a way that we are left in no doubt that no more will be said about it.

We pass the weekend not mentioning the cough but making sure that we plan in plenty more benches and some cafes. He seems to get worse as the weekend goes on. He walks slowly and gets out of breath easily. We wave him off on Sunday afternoon. As his car goes around the corner and out of sight, Rob and I look at each other.

'I'm worried about him. Has he told you anything?' I ask.

'No, nothing at all. He's a stubborn man.'

'Like father like son then.'

Then Harlee tries to run into the road and we are back in the house sorting out who has emptied whose toys over the floor, who has trodden the chocolate bourbon into the carpet and whether the lawn will ever get mowed or the dirty laundry washed.

As the weeks go on David sounds worse on the phone. Then one evening Rob comes home from work when I am giving the children their tea; he looks awful.

'Dad rang me today. He's been to the hospital for some tests. He's got a lung disease. I need to go on the internet and do some research. He wouldn't tell me much but…' He looks at me. I give him a hug but he shrugs it away. Then, 'Mummy. Mummy. Mummy? *Mummy. Mummy. Mummeeyah!*'

Jaymey hasn't quite finished his tea. I turn around and ask him what he wants. He hasn't thought of a question yet and has to think on his feet.

'Mummy…what is…for pudding?'

I am cross at his intervention, although I know it is about competing and being jealous of the attention Rob is getting.

'Nothing,' I say. I turn back to Rob. 'So did he tell you what the disease is called?'

'*I not eat my tea then!*' shouts Jaymey, putting down his cutlery and crossing his arms in front of his chest.

We ignore him.

'I can't remember exactly. I've got it written down. I'm going up to get changed.'

Jaymey pushes his plate away from him and it catches on the cutlery and tips over, spilling baked beans on the plastic tablecloth. I scoop it all back on to the plate.

'You need to eat this.'

'No. I hate you…you go live…in…Africa…on your own and be lonely. I stay with Daddy here. Not with you!'

His face is bright red and he spits the words at me. It seems to have flared up from nothing, from me diverting my attention from him to Rob for a moment. Harlee keeps eating as though she hasn't heard any of it.

'Well unfortunately I'm not going to Africa, so you are stuck with me. And you can have a yoghurt when you've finished your tea.'

He takes a while to assess his options and then eats most of his food. He leaves just enough to see if I am up for a battle and then looks at me provocatively. Tonight is not the night.

'Here's your yoghurt.'

'Don't want strawberry, want peach.'

'Well that's a shame because we've got strawberry. I'm sure Harlee will eat it if you don't want it.'

She reaches out for it but he grabs it first.

After tea I take them both upstairs and shut them in the bathroom with me while I run their bath and get them undressed. Then when they are both in the bath I find Rob in our bedroom, using the laptop.

'I'll do bedtimes tonight.'

'Thanks.'

Bedtime is stomping and shouting and aggravation. Harlee goes into her cot happily but is kept awake by Jaymey who lies in bed and shouts about the unfairness of having had to share a bedtime story with his sister. Normally he gets a story with Rob one night and then me the next night and this little change in routine evidently means that we don't love him anymore. As I am going down the stairs I hear him shout,

'I go back and live with Thelma!'

I feel a rush of anger and storm back up the stairs.

'You are not going back to Thelma's – you are living here now. Now be quiet and go to sleep.'

I shout too loudly and slam the bedroom door too hard. Then I storm back down the stairs, whisk into the sitting room and drop into the sofa. I try to breathe out my anger. After a few moments a wave of guilt hits me. Shouting and slamming doors is not something I have done since I was a teenager. And I have just lost control in front of a four-year-old. Somewhere in my thinking I know why he played up at teatime and I know why he couldn't sort himself out. The images of the baby birds in the nest, fighting for survival, returns to me. But my anger had blinded me.

I cook some pasta for Rob and call him. We eat in front of the television.

'Have you found anything on the internet?'

'Yes, it's not looking good. He's taking some steroids and he told me they have helped a bit.'

We both sit in silence for a while.

'Do you want to go and see him this weekend?'

'Yes, I think I should. Do you mind?'

'Of course not.'

I am immediately filled with dread at coping on my own for two days and then filled with guilt that I could be so selfish.

I explain to the children that Daddy will be away for two sleeps, that he is going to visit his daddy who is poorly and that he will ring them before bedtime. I look at Jaymey's face as I talk and sense that he doesn't get it, doesn't understand what two sleeps is, doesn't really believe that this is a temporary state of affairs. Rob comes into the kitchen to kiss them goodbye. He lifts Harlee out of her high chair and she giggles and then kisses him. Jaymey acts as though Rob is a complete stranger to him, a punishment for going away and leaving him. Harlee and I go out to the car, give Rob a kiss and wave until his car has disappeared. I am left feeling teary, bereft and guilty.

Despite Jaymey's anger, I manage to get him ready, into the car seat and off to pre-school for the morning. I leave him there looking as though he wants to kill me, feel relieved to have three hours without him and then feel immediately guilty again.

Rob rings that evening. Jaymey won't speak to him, despite me trying to persuade him, then bribing him and then getting cross with him. Harlee takes the phone and breathes deeply into the receiver and then makes some noises. I desperately want her to make a sound that is something like 'da da' but nothing comes. I talk to Rob whilst Jaymey stands in front of me saying 'Mummy' over and over again. Fleetingly I know what he is really saying is, 'I'm here, I'm here, please don't forget about me,' because a chick's survival is in the balance when its mummy has something else to focus on.

'Dad is in hospital. He got suddenly worse.'

I struggle to hear him over the top of Jaymey.

'He's on a ventilator. The doctor is hoping they can stabilise him.'

'So he's going to be in for a while then?'

'Looks like it.'

We say our goodbyes; Rob's is drowned out. He seems a million miles away.

David's condition worsens and there is little sign that he will be out of hospital. Rob does the 500-mile round trip to visit him every weekend. I stay at home with the children, wishing I could be with Rob but knowing that this division of labour is the only way we can manage. We both feel as though we are in a 'no-win' situation. Rob is doing his best, trying to fulfil his roles as a son and a father. But he still feels as though he should be spending more time with his dad and more time with Jaymey and Harlee. And he still has a demanding full-time job. Jaymey, in particular, responds to this change in routine very badly and it is clear that the last thing he needs is his new daddy suddenly disappearing for some reason. He seems to want to punish Rob for being away by cutting him off, staying aloof from him. During the May half term there isn't even the routine of pre-school to fall back on and I start to feel as though I am losing control. Jaymey scribbles on the front of the house and the front door in blue crayon. He makes the classic mistake of writing his name and then saying, 'Mummy, look what Harlee has done, she is very naughty.' It seems that he is in some way happy when he thinks Harlee is in trouble, as if love is rationed according to who is good and who is bad. Every single journey in the car is interrupted two or three times when I have to stop in a lay-by to refasten Harlee's seatbelt. The unfastening is carried out deftly so I don't see who does it. Jaymey is always very convincing when I challenge him, looking out of the window and then acting as though I have interrupted him in deep thought. Then, on a journey home from my sister's house, I happen to look in the rear view mirror at the very moment that he leans across, undoes his sister's seatbelt, throws her a knowing glance and then nonchalantly looks out of the window. ('That's definitely more love for me now.')

'Jaymey, why did you undo Harlee's seatbelt?'

'It is undone?'

'Yes it is. Why did you do it?'

'I think Harlee did do it. Harlee did you undo your seatbelt? You is naughty girl.'

'Jaymey?'

'Yes Mummy.'

'I saw you do it.'

There is a brief silence and his cheeks flush red.

'*I did not do it. I did see Harlee do it!*' he shouts.

'I saw you do it.'

'I hate you. I go with Daddy and leave you horrible Mummy. You be lonely!'

He has a plastic policeman grasped tightly in his hand, which he raises up. I prepare for it to be lobbed at my head, but it is Harlee who gets it thrown in her face. She starts to cry and Jaymey continues shouting at me. We are ten minutes from home and past the last lay-by, so I continue on, trying to tune out the cacophony of high-pitched noise, trying not to brake too hard and propel Harlee through the windscreen, trying not to kill us all.

We pull into the drive. I get out of the car and close the door. Sudden peace. I take a breath. I can see the fracas taking place in the back of the car and hear the muffled sound effects. I try to convince myself I am feeling calm and in control. I open Jaymey's door first. He screams at me that he will not get out and describes what he will do to me if I make him. I decide I will remove Harlee first. As I walk around to her side of the car I see Jaymey reach across and grab her jumper. I open her door.

'It's OK, Harlee, come with Mummy and we can have a look at your hurt. Jaymey, let go...Jaymey...'

I use force to unpeel Jaymey's fingers from the jumper. Then he screams,

'You hurted me. Mummy you hurted me!'

I lift Harlee out, balance her on my hip and as I turn I am face to face with Jean, our next-door neighbour.

'Having trouble, dear?'

'Yes, you could say that.'

'Never mind, dear. All children have tantrums. Terrible twos, I expect.'

I expel some air through my clenched teeth, which I intend to sound like a complicit kind of 'Yeah, what a nightmare,' but which sounds more like 'Don't fuck with me now.' I do the lopsided one-handed key turn, Harlee kicking me in the kidney, and then I quickly strap her into her high chair. I wipe her tears with a tissue and go into the food cupboard. This causes an immediate cessation in crying. I open a packet of teddy crisps and give her the whole packet, something that has never happened to her in our house. She is ecstatic. I purposefully walk back out to the car, with my head down, to avoid Jean.

'Come on, Jaymey, time to come in.'

'*I not go into horrible house with you, you hurt me and I tell Daddy and I tell Thelma and I tell policeman. And you go prison!*'

'So I'm the bad guy am I?'

I know that this is my final attempt at keeping my cool.

'*You very, very, very, very baaaaaddddd!*'

He says this right into my face.

I want to shout back at him, but I'm aware of Jean's continued presence. An intimidating, low, slow voice comes out of my mouth and surprises me with its venom. I have never heard myself sound like this before.

'You are coming with me right now and you will never speak to me like that, ever again.'

We are then in a struggle, me to get him out of the car and him to cling on to anything he can. I use my strength over him and carry him like a roll of carpet, into the house with his arms jammed into his sides to avoid him hitting me or wriggling free. I try to sit him at the bottom of the stairs next to the kitchen, but he lashes out with his arms and feet, his face now purple with anger. Then I pick him up again, run up the stairs with him, open his bedroom door and drop him on to his bed.

'*I hate you!*' he shouts as I leave the room and go down the stairs.

I daren't open my mouth.

Harlee has finished her crisps and is licking the inside of the bag. As I get the juice from the fridge and her cup from the draining board, I can hear destruction taking place upstairs. I sit with Harlee as she drinks and we both listen nervously to the crashing and shouting. I am out of my depth.

When Rob gets home, it is like some catastrophe has swept across the house. I feel like a disaster movie victim wandering around aimlessly in a state of blank bewilderment, unable to take in events. Jaymey greets Rob more enthusiastically than he has for weeks. This narks me – that he is turning on the sweet and cute after all that has happened. It feels like a calculated move to get between Rob and me – to divide and conquer – so that Rob could not possibly believe what Jaymey knows I will tell him. And yet I know that his anger was not deliberate, and even the cuteness comes from a place of fear, 'Please love me, don't leave me.'

'Daddy, you want play tractors with me?'

'Just let me get changed. What have you been up to today then, Jaymey?'

'I…' he glances across at me, 'I played in park with Aunty Alice and Luke and Harry.'

'I'm sorry to have missed that.'

I follow Rob upstairs, wordlessly and then indicate that he should look in Jaymey's room. It looks as though a burglar has been through it. His bedding is on the floor, the drawers are all open and emptied of clothes, furniture is upturned and his curtains, curtain rail and a shower of plaster crown the destruction.

'My god, what happened here?'

'It's a long story, but it started in the car on the way home from Alice's. He just lost control, completely, he was so angry. It went on and on.'

I am so drained that I cannot recall the sequence of events, the things that were said. I jumble things up and skip back and forth. It ends up sounding like a big fuss about not very much, something that I should have been able to quash, which I allowed to get out of control. I get frustrated with myself, my inability to reach and convey the essence of what has happened.

It is bread and cheese for tea. Rob takes care of the bedtime routine. I sit and stare into space again, echoes of the afternoon coming back to me in little sharp fragments. I remember things I have thought and said and feel guilty, yet again. I know that Jaymey is not purposely trying to hurt me or Harlee and that he didn't really want to create havoc in his bedroom. But it is not that easy to intellectualise about the causes of the storm when the storm is directly overhead. Tomorrow is Friday, the day of the Freeing Order; the day when I hope the path will be made clear for us to become a family – a proper, legal family. I feel a need to mend things with Jaymey, before he goes to bed. I find him and Rob cuddled up under the duvet reading a book together. I reach over and kiss Jaymey. 'Mummy loves you, do you know that? And tomorrow is a brand new day.'

'Night night, Mummy. Love you too.'

CHAPTER 11

After we have taken Jaymey to pre-school, Harlee and I go into the garden. It is hot so we sit at the table under an umbrella, her on my lap. I am waiting to hear news of the Freeing Order from Lorna so I guard the telephone handset, making sure it is out of Harlee's reach. She drinks juice from a plastic cup with two handles, although she is far too busy to use both hands. With her left hand she drags a blue crayon across a piece of paper. I take a red crayon from the box and using her squiggle as a shoelace, I draw a training shoe. She looks at me, beams so that juice runs down her chin, lifts her leg up on to the table and points to her new pink, canvas shoe.

'Well done, you got it, it's a shoe. Can you say "shoe"?'

She makes another mark on the paper and then indicates that it is my turn again. I swap my red crayon for a green one and then turn her v-shaped lines into the stalk of a bunch of grapes.

'Mmmm…' she nods approvingly.

'You got that one too, it's grapes. You're doing very well at this game.'

I am given another squiggle. This time I turn it into a hand, with fingers splayed, long nails, nail moons and knuckle creases. I pass Harlee the paper and she smiles and holds out her hand.

'Fantastic, it's a hand,' I say, grabbing her hand and blowing into her palm. She laughs, pulling it away.

'Go on, let me have that hand.'

She puts her arms behind her back and I tickle her, then grab her hand again and pretend to bite her fingers. She looks at me with wide eyes and then takes the piece of paper.

'Mo, mo mo.'

She looks at my face very closely and then raises her eyebrows. 'Mo? Mo? Mo?' she nods.

'More, would you like me to draw more pictures?'

She settles on my lap and watches as I draw a semicircle, with a bob of curly hair on the top and small eyes and nose and a rosebud mouth. She gets excited and points at her chest. Then I draw a body wearing her t-shirt with the cherries on, her shorts and new shoes. She looks down and touches her shorts and shoes, then points to the hair on the drawn girl and touches her own.

'Well done again. It's Harlee.'

She attempts to colour in the picture, energetically scribbling over the eyes and mouth and I lazily draw grass and flowers around the edge and some rabbit ears appearing out of the undergrowth. Just as I contemplate adding a tail, the phone rings. I shift Harlee on to the chair and stand beside her.

It's Lorna. 'Good news. The Freeing Order has gone through.'

The relief floods me and I pump my fist and mouth a silent 'yesssss'. But she sounds shaken.

'Was everything alright?'

'The birth family weren't easy to deal with. They made threats, not against you. You can put in your adoption application now, if that's still what you're planning to do.'

'Of course. I can't wait to get the forms in the post.'

'I am pleased for you all. Jaymey and Harlee are so lucky to have you and Rob.'

'Lorna, it's we who feel lucky.'

I put the phone back on the far side of the table, lift Harlee out of her chair and spin her about so her legs fly out behind her.

'You are my best baby girl.'

I slow down and stand her on the grass, to stagger around for a bit. She falls on her bottom.

'Shall we ring Daddy?'

She gets up and makes her way back to the table where the phone is. I sit down and Harlee sits on my lap again.

'Rob, it's good news!'

I tell him what she said.

'Sal, don't dwell on the threats, let's just get those adoption forms from Mel and get them in the post.'

'What time are you leaving?'

'Lunchtime. I want to get to the hospital for evening visiting. I'll ring when I get there.'

Harlee has been trying to grab the phone from me.

'Harlee would like to speak to you.'

I hold the handset to her ear and she looks startled to hear Rob's voice. I can hear him asking her questions. Are you having a nice morning? Are you looking after Mummy? Did you take Jaymey to pre-school? She is silent and then starts to make a few noises.

'Wa, wa, wa.'

I wonder if she is about to find her tongue and whisper 'Daddy', but she loses interest in the phone call in an instant and drops the handset on the table, simultaneously picking up a crayon. I say goodbye to Rob and we continue the drawing game. Harlee doesn't get much of a look in when Jaymey is around, so when he is at pre-school she wrings every drop of attention out of me that she can.

The weekend is long, oppressively hot and endless. We are up so early in the morning that the days stretch out like a series of endurance events. We go swimming on Saturday morning and when we get back home it is only ten o'clock. We walk to the park and I follow them both around lifting them on things, then off things, then back on, then follow them on to something else, then back to the first thing. I look jealously at other mothers, sitting in groups on benches, chatting and sunbathing, organising their fabulous social lives. They occasionally get up to wipe a snotty nose or nurse a grazed knee, then return to their friends. Jaymey has a knack of being able to make friends in any situation. Before long he has teamed up with another little boy, Liam. They both head for the swings so I take Harlee too and put her in the baby swing next to them. I push Harlee and Jaymey and wonder if I should be pushing another woman's child.

'Liam, you want my mummy to push you?'

Liam doesn't understand.

'Mummy, push Liam too.'

I glance around the park but can see no sign of a protective mother looking warningly at me so I push all three swings, one after the other, keeping them going in a cycle. Harlee screeches to be let down so I lift her out and let her go. The swings barely miss her head as she veers in front of them, en route to the climbing frame. I watch her with half my attention, still pushing the boys who are giggling. In a moment she has climbed to the top of the ladder and is attempting to cross the horizontal bars. I leave the boys, run to her and watch as she inches her way across, only accepting help when she needs lifting down from the platform at the other end.

'My word, you're a little monkey.'

She's off again: this time she climbs the net, little feet slipping on the rope, little legs straining to reach each level. I see a degree of determination I have never seen in her before, outside the kitchen. She watches older children overtaking her on either side and this only spurs her on, strengthens her resolve. When she gets to the top I lift her down and she runs to the slide – the big one, not the one designed for children of her own age. It is set into the side of a grassy mound and again she climbs it – slowly but effectively – as older children run ahead of her. At the top, I watch as she carefully sits, unfolding her legs so her feet are out in front of her. I position myself at the bottom, legs astride the slide. She looks down at me and for a moment I wonder if she is thinking it all looks too frightening. I have to physically stop myself pointing out the danger, offering a get out. And then she is off and comes to a stop just ahead of me, laughing. I lift her off and up she goes again.

Then, 'Mummy, I have been shouting for you, for a long, long time. You push me and Liam now.'

'OK, in a moment, just let Harlee have another go on the slide.'

'You leave Harlee and come now.'

'No, I'll be with you in a moment.'

I look over at the swings and Liam is looking across at me, smiling hopefully. Jaymey stands next to me, frowning.

'You've made a nice friend.'

'*Push now!*'

Harlee hurtles down the slide again.

'Good girl, very clever. Right, would you like me to come and push you on the swings now?'

He marches off ahead of me.

Back at home again and lunch over and done with, it is still only one o'clock. I wonder how I am going to fill the rest of the day. I remember the bottles of bubbles in the cupboard under the sink. I open one bottle, fish out the blower and crouch down to blow a bubble as they both stand beside me. By mid-blow they are both grabbing for the bottle so I blow some bubbles down towards them, explaining how it is done and give them a bottle each. Jaymey puffs too enthusiastically at first and then gets the hang of it. I help Harlee to blow some, which she pursues until they float out of her reach. I decide now is the time to put the kettle on and attempt five minutes of actual sitting. I run inside and quickly make two juices with lids on and a cup of tea. I am back in the garden in record time to see Harlee tipping the bubble mixture into the sandpit and then mixing it with the soil, which she had added earlier. At that moment next door's cat saunters across the lawn.

'Cat, Mummy, cat,' says Jaymey, pointing at it with the hand that is holding the bottle of bubble mixture. It is like watching a drunk person clutching a pint of beer and checking their watch. As the soapy liquid gently soaks into the grass, his expression goes from puzzled to disappointed to upset to angry – very, very angry. His face goes red, his foot stamps on the wet grass, he checks in the bottle, finds it is completely empty and then throws the bottle into the hedge. I don't catch what it is he shouts, but it is something about not wanting to live here anymore.

'Jaymey, it's OK, we can buy some more.'

He calms a little.

'Buy more now?'

'No, we aren't going to the shops now.'

'*Yes now!*'

'No, another day,' I say patiently.

'*I hate you Mummy…fat head…*' and he darts in all directions kicking furniture, plant pots, toys, anything.

'Come on, let's go inside.'

I pick him up as he tries to push and kick me away. We are in through the back door, through the kitchen and into the hall. I sit on the bottom step and clamp him on to my lap as he almost explodes with the effort of trying to break free from me. I know I shouldn't leave Harlee alone in the garden so I leave Jaymey on the stair whilst I bring her, complaining, into the kitchen and sit her at the table with her juice and a biscuit. When I get back to Jaymey, all the clean laundry, which had been neatly folded and stacked on the stairs, has been strewn across the floor.

'No, you do not do that.'

I attempt to gather the clothes, but he wrestles me for them. I see the care I have taken, in washing them, pegging them on the line, folding them, putting them in the correct piles – trousers and shorts on the bottom, then t-shirts and pyjamas and then pants and socks on the top. Each one of these tasks has been undertaken, staccato fashion, in quick opportunistic spurts, through a fog of adrenaline and exhaustion, when maybe they are in the bath, or on the toilet or eating yoghurt. I see him gathering my effort up in armfuls and flinging it at the floor.

'*Get up to your room now!*' I shout at him.

'*No!*'

'*Now.*'

He doesn't cry, doesn't look scared, doesn't flinch when I scream so loudly that my throat tears. I grab him and he gets away and runs up the stairs as I chase after him, screaming. He runs into his room and I pause, listening to the sound of Playmobil vehicles being thrown. I head back down the stairs and crumple into the bottom stair, my head in my hands. I hear him run out of his room and stand above me on the landing, bearing down on me.

'*I going to chop off your head, chop your head all off and peel your skin all off. I going to peel your eyes out. I hate you Mummy!*'

The brutality of the words cut and dislocate me; they fill my head with images I don't want to see. I am lost. I think of Harlee in the room next door listening to this; I think of my neighbour Jean maybe overhearing as she deadheads her roses. My mind flits around as I try to decide what my options are – sit here and let him shout like that and then destroy his bedroom or run up after him and...then what? I feel the emotion rising up, my throat constricting, my eyes filling with tears. I run into the kitchen and close the back door and the windows, then run back to the stair. And then an unholy noise comes out of me – a wail that bends my body in two. It comes and keeps coming. It makes me thrash my arms about then clasp them around my bended knees as I rock and wail and wail, surrounded by a jumble of sheets, shirts and trousers. I am flooded with self-pity, alone, exhausted, failing, guilty. I need Rob, who is away; I need my mum, who is on holiday. I need Mel. I need the quietness of a Cumbrian mountain, the abandon of a Cornish beach; I need the joy of being with friends. Then I hear a sound from the kitchen and then the downstairs toilet. Harlee is beside me. I uncurl and look up at her through a glaze of tears. She is holding a tissue out to me. I take it and she puts her hand on my head. She looks scared.

'Thank you, Harlee,' I sob.

I wipe my eyes and mouth and she puts her head close to mine and breathes into my neck. I put my arms around her body and she puts her arms around my neck. Then she breathes into my ear, 'Mu mu mu.'

It sounds as if she is trying to say 'Mummy' but she is barely audible. I am aware of Jaymey listening silently at the top of the stairs.

'That was a very kind thing to do.'

She pats me on the head.

Then from above me I hear, 'I very sorry Mummy.'

I can't look at him.

'Mummy, I very sorry.'

'Come here then.'

He slowly and quietly makes his way down the stairs and sits on the stair above me.

I look at him, and he is clearly spooked and scared. I am supposed to be the rock in the stormy sea that he and Harlee can latch on to, can rely upon not to wobble, not to crumble. And I have shown myself to be flimsy and breakable.

Jaymey puts his arm across my shoulder and I draw him and Harlee into me, into a tight hug.

'Mummy loves you both, very, very much. You are my best boy and my best girl and I love you more than any other boy or girl in the world.'

They hold on to me silently. We pass the rest of the day in shock.

At half past eight that evening, I hear Rob's car pulling up outside the house. He comes in looking exhausted. I am sitting in my pyjamas eating an Aero.

'Ready for bed already?'

'It's a long story. How was the journey? How's your dad?'

'Not good.'

'Do they know when he's likely to be coming out of the hospital?'

'I don't think he will be.'

There is nothing to say. I give him a hug, but he is far away.

*****

Mel visits and I show her into the kitchen. She has brought the adoption forms in a big, brown envelope. Social services has completed its sections and now I need to fill in the application form.

'Have you decided on the names?'

'Yes, we're going to change the spelling of Jaymey's name to J-a-m-i-e, so that he doesn't have to spend the rest of his life explaining the "y"s. And we are going to give them each a middle name. Jaymey will be Jamie David – it's a Donovan family tradition for the men to have David as a middle name. And Harlee's middle name will be Rose.'

'That's lovely. It's nice to have a bit of a say over your children's names. And I've spoken to my supervisor. We are both of the strong opinion that we must apply to have the adoption hearing out of this county and in a city court, where you won't be seen by anyone who will know the birth family. We are still concerned for your security and at least that way you can all enjoy the day without looking over your shoulders.'

'You're right. I'm tired of worrying about them and I don't want it to ruin the occasion.'

'And we can all have a nice day out,' Mel smiles.

'So once the children have been formally adopted, will you continue to support us, or will someone else do that?'

'I will always be happy to speak to you if you have any problems, but your file will be passed to the post-adoption support team. You will be given a support worker. I'm not sure who it will be, but they will be in contact with you soon, I'm sure.'

I feel a bit of dread creeping at the thought of being without Mel.

'Are the support workers qualified social workers?'

'No. They are part-time workers who can support you over the phone and come out and see you.'

This is not sounding ideal.

*****

On Monday morning, Rob gets up and goes off to work. I suggest that he take a day off – or maybe just the morning – but he would prefer to stay busy. As we kiss him goodbye, I notice that Jaymey's face is looking a bit blotchy. I lift up his t-shirt and his chest is blotchy too.

'Are you feeling alright, Jaymey?' I ask.

'Yeah, I not poorly.'

I keep him home from pre-school just in case, but he carries on as normal, playing outside, wanting me to kick a football around. Then when I put Harlee to bed for her afternoon sleep I cuddle up with him on the sofa and we watch some television together – Big Cook, Little Cook, which he loves and I find bearable, then Balamory, during which I fantasise about being on a silent yoga retreat. Then Mr Tumble comes on and as I turn to Jaymey to acknowledge our shared respect for Justin, I notice his eyelids drooping and his head nodding. I lay him down on the sofa with a pillow and a blanket, and he goes straight to sleep. I quietly wheel over the footstool, put my feet up, switch over to a Grand Designs repeat and my own eyelids close. It is blissful. I sink into a lovely place, with Kevin McCloud and plenty of light and a sense of the outdoors coming in. Then a little sound from upstairs invades my peace. I ignore it for longer than I should. I am so, so tired. I wonder how I might get just a little bit of rest. Not active rest – bed rest. I don't want a horrible disease, just something temporarily disabling. It would have to be something serious enough that I wouldn't be able to battle on in pain. So a broken arm would just make my life even more trying. But a broken leg…now we're talking. A broken leg could put me into hospital for a couple of nights. I wouldn't be able to shop, cook, hang out washing. Everyone would have to be nice to me, help me out, a lot. I wouldn't feel so bloody lonely. The little noise increases in volume to an unhappy, 'I am awake you know and I'm not impressed with being left up here on my own.' I drag open my eyes and dizzily force myself up from the sofa and up the stairs, stepping over the laundry and toys that someone is meant to carry up.

The next morning I wake up early – very early – feeling terrible. I am hot and itchy, itchy, itchy, all over my body. I get out of bed and lift up my pyjama top – I am covered in small pinpricks of dark red. They literally cover every square centimetre of my skin. My vision clouds over with flashing puffs of purple and orange, and the noisy world in my head drowns out Rob, who is sitting up in bed mouthing something at me. I fall back and breathe too much – hot but cold and the noise, the noise is dreadful. The itching.

I lay my hand on my stomach for the relief of a different sensation. I open my eyes and Rob is standing over me.

'Are you OK?'

'No,' I manage pathetically, pointing to my stomach.

'Oh my god, you are covered.'

'Hot, very hot, itchy.'

He takes the covers off me, disappears downstairs and then comes back with a cold drink and a paracetamol. He sits me up and I swallow the pill. It takes a mammoth effort. He looks at my back.

'I think I'd better stay off work.'

I am left alone for what feels like an age. I lie completely still as any movement drags the sheets against my skin, which responds with a flame of heat. Rob appears.

'Jaymey is at pre-school. I called NHS Direct. It might be a virus. You have to take paracetamol and drink lots of liquid. Mel rang. She wants to discuss the adoption application.'

'I can't talk to anyone.'

'I'll deal with it.'

The words are like honey. I mentally collapse into the resolve of another and remember my idle thought from the day before. I wished for a broken leg and have been punished for my selfishness with this inferno.

After two days of itchy torture Rob takes me to see the GP – a German locum doctor. He says it is a bad idea to seek help for a rash over the phone and then he takes a look at my legs and stomach and says that what I have is a form of German measles. My mind meanders and dreams over the chances of a German doctor diagnosing German measles. I forget to listen to everything he says but remember having German measles as a child and it was a breeze – a few days off school, some bike riding, some skipping and lots of ice cream.

'With adults it is different,' he says, 'much worse.'

He writes a prescription for something that will stop the itching. They will make me feel tired. Nothing could make me feel more tired. I am the Queen Mother of tired. I am stupidly grateful. No itching and sleep – lots and lots of beautiful sleep. I take the first dose of pills in the car and then some more later in the day, and by the late afternoon I feel the itching starting to ease. The prickles are less frequent and less sharp, and a heavy fog hangs over me. Occasionally I open an eyelid and see a child standing over me, staring. Then I will open the same eyelid again and they will be gone. I hear meal noises and then suddenly it is dark. I take pills and sleep, wake up, take pills and sleep in an endless beautiful cycle of abandonment.

A few days pass before I start to recover and lose the burn victim look. Rob goes back to work and my mum comes and feeds me homemade pasties, does some laundry and tidies the sitting room. Then, before I feel fully returned to the real world, Rob is back in Manchester and I am coping alone, dragging myself through endless hours engulfed by a heavy blanket of tiredness. On Saturday evening Rob rings.

'Hi, was your journey alright?'

'Yes, long, slow.'

'How's your dad?'

'Really not good.'

He stops talking.

'We all miss you. Jaymey's been playing with his trucks on the blanket in the garden. Harlee's drawn you a picture.'

'That's nice. I'm aiming to be home by mid-afternoon tomorrow, so I can spend some time with you all. And I'm looking forward to our holiday. It's only a month away now.'

'Yes, I can't wait.'

'Must go now, see you tomorrow.'

'Bye.'

The holiday is out in the distance like a gorgeous snowy peak. I have my head down, trudging towards it, one step at a time. I have booked a house in the centre of Wadebridge in Cornwall. It looks old and roomy and relaxingly shabby. I discounted anything that looked like a Grand Design. It would just show up the spills and the crayon.

On Sunday morning the three of us are drawing at the table. I draw a picture of me, Rob, Jaymey and Harlee standing in front of our house. Harlee watches me and occasionally adds a mark. Then as I finish with a sun and a puffy cloud, Harlee points to the drawing of herself and then points to her chest.

'Yes, that's you. And that one's Jaymey with his football and that's Daddy and that's Mummy.'

She points to the picture of me, 'Mu-mmy mu-mmy.'

'Mummy, yes, Mummy, did you say Mummy?'

'Mu-mmy.'

'Fantastic! That's right, Mummy. Jaymey, did you hear Harlee? She just said Mummy.'

He looks up, mutters 'well done' and then pretends to be engrossed in what he is doing. I clap and cheer, anxious that Harlee is aware that this is something to be rewarded and repeated. She claps too, with a big dribbly grin. Whenever she would sit still long enough, I have grabbed the opportunity to encourage her to make sounds. 'Mu, mu, mu, mu, Harlee, can you say mu mu mu?' 'Harlee, du, du, du, du.' I would let her look into my mouth so she could see how I was making the sounds. All this whilst other children of her age are saying 'Mummy, please pass my Dante, it is over there by my chess set.' I'm aware that I have to make up for the months she spent in her cot staring at a blank ceiling, when other babies were being bounced on the knee, being sung to, having the palms of their hands tickled 'round and round the garden', never much doubting that the world is a safe place, full of loving and caring people. So when we meet acquaintances in the street, or Jean from next door and they say, 'Ooh, isn't she talking yet?' I say, 'No, not quite,' and not, 'You have no idea, idiot, of the time we have spent emming and effing and essing during every spare moment so that it is another thing which is on my mind all the time, that I must teach her to speak before I move on to try to fill other parts of the void that grew out of months of neglect.'

That evening in the bath, high on her earlier success, Harlee scoops up some foam in her hand, holds it close to her face and says, 'bu-bble'. We clap and cheer again and she says 'bu-bble' again and again. I know what the next word needs to be.

'Harlee, can you say daddy? Da-ddy… OK then how about da, da, da, da.'

'Bu-bble.'

'Very good, there are lots of bubbles on your hand and oh look, some on your nose.'

She points to her nose. She is good at the body parts pointing game. Elbow is her favourite, and knee.

'Try da da da da.'

'Mu-mmy.'

I reach for the towel, lift her out of the bath, wrap her up and sit her on my knee. She is wet and shiny and perfect.

*****

There is a pile of mail on the doormat. Double glazing offers, animals to be rescued, three for two on barbecue items at Somerfield. And then, underneath it all, a lovely, gleamy, white envelope. I know what it is.

> Dear Mr and Mrs Donovan,
>
> Would you please be present at the County Court at 11.00 am on Tuesday 10 July for the adoption hearing of:
>
> Jaymey Smith
> Harlee Smith

Directions to the court are below. If for any reason you cannot attend at this time then please contact the court to rearrange the hearing.

Yours faithfully,
The Clerk to the Court

It is one month away, the week we are away on holiday. I ring Rob at work.

'Rob, we've got the date for the adoption hearing – 10 July.'

'10 July,' he says, contemplating his diary, 'we're on holiday. We'll just have to take a day out. I don't want to delay it.'

'No, definitely not. How long do you think it will take us to get there from Wadebridge?'

'Mmmm…it's going to be a long journey. Good job we're early risers now.'

'I can't wait.'

'No, nor me. We'll finally be legal.'

The following weekend it is hotter than ever. I take Harlee and Jaymey swimming again and we meet Anna and her children in the pool for the fun session. The boys play with the balls and the floating crocodile mats. We swim around and chat.

'How is Rob's father?'

'Not good at all. Rob's just trying to spend as much time as he can with him. The doctors say that he doesn't have much time left.'

'It is so hard on you all. Are you still planning to go on your holiday?'

'Yes, we all want to and we need it. Rob needs a break, even though it won't be much of one.'

'And it's hard for you, having to look after the children all week and all weekend as well.'

'It is hard. The children have only been with us for six months and I worry that they are unsettled by Rob being away. I am tired and crabby all the time. But we don't have any choice – Rob has to be with his dad.'

After swimming we make the traditional visit to the bakery. Jaymey chooses his customary gingerbread man and is concerned that we don't forget Daddy, so I make a big point of buying an iced bun for Rob.

'We save that for Daddy,' he says, 'when Daddy home?'

'Daddy will be home tomorrow, just after lunch.'

'I give Daddy his bun?'

'Yes, that would be a very kind thing to do.'

That afternoon, Rob calls.

'Dad passed away.'

He sounds distant and broken. I can't believe that I'm not with him.

'I'm so sorry, Rob. Are you alright? Are you still at the hospital?'

'No, I'm back at Pam's. I'm preparing to make some phone calls. I'm going to need to stay up here for a few days to sort things out.'

'Do you want us to come up?'

'I just don't think it would be practical.'

There is a long silence. My throat constricts and I swallow back the sadness.

'Keep in touch, ring me tonight, whenever you need to.'

'Bye then.'

'Bye. Love you.'

I put the receiver back down and am suddenly aware of the children, both sitting at the kitchen table, looking at me, silently. They look uneasy. I sit them both on my lap – one knee each.

'Do you remember that Daddy's daddy was very poorly and in hospital?'

They both nod. Harlee looks very closely into my eyes.

'Well, he died today.'

As I say the words, I choke up.

'And Mummy and Daddy are going to be sad for a while.'

'Who is Daddy's daddy?' asks Jaymey.

'Your granddad, who came to stay.'

'Granddad what did give me tractor jigsaw and who did give Harlee dog?'

'Yes, that granddad.'

'Oh.'

'So we're going to have to look after Daddy.'

'Yes. I make him card.'

Tears roll down my cheeks and they both put their arms around my neck and lay their heads on me.

'Poor Daddy. Poor Mummy.'

The sight of the stale iced bun unexpectedly saddens me. I open the bread bin and see it there, leaching into its paper bag.

*****

The children become more difficult. Jaymey starts to make noise all the time. It is mostly nonsense. I know why he does it – to hang on to his brittle sense of existence, to say, 'Mummy, don't get lost in your sadness, don't forget about me.' But at times it drives me insane.

'La la la-la, I need a car for my dar for my bar for my yar yar, blah blah my teddy ted ted on my…mummy, mummy, mummy, mum, mum, I drink I drink drink, what that, what that there that dirt on my finger finger pointy point point…'

It is as though he is wound up tight inside and can't stop. Sometimes I ask him to stop or I try to engage him in a conversation, but nothing seems to work. When I am close to exploding I walk into the hallway, out of sight, and breathe deeply then look at my watch and plan my way to bedtime. I need someone to share this burden with – to take a turn so that I get some recovery time. Football helps. I drag out reserves of energy and run him around the garden, just as a relief from the noise. Then in the evening, when silence hangs over me, the frazzled feeling remains and is still there when I wake up in the morning, crackling and fizzing.

One afternoon, I decide to talk to Jaymey about our holiday.

'Soon we are going on holiday by the seaside.'

'How long is holiday?'

'Seven sleeps and then we come home again.'

'And when I go back to Thelma's?'

The question takes me by surprise.

'You aren't going back to Thelma's. You are staying here with me and Daddy and Harlee, forever.'

His eyes fill with tears. I sit him on my knee and put my arms around him.

'I know that makes you sad. You miss Thelma and Bill very much, don't you?'

He cries and cries. It seems we are all grieving.

*****

Rob insists that we still go on holiday and so we pack up the car with deckchairs, a rug and brand new buckets and spades. I buy the children some sweets and sticker books for the long journey and a copy of Topsy and Tim Go to the Seaside, a book that I read as a child and that fed my lifelong excitement about a trip to the sea. The house is perfect. We spend some time packing away the trinkets and barricading the fireplace with footstools. After that it is surprisingly child-friendly. It has a long, empty hallway, which we roll soft balls up and down, a game that keeps us occupied for ages. On the beach we dig enormous holes, build mountains with road tunnels through, dig out water channels and bury little feet. The children actually seem content. They play all day. We play with them, but in shifts so that we each get a chance to sit or, more often than not, lie and doze off. It feels wonderful to have Rob back – another adult to talk to, someone to share the load. Some days we walk into the town and meander and buy pasties for a quick tea. Despite the warnings about taking newly placed children on holiday, it goes remarkably smoothly. The loss of Rob's father is there with us through the week, but it is as though we park the grief, knowing that it will be there waiting for us when we get home. During this brief interlude, we enjoy ourselves and our children; it feels very much needed.

*****

The night before the adoption hearing I manage only short breaks of sleep. My mind flits around timings, worrying that we will oversleep, recalculating the time we need to get up and leave, checking I'd packed the smart clothes, the directions to the court. And on and on until eventually I lie there, listening to the alarm clock clicking on to five o'clock before it beeps. I creep downstairs and drink a cup of tea whilst I gather the sweets and things for the journey. I use the bathroom, get dressed in peace and wake up Rob and then Jaymey. Jaymey has his breakfast whilst he is still in his pyjamas to avoid Weetabix staining, then I dress him in his new orange checked shirt and beige shorts. He looks lovely, like a catalogue child. Rob brings Harlee down for her breakfast and then I dress her in her new turquoise, flowery dress. Her auburn curls and golden skin with the dress are a picture. Finally we are all ready – all looking clean and smart, at the same time. We go out into the empty street and get into the car. It is six o'clock in the morning.

We park in the shopping centre and walk down a few city centre streets to the court. It is a big, solid building that rises up from the narrow dark street. Litter blows around the steps and some thin men hang around smoking and looking nervy. The reception area is dim and cramped but the ladies behind the desk stand up when they see us and smile. They take Harlee's pushchair, show us where the toilets are and direct us up the two flights of stairs to our courtroom. They confirm that Mel and Lorna have not yet arrived, but not to worry – we are 20 minutes early. We climb the imposing limestone staircase and come into a corridor, typically municipal with an old, lino floor and dirty grey gloss walls. We sit on a narrow, wooden bench. Lots of people mill around. Most are dressed drably in baggy denims or tracksuit bottoms, t-shirts and trainers. A chesty cough echoes from an adjoining corridor and morphs into unconvincing, drunken-sounding laughter. The smell is of old cigarette smoke, with a bit of stale alcohol thrown in. These people don't look as though they are here for a good reason. We look very out-of-place in our best clothes – as though we are going to a wedding. It doesn't feel as though it is the correct place to be marking the legal starting point of our family. I look at my watch. Ten minutes to go.

'I'm getting worried that Mel and Lorna aren't here yet.'

'They've still got ten minutes, but they're cutting it a bit fine.'

A flutter of nervousness passes across my stomach and Harlee gets down from the bench beside me and starts running up and down the corridor.

Then five minutes, and then one.

'Where the fuck are they?' whispers Rob in my ear.

'I wonder if we can be adopted without them?'

'I hope so. I'm not leaving here…' then his face changes. 'Mel, Lorna – we were worried.'

They both look very flustered. I sense that their lateness is someone's fault and that they have had a tense journey.

'We are so sorry,' says Mel, putting her bag down beside me. Just as she sits down, the door of the courtroom opens and a smiling lady dressed in a dark suit and a white shirt welcomes us in.

'You cut that fine,' I whisper to Mel and we all take a deep breath.

I have never been in a court before and am cowed by its size, darkness and seriousness. It looks like a set from a television legal drama, but much bigger. Every surface is wood; rows of solid wooden tables and chairs, pew-like seating to the side and, at the very end, an enormous high-backed chair behind an enormous table. This monumental room of English oak is definite in its purpose – solid, durable, strong, inflexible, dependable. We are shown to a table at the side of the room. The judge, in his gown stands to greet us and shakes our hands.

He bends down to the children, 'And you are?' he says to Jaymey.

'Jaymey.'

'And who is this?' he asks, taking Harlee's hand.

'Mine sister, she is Harlee.'

'Pleased to meet you, Jaymey, and pleased to meet you, Harlee. My name is Paul and I am a judge. Would you like to sit down here with your mummy and daddy and these kind ladies?'

We all sit at the enormous table and the children look in wonder around the room.

'Is that your throne?' asks Jaymey, pointing to the big chair.

'It looks like a throne, doesn't it? That's my chair and it's where I sit when I am doing important business. Now we are here to do something important today. Do you know what?'

'We are being adopted today?'

'That's right. Today is a very special day because you and your sister are being adopted, which means that, by the law, this is your mummy and by the law this is your daddy.

And they will be your mummy and daddy forever. Isn't that a good thing indeed?'

'Oh yes,' nods Jaymey earnestly.

'And your name is going to be spelt a little bit differently. Is that right?'

'Yes,' says Jaymey.

'And your last name, your surname, will be Donovan now, the same as Mummy's and Daddy's surnames.'

Jaymey nods again.

I look at Harlee on my knee. She stares at the judge in wide-eyed bemusement. I wonder what she makes of this strange holiday – one day we are digging on the beach and paddling in the sea and the next we are in our finery, in a vast wooden room, talking to a man wearing a cloak.

'And all I have to do to make that the law is sign my name right here, on the front of this file. And there, it's done. You've been adopted and this is a happy day. Congratulations, Jamie Donovan and Harlee Donovan.'

I breathe a secret sigh of relief at no longer having to explain away the stray 'y's in the middle of 'Jaymey' and why we have different surnames.

The judge reaches across the table and shakes our hands and congratulates us. He genuinely looks as though he is enjoying himself, as though this is a part of his job that he finds satisfying. I know that he won't have presided over any of the hearings involving our children, but he will no doubt have made judgements on many cases of child safety, deciding when children are removed from their parents or returned back to them.

'What is that?' asks Jamie, pointing to something on the table.

'That is my wig. I wear that when I do serious business but I didn't want to wear it to see you because I thought you might find it a bit scary. Would you like to touch it?'

Jamie reaches out his arm and strokes the wig.

'Can you guess what it is made of?'

'Mmmm…'

'It's an animal's hair.'

'Dog?'

'No, it's made from horse hair.'

Harlee touches the wig too.

'And I have something to give you both so that you can remember this day forever. It is a certificate, signed by me, to say that on this day, you were adopted and in this envelope is a card for you each. And maybe if you give those to Mummy or Daddy to look after, I could show you my big chair and maybe you would like to sit on it. It spins around.'

Jaymey and Harlee both get down and we follow the judge to the front of the court and on to the platform. The children both sit on the chair and Mel pushes them round. Harlee isn't sure and gets down and holds my hand. Then we take photographs. Strange photographs. We are posed almost like a wedding party, but instead of a vicar and a best man, our new family is framed by two social workers and a judge.

The judge sees us out and we say goodbye to him. We make a point of thanking him because he has gone beyond his duty – I have heard stories about adoptions being short, sharp, unfriendly affairs. And then we are back down the steps and into reception. The ladies behind the desk congratulate us and return our pushchair. We stand in front of the brass plaque outside the court building and take some more pictures. We pause whilst a policeman waves out a fleet of white prison vans that emerge from an underground entrance beside us. Those hanging around the building anxiously awaiting their moment look sideways at our motley party celebrating our day in court.

'Do you have to get going or shall we find somewhere to have some coffee and cake?' Rob asks Mel and Lorna.

They look at each other and nod.

'Yes, let's do that. Let's celebrate.'

We find a cafe nearby and gather around a big table.

'No going back now,' laughs Mel.

'No. We have waited a long time for this day.'

'I think we did a pretty good job, Lorna, matching these guys up – what do you think?' asks Mel, smiling.

'I think you are right. You were all made for each other. When I think back to when I first met the children I can hardly believe they are here now, part of a new family. It's brilliant. It makes my job worthwhile,' says Lorna.

'Well, we couldn't have done it without you,' I say. And I look around the table at Rob and Lorna and Mel smiling and at Jamie, without the 'y's, playing with his new Playmobil police motorbike and at Harlee, deep in chocolate cake, and I know that I wouldn't have our family any other way.

PART 6

Getting Educated

Learning the Hard Way

CHAPTER 12

He is quiet at the back of the car, preoccupied. Alice has invited him to play and have tea with his cousins so we are driving to her house.

Then, 'Mummy, there was hot water in kettle, it did spill on mine arm. It did hurt really, really a lot. Did I go hospital?'

'Was this in your first house?'

'Yes, was man and big children and the kettle did spill and did burn me.'

'You had to go to the hospital because the burn was a bad one. Do you remember being there?'

'I did go in the kitchen in the morning and I did ask for Weetabix and the lady she did say, "*No no no go away!*" and I was really hungry and my tummy was hurting.'

The town centre is busy with traffic and shoppers and I must not lose concentration. At the same time this revelation, like the last, is a precious glimpse into Jamie and his past and must not be squandered. His vivid recount of two weeks ago – the blood, the pain, the missing tooth – has haunted me. I haven't revisited it with him for fear of upsetting him, but at the same time I don't want him to think his bravery has been met with embarrassed avoidance or ambivalence. The truth is I feel out of my depth and dread making things worse.

'And I was in mine pushchair for long, long, long time and I was not let out to move about.'

'That must have been very hard for you and not fair either.'

'No not fair at all.'

'It is awful to feel so hungry and not to be given something to eat.'

'Mummy? Is those people in prison now?'

They are not in prison and never were, but how can I let him worry that they are out there somewhere? I decide to lie again to help it make sense to him, in his black and white world of good and bad.

'Jamie, those people are in prison and you will never see them again. What they did to you was very bad. At our house, there is always food to eat and time to run around.'

'Mummy?'

'Yes.'

'I go be a soldier when I grow up so I can have a gun and I go shoot Trudy and shoot that man so they be dead.'

He says this with such certainty that it makes me shiver.

'You are very angry with them and so am I, but we are not allowed to kill people or we will have to go to prison.'

'I don't care if I go prison.'

A surge of panic that I have pushed Jamie towards associating himself with prison. Amateur psychologist throws away a chance, ruins a life.

'You are not going to prison. You are going to stay with me and look after me when I get old.'

'No, I kill Trudy and that man and then I go to prison.'

He sounds very sure and I don't want to further his resolve by disagreeing again.

'Well, thank you for telling all me that. It was brave of you.'

'That alright Mummy. How long till we be there?'

'We'll be at Aunty Alice's in about five minutes. Do you still want to go?'

'Yes,' he says, as though it is obvious.

I drop him at Alice's and he kisses me and runs off upstairs to play. I drive back home, my mind turning over what he has shared with me. He was removed from his birth family when he was two years old, so these memories are early ones. I can't remember anything from that far back, but then maybe nothing happened to me that etched itself so clearly on my memory. When he had shared the memory of his tooth being knocked out, I was struck by how present and clear it was, how genuine and convincing the details were. I recounted the tooth incident to Mel. She told how once she had been out walking with her brother and niece and a pony had kicked back and knocked her niece's front tooth out. She had been struck by just how much blood there had been and had thought that the imagination alone would not have got that detail correct. And surely a child could not dream up being so hungry that their stomach hurt, or think up a story about being strapped in a pushchair when all they want to do is move around. It frustrates me that there is nothing practical I can do with this information. Mel has advised keeping a note of Jamie's memories but she left me in little doubt that nothing can be done. Maybe my world is too black and white like Jamie's, but I have a lingering sense that justice has not been done. No one has been brought to account for their mistreatment of him and Harlee. Their young voices are not strong and consistent enough ever to be used to convict anyone. But still, it doesn't seem right and I feel angry for them.

Our new support worker rings to ask how we are. I tell her about the conversation I had with Jamie in the car. She makes the right noises of concern and sympathy but somehow I don't feel a substance behind it. She mentions his lifestory book, but I tell her he won't go near it. Then she's out of ideas. The phone call fizzles out and I am left in the silent house casting around in my mind for someone to ring and share this with. Perhaps I should be strong enough to deal with it on my own but I can't seem to organise my thoughts without bouncing them off someone else first. Rob is away dealing with the aftermath of his father's death and I can't burden him with any additional misery. Talking to my immediate family will only burst their bubble, force them to look at the ugly side of adoption when what they deserve is to grandparent or to aunty the nice bits. They didn't decide to adopt children into their family, after all. And my friends, who have been my friends forever? I have barely had a telephone conversation with any of them since I told them of our intention to adopt. And I know they are all busy working and building their own lives. But if I rang any of them now I couldn't launch straight into scars and hunger because the foundation stones for a conversation of that difficulty have not been laid. And I feel too sore to make the effort to ring them. In the early weeks of the children being with us when we were in the depths of uncertainty and tiredness, I had held a secret little hope each morning that the postman would bring powder blue and sugar pink envelopes containing congratulations cards, best wishes, thoughts and promises to visit with presents of little children's clothes, toys and blankets. We received a few cards from unexpected places – a neighbour of my parents, an aunt and uncle, an old family friend whom I hadn't seen for years. And, of course, presents from my parents and my sister. But the virtual silence from my friends has left me adrift. I wonder if it is the absence of etiquette surrounding the arrival of adopted children into a family that is behind the silence – not knowing quite what to say or do, not wanting to offend or interfere. I think about talking to Anna, who is aware of the bare essentials, but I worry about scaring her off and ruining the beginnings of a friendship. I should build on my friendship with her and make more local friends, but I am sapped of the energy and confidence I need to get out and do it. That evening I decide to ring Alice.

'Hi Sally, Jamie had a lovely time with Luke and Harry this afternoon.'

'Thanks for that, he loves going to play.'

'Is everything alright? You sound really tired.'

'Yes, you know, life as normal at the moment. Rob is still away but hopefully he'll be home the day after tomorrow. And Jamie has started talking about some memories of being with his birth family.' I tell her about the incidents he has described to me.

There is a pause and for a moment I feel bad for dumping this on Alice.

'Oh my goodness. But how amazing that he's told you – incredible. I know it must be very hard to hear all that but I think you should see it as a positive thing.'

'I do feel privileged that he's shared it with me. It's like he needs to get it out, for his own sake and also to test the water, to see how I'm going to react. And then he quickly moves on and plays or something and I'm left with this awful knowledge and this feeling of powerlessness.'

'Have you spoken to your support worker about it?'

'I have but she couldn't do any more than sympathise. She's not qualified for this sort of thing so it's not her fault. But I need to know how to handle it properly. I'm stumbling through it.'

'You are doing a fantastic job – don't lose sight of that.'

And I get a pep talk from my younger sister and am glad that I have her.

*****

The local primary school is just a five-minute walk from our house. Everyone I speak to sings its praises and says how good it is and what a lovely atmosphere it has. It is a first school, so has children from four to nine years old. I have had a brief phone conversation with the head and she has space for Jamie to start in September. We attend an open day and are shown around the classrooms, the hall and the playground. Apart from the occasional computer, it looks much like the school I went to. There are rows of pegs with PE bags on, a shelf for lunchboxes and displays called 'Where we live' and 'The weather'. We are shown into a classroom where the children are singing Jesus Gives Us the Water of Life to a tape-recorded track. Jamie stays close to me and holds my hand tightly. Harlee is off at every opportunity, delving into boxes of coloured cubes and beads, picking up handfuls of rubbers and pencils. I try to hold her hand and she twists and writhes to get out of my grip. Other children – shy and nervous – stare at us. We are shown into the playground where coloured hoops have been laid on the ground and the children are given beanbags to throw into them. The teacher is very encouraging and Jamie proudly shows off his skills. The visit concludes with drinks and biscuits in the classroom and we are asked to sit in a semicircle on tiny plastic chairs, while the children play in an area behind us. There are about ten of us. I smile across at Anna, who is there with her youngest son. A lady of about 55 with lead-grey hair, drapey clothes and chunky silver jewellery introduces herself. She is the head teacher, Mrs Jenkins. She talks for a while about the school and I struggle to listen as Harlee rummages through boxes of noisy, plastic toys.

Mrs Jenkins opens up the floor to questions. There is one from a nervous-looking woman about whether her son will be in trouble if he doesn't eat his fruit during fruit break – you see he eats lots of other things but he really doesn't like fruit. Then there is a question about a child who wears glasses (we all try not to look at the child with the glasses but we do anyway) and how the school is going to manage this, because the child is very sensitive about it. Then a question about phonics, which gets us all sitting up straight. Which system of phonics does the school use and how can this be supported at home before school starts in September? Mrs Jenkins starts to answer but is interrupted, 'Yes, we've started using flashcards already.'

Mrs Jenkins sighs almost imperceptibly. 'The most important thing that all of you can do with your children is to read with them, every day if possible. Make it enjoyable.'

'Which reading series do you use?'

I have a good look at Pushy Two Shoes. She is turned out casually but tastefully in slim-fitting jeans, a long cardigan and leather flip flops. She is Diesel and cashmere and not Asda and M&S. Her long, curly hair is pulled to the side over one shoulder. She occasionally strokes it and looks at it. She speaks softly and looks serious, as though she has an unpleasant smell under her nose.

'We use the Oxford series mainly but at this stage I would recommend that you share stories for fun. You can go to the library – they have a good selection there and they run a story time I think, don't they, Mrs Rendell?'

We all look at Mrs Rendell, the reception class teacher, who nods self-consciously at her hands, which are clasped in her lap.

'And what are your provisions for gifted and talented children?' (That's what she is broadcasting to the gathering: 'The fruit of my loins is a gifted child.')

'We are strong in individual learning, so each child will be treated as such and given work according to their abilities to reinforce learning and to stretch them as well, whether they be gifted and talented or have a special educational need or, indeed, whatever their level.'

Pushy Two Shoes nods in a most sincere way as Mrs Rendell is delivering her answer. Every third or fourth nod is aimed at her daughter sitting next to her. Anna glances over to me and raises her eyebrows.

'And do you offer instrument lessons?'

'Yes, we have visiting teachers for the piano and guitar and the lessons are offered from Year 3.'

'Why not earlier than Year 3?'

'Because the music teachers consider that the younger children struggle and get put off. And we do cover music in our curriculum from reception class.'

Pushy Two Shoes shuffles disapprovingly. Just as I think she has asked all her questions, she comes in with another.

'And what after-school activities do you offer?'

'We have a sports club and then a computer club and dance club, which we run at lunchtimes. These are all for the Year 2s and upwards.' She senses the next question coming and quickly adds, 'The younger ones find school tiring enough without going to clubs as well.'

I marvel at the questions. Pushy Two Shoes has obviously prepared, whereas I, bouncing from one crisis to another, have not. And I marvel at her commitment. She is like a mother project manager. Were my life less crisis-ridden, I think I might be more like her.

The session finishes and I wait whilst other mothers crowd around Mrs Jenkins asking her questions. A couple of the mothers have looked uncomfortable throughout the tour and the question-and-answer session, and can't get away soon enough. Finally the questions about inhalers and playtime and Ofsted results dry up and I am the last mother left.

'We spoke on the phone. I'm Jamie's mum. We haven't applied for a place yet. Jamie is our adopted son and has only been with us for seven months.'

'OK, yes, I remember. Well, we have a few places left so you need to contact the Local Authority. Where do you live?'

'Just five minutes' walk from here.'

'You are well inside the catchment area so there shouldn't be a problem at all.'

'He's had a difficult time – lots of change and upheaval. It might be a tricky time for him, starting school.'

'We can manage that. The reception class is quite small and we can keep an eye on him. And if he finds it too much at first then he can have a few afternoons off during the week. We often have to do that.'

'He's likely to have some attachment issues,' I offer, testing the water.

Mrs Jenkins doesn't really look like she knows what I am talking about. I know that I should be more confident of what I am saying, that I should ask her outright – does she know what attachment disorder is and how will she manage it in the classroom? But I feel intimidated and worn out. My question is brushed off with an 'everything will be alright' smile, which makes me feel as though I am ranked somewhere just below the fruit worrier.

As I remove layers of fairy witch costume from Harlee, which she has helped herself to from the dressing up rail, Mrs Jenkins chats to Jamie. She has a lovely way with him and he seems comfortable with her.

We walk back from school with Anna and her son.

'It is a lovely school – my eldest has been very happy there and he's doing well,' she says.

'To be honest, I haven't really thought about what I was expecting. When I was a child we went to the nearest school and that was it. You didn't have your parents coming in fussing about whether you would have to eat fruit, or how soon you'd be learning the tuba.'

'Fruit at our school came out of a tin and had custard all over it. And if you didn't eat it, you had to stand in the corner.'

'We had semolina on our fruit and that was only if we'd finished up all our mashed swede.'

We laugh and then head off on our separate ways. On the last stretch home, I feel a small cloud descending on me. When I get back home I ring our support worker.

'Is there anything I can do with Jamie's school to make sure they understand his problems?'

'You could warn them about the security issues – make sure that they don't put any pictures of him in the newspaper or on the internet and they need to know that no one other than you or Rob should be allowed to collect him from school. But other than that, I don't really know what to say.'

'There's no guidance – a leaflet or anything?'

'Not that I know of.' She pauses. 'My eldest has had a terrible time at school; he's always in trouble, can't sit still, fights with the other children. He doesn't have any friends; no one wants to play with him. The teachers have tried their best, but they don't know what to do with him. I just don't know what's going to become of him.'

She has already told me something of her son – her adopted son – who has had a chaotic little life, who lies in his bed at night and rocks himself to sleep, like a child in a Romanian orphanage. I let her talk on, offer some platitudes and then ring off, resolving to go into school and have a meeting with Mrs Jenkins.

I get Harlee settled with a plastic farm and some farm animals, Jamie plays with his bricks and I get the post. There is one letter in an envelope bearing the social services frank mark. I open it with mild interest and inside is a handwritten letter. I immediately recognise the rounded script. It is from Trudy.

> Dear Temporary Carers of Jaymey and Harlee,
>
> I am sure that you are nice people and that my children are being looked after well. Nothing against you personally but my children were stolen and I will never give up the fight for them. I can't wait to see Jamie and say to him 'I love you' when we are all back together again, like the family we are.
>
> From Jaymey and Harlee's mum

I can't put my finger on how I feel. I don't quite have the emotional vocabulary. It is something between anxiety and fearfulness but with an underlying protectiveness and anger. I pace around and then have a need to put the letter back into the envelope, but still it sits there on my kitchen table, next to my daughter's tin of crayons, like a threat. A threat that ought to feel meaningless. I want to burn it, to get it out of my house, but then I've been told how important contact with the birth family is for the children. They need to keep that connection so that they have a sense of identity. I'm confused about what I thought I knew. Why it is so important when Jamie is content to think that they are in prison. And why am I the only one who has no right to a voice? Am I really expected to write some hogwash of pleasantries back to this woman, again?

Lorna rings. I am surprised to hear her voice.

'Sally, I need to come and see you. Another security issue has cropped up and I want to explain things to you in person.'

And again, there I am pacing around the house, feeling unsafe, wondering how real this threat really is and whether I am strong enough to fend off whatever it is.

She arrives that afternoon, on time and comes in purposefully and seriously.

'The birth family has been leafleting about the injustice of their children being removed and how they will never give up looking for them.'

'How can they see it as an injustice, or am I missing something?'

'Families often don't acknowledge what they've done wrong. It's a complete denial. They blame social services and paint themselves as perfect parents, victims of the system.'

'Have they been using the children's names in these leaflets?'

'Yes, and some photographs.'

I sit opposite her, my hands in my lap, staring at the chequered tablecloth. Behind me on the dresser is the letter from Trudy. My mind has gone into some kind of lockdown. I can't think of a single word to say. I can't even think of what someone else would say – what one should say in a situation like this.

'I was expecting you to be really upset.'

Slowly I look up at her.

'I am like a boxer who has been punched over and over, so many times that he just stands in the ring taking the punches.'

'I know, it's been tough. But Trudy is the sort of person who never sticks at anything for long. She has to do this and soon she will move on to something else. Perhaps it's part of the grieving process.'

I get up from my chair, cross the kitchen, pick up the envelope and put it in front of Lorna.

'I got this yesterday.'

She reads it.

'Just put it away somewhere and forget about it.'

But the letter has already landed its punch.

'And if Trudy and Mike are successful and find us?'

She goes through her spiel about photographs and saying their names in public. Punch. Punch. Punch.

That night my paranoia dreams return. Rob is at home with the children. I am away somewhere, alone, being pursued through a crowded street. I attempt to ring Rob and warn him to keep the children safe. My phone is out of charge. I run into a police station, hysterical. Policemen surround me. They are telling me to calm down. They think I am mad. I can't make myself heard. But I need to warn my husband. They are after us.

Everywhere I go, whether it be to the supermarket or the town centre, my brain is in overdrive, assessing the people around me, thinking every other person looks like Trudy or Mike, looking out for people giving out leaflets, people with cameras, people looking shifty. I am taut and twitchy.

After a few days my fear hardens into red raw rage. The rage has nowhere to go, so one evening I lie on the bed and write a letter. I know that it will never be sent but it feels good to write it.

> Dear Trudy,
>
> I received your second letter. You write again about how badly treated you have been, how your children were stolen from you by evil social workers. You clearly see yourself as the victim in all this, now rising up to fight the bureaucracy for your rights.
>
> You imagine a wonderful, fairytale reunion with your children, a reunion that puts all the wrongs of the past right. Maybe you picture a televised reunion, you get to tell your side of the story. Your children will run into your arms, your tears and theirs will mingle, you will never again be separated. I, their temporary carer, will be written out of the story. It will be easy to do because I have no voice. I cannot write you the truth, or give out leaflets in the street, or talk to the newspapers. I can't do that and I wouldn't.
>
> But there is one small problem with your plan. My son, your third born, has expressed his intention to murder you. He is going to track you down, just like you are trying to track him down now, and gun you down. He is only five years old, so with a bit of luck, the years of therapy that he will need may help him to change his mind. You probably thought that your secrets were safe, didn't you? If the mask of self-delusion ever slips for a moment, you must put it back on and think 'Well, he was so young, he'll never remember and if he does, no one will believe him.' Guess what? He does remember. He is believed.

> When I first laid eyes on the photograph of you, I was still feeling so liberal and so understanding. I was fresh out of adoption training. All politically correct and compliant. There but for the grace of god and all that. I could sort of excuse your behaviour and put it down to the bad childhood you must have had, the lack of positive parental role models around you. And even now, I know that is probably true, but enough is enough. They fuck you up, your mum and dad, but at some point we have to take responsibility for ourselves, try to be better people.
>
> I don't want to admit this to you, but I have worried that you might find us and I even have a plan if you do. So well done for that. But I really don't think you will be bothered to. I expect you read my last letter. Wasn't it newsy? But do you know what? My role isn't to write to you about the children, to make you feel better. My role is to help them to feel safe, to protect them, to help them mend. So you have had your last letter from me. And I am not going to read any more letters from you.
>
> Jamie and Harlee's mother

The next day I ring the social worker who is responsible for the letter exchange system and I explain why I can no longer take part in this fucked up pen-friend scheme. I am prepared for a big dose of gentle persuasion but she is understanding and agrees with me. I put the phone down and feel a small burden being lifted.

*****

Jamie starts school. Other children have to be peeled off their mothers in the mornings but he runs straight into class without a kiss, without a backward glance. His teacher Mrs Rendell says he is doing well. He plays constantly. He interacts well with the other children. He brings a reading book home every day and at bedtime we lie in his bed and he learns to sound out letters and put together some rhyming words. We read about dogs and frogs on logs. We move on to boys and toys and trucks in the muck. He often seems distracted when he comes home from school and will try to pick a fight with me over something trivial. But I put my faith in the school and guiltily enjoy the six hours of relative peace that fall upon the house every weekday. I soon find that, although the school and the pre-school had both advised that no advantage is to be gained from teaching your child to read before they start school, a good quarter of the parents have done just that. Every afternoon at picking up time, several of the mothers, including Pushy Two Shoes, publicly remove their child's reading book from their book bag, wave it about and loudly declare, 'Haven't they moved you on from bullfinches yet?' or, 'Oh well done darling, you've made it to centipedes.' We haven't made it on to an animal-related series yet. Even if I had the brightest child in the county, I don't think I would brandish their reading book like a badge of honour ('Oh marvellous, Lord of the Rings.'). There is something barefaced and coldly competitive about it. And the same women gather around the teacher at any opportunity, soaking up her time and energy over trivia. They stand in the playground and moan about how there is too much play and not enough work, how the naughty ones are distracting the ones who really do want to work and how if they were the head those children (*those* children) would have been expelled a long time ago. I have plenty of time waiting in the playground to muse over this shameless display. It seems some of these women would climb over their dead grannies to get their child ahead. And we are not mothers fighting to feed our children in the midst of war and famine, scrapping over handfuls of grain; we are rich and privileged, like spoilt children vying for attention. I notice that some mothers do one-upmanship in a more underhand way – they will slip in a boast, dressed down as tutting criticism.

'Hello, Milly darling, have you had a lovely day? Yes? Daddy's at home. You wanted to show him your *Head Teacher's Award* sticker, remember you wanted me to remind you. You don't? Well, it's a good job I reminded you then, isn't it, you silly Womble.'

All this is punctuated with glances at any mothers who are unlucky enough to be within earshot and who are not strong enough to deflect the eye contact. Glances that say, 'Aren't they silly, forgetting things all the time, my my, whatever next.' The real meaning shouts out loud and clear: '*My child won the Head Teacher's Award yesterday. Did you hear? My child is fantastic; my child is more fantastic than your child. My child is heading for a First at Cambridge. My child is an extension of me therefore I too am fantastic!*'

Pushy Two Shoes, being well brought up, might sometimes try a little fake interest in someone else's child. She says to Jamie one afternoon, 'I liked the picture you showed in assembly – you are very good at painting.'

This was the assembly that Jamie stood through, staring at the ceiling, flicking the side of his nose, whilst all the other children sang. The other children held up their drawings of a rainbow; Mrs Rendell had to hold up his splat of khaki because he refused to.

'You have no fucking idea,' I want to say. Then I check myself. Am I just feeling sour because I am jealous of the mothers with children who sing solos in church and paint beautiful rainbows?

The playground, I've found, is the perfect place to indulge in some wild generalisations. There is a small group of mothers who stand together miserably; they shout at their kids a lot and generally have the children who are judged by others to be 'the naughty ones'. One of them looks a bit like Trudy. Then there are a couple of grandparents, who I quite like to chat to. They have been there and done that and are not interested in the 'Reading Scheme Jousting'. Then there are the competitive mothers, who are generally, but not always, the mothers of the well-behaved, the polite, the compliant. And their darlings are often whisked off, publicly, to swimming lessons, ballet lessons or gymnastics. The girls in particular have lots of play-dates together, organised in loud voices in the presence of a red-faced child who is not included and who aches to be. Play-dates would be an added complication that I don't need right now and Jamie seems content to play with Anna's boys occasionally.

*****

The school nativity is held in the church. I look forward to it. There is something about hearing a group of young children singing Little Donkey that melts my heart. Despite bringing things for Harlee to do, I struggle to keep her amused and quiet. She climbs up on my legs, tries to stand on them, then slides down and tries to crawl out over people's handbags and feet. The head teacher introduces the play and Harlee climbs up on to the pew and stands. I quietly wrestle her down and clamp her on my lap where she writhes and says 'no no no' over and over again. I notice disapproving looks. Anna gives her a biscuit, which buys me a few seconds of time.

Jamie stands at the back of the group, shorter than most of the others and wearing an animal mask. I can hardly make him out. I catch his eye and give him a little wave. He waves back. I am relieved that he knows I am here. We then endure half an hour of nativity vignettes acted out very earnestly and inaudibly by the older children. Some of the younger ones are given starring roles, most of the drama around which has been acted out in the playground by their parents; and then we have to watch one of the girls, in full leotard and tutu, perform as though a twirling dancer in a musical box. It goes on far too long and has no bearing on the story. Anna leans towards me and whispers,

'Her mother complained that she didn't get the part of Mary, so they let her do this instead.'

We snigger. Throughout the dancing I watch Jamie, who is now sitting in a pew at the front of the church with the rest of his class, banging his head repeatedly on the pew in front. I itch to reach out and stop him. Eventually a classroom assistant notices him and silently, but rather angrily I think, asks him to stop. He ceases for a moment and then continues. Harlee wriggles in my lap and then bashes my foot with a plastic horse. More looks. One woman sitting a few rows in front of us keeps turning around, frowning and tutting and giving her neighbour a pursed-lip shake of the head. They whisper to each other. Unbelievable. So badly behaved. Ruining it for everyone else. She looks back at me again. I don't think Harlee is being that noisy so I throw half a smile. Anna says not to worry, to ignore her. I have noticed this woman in the playground – Frumpy Mum. She is one of the most accomplished players of Reading Scheme Jousting and has two very shy, pale, studious-looking girls, one of whom is in Jamie's class and the other is in the same class as Anna's eldest son. I've watched her antics in the playground and marvelled at the fuss she can create. It appears that nothing is good enough, safe enough, stretching enough or wholesome enough for her girls. They are her life's ambition and will now be her life's work. And she is in a state of permanent disappointment that her girls are not everyone else's be-all and end-all. In other respects this mother is very sensible. She has a sensible haircut, which doesn't need styling, she wears sensible shoes from the far end of the Clarks shop and mid-calf-length gathered skirts from the M&S Classic department. To avoid bother, she keeps to a narrow palette of creams and navy. She is also somewhat of an expert on hidden sugars and other nasties in food. She can reel off the most evil breakfast cereals and yoghurts and will bore anyone who wants to listen on the dangers of a Fruit String or a Babybel.

To raise money for the school, on the last day of term the children bring in unwanted toys plus the maximum of £1.50 in change, in a named purse, with which to buy said unwanted toys. I squirrel a few things out of the house. As I stand in the playground at the end of the day, children start coming out of their classes with toys they have bought, to show their parents, who mostly look dismayed by the purchases. I see Jamie coming towards me holding Mrs Jenkins's hand. Frumpy Mum's sensible, unpierced ears flap as she strains to hear what the head teacher will say.

'Mrs Donovan,' says Mrs Jenkins, holding out a Barbie wearing a green bikini, 'Jamie bought this for his sister this afternoon at the sale. It touched me so much I just wanted to come out and tell you. He was the only child who bought something for someone else.'

She puts the doll in Jamie's hand and he holds it out to Harlee.

'Harlee, is for you, is Barbie.'

CHAPTER 13

Miniature grey plastic chairs line the dark corridor outside the classroom. We perch awkwardly and flick through some of Jamie's exercise books. The work inside is sparse and scratchy and some pages are ripped. We have no concerns about parents' evening; at the previous one we had been told how well Jamie was doing – how good at reading and maths he was. Laughter comes from inside the classroom, we hear some muffled words ('pleasure to teach') and then the door opens and Pushy Two Shoes appears, immaculate in cashmere. She thanks the teacher, Mrs Watts, loudly and confidently.

Mrs Watts, Jamie's new teacher for this year, turns to us and her expression appears to change. 'Mr and Mrs Donovan, would you like to come through?' she says seriously.

We follow her into the classroom and she beckons us to a tiny table and more tiny chairs. We squat down. My coat drags on the floor. In front of us are some more exercise books.

'There have been a few problems this year. Jamie seems to sit on the outside of things, doesn't really engage, is easily distracted.'

She looks straight at us as if she is searching for an explanation.

'And he doesn't seem to really grasp numbers,' she continues.

'I thought he was doing alright,' says Rob.

'He distracts others as well,' she ploughs on.

'How long has this been going on for?' I ask.

'Since the beginning of term.'

It is December and we are three months into the term. There is a short silence, which Rob and I are clearly meant to fill with something.

'Is there anything we can do to help him at home?' Rob asks.

'Yes, you can practise his numbers with him – counting beyond 20 and he needs to learn his number bonds. They're the pairs of numbers that add up to ten, like two and eight, seven and three and so on.'

Her tone is slightly accusatory, because to Mrs Watts this is a basic task that every parent would be expected to carry out. She doesn't appreciate – because it is outside her experience – the almighty battle that would ensue, if we were to pick the wrong moment to attempt to instil this knowledge, the anger that would boil up, the head that would bang on the table in frustration, the pencil thrown, the paper torn up, the evening disrupted, the bedtime screwed up. I cannot begin to explain this to her without it sounding like a cascade of excuses from a flaky parent. As she shows us some more work Jamie has done I notice a felt board behind her on which is stuck a collection of frogs, cut out of thin card and laminated. They are gathered in a pond. Each frog has a different child's name across the bottom. Two of the frogs are not in the pond, but crouch some distance away, and one of these has 'Jamie' written on it. I wonder how long his frog has been banished from the bright blue, felt-tip waters. I think of the other parents who have sat in my chair this evening and seen my son's shame and I imagine him coming into his classroom in the morning, full of hope, to see his frog sitting on the outside looking in.

Mrs Watts sees me looking at the frog board.

'Whenever a child misbehaves we move their frog out of the pond, until their behaviour improves. Jamie was running around this afternoon and not sitting still.'

He is six years old and has been with us for a year and a half.

*****

Over the next few weeks I make a point of glancing through the window of the classroom to monitor the frog situation. Every morning and every afternoon I check. Jamie's frog is always outside the pond. I get increasingly cross about it but don't feel confident enough to confront the teacher; she must know better than I what works for the children in her class. But surely it can't be working, otherwise he would, now and again, make it in for a quick swim at least. I become almost obsessed with the bloody frog. I wonder if a more unsuitable system could possibly be designed for a child who experiences shame and abandonment so keenly. Eventually I am carried into the classroom on a wave of raw frustration.

'Mrs Watts, could I have a word, please?'

She is polite.

'The whole system with the frogs, I was wondering if it is the best thing for Jamie – I think it may be reinforcing his view of himself as someone who is bad.'

She bristles.

'Well, that system suits most of the children – it is clear and they understand it.'

'But the same two children are constantly out of the pond, so can it be working for them?'

I have tried to phrase my point so as not to be accusing.

'I can have a think about it, but I have to cater for the majority.'

Her voice is clipped and short and it is clear that the conversation is over. I walk home feeling stung and the conversation rattles around in my head as I play with the children and make tea.

The next morning I ring the support worker. Again she displays some interest before talking about her own children, so the conversation is short and unsatisfactory. I decide to leave my frog crusade for a while.

*****

Harlee and I sit at the kitchen table amongst a criss-cross of coloured pencils, drawing a vast underwater scene. She adds little blobs with tails and, as she draws, carefully opens and closes her mouth making the universal sound of a fish. Watching her lips and her cheeks puffing is the sweetest thing. I draw a mermaid and see her excitement as she colours the face orange. I add a fishing boat with a net, some anemones attached to rocks and a jellyfish.

'That's a jellyfish.'

Harlee rubs her tummy and says 'mmmm'. She likes jelly. I laugh and she looks into my eyes and laughs as well, as much to join in with me as to share in the joke. It seems to amuse and puzzle her that she has made me laugh. I put one arm over her shoulders and rub her tummy with my other hand.

'You are funny.'

She puts both her arms around my neck and nuzzles into me.

'Mummy loves you,' I whisper into her ear.

*****

Rob has been working long hours for the past few months, and we have both been struggling, even with the basics of our lives. The death of Rob's dad hangs over us, like a heavy grey blanket, which we try to ignore. We are so emotionally crowded out, it doesn't feel as though we have the time or space to grieve. Jamie's troubles at school persistently tug on me and suspend me in a perpetual state of uncertainty and discomfort. He will employ all the tactics he can to delay us in leaving the house in the morning. He will suddenly remember something vital that is upstairs somewhere, suddenly need a wee, refuse to put his shoes on or start an argument over something trivial. I worry about him through the day but it is a worry I can't quite put my finger on. After a day I know nothing about, he comes home and shouts and rages at me. It will start with nothing – maybe the wrong juice or the wrong colour of cup – and then this will become the focus of his anger, this and my inability to do the right thing for him. Sometimes it will start with him chattering, but not the sort of chatter I have heard from other children – it is a wild nonsense. The words pour out of him in agitated waves making little sense but demanding response. If I ask him to be quiet for a moment, he becomes louder and more insistent and ruder. His rantings often continue for long periods and start to become the theme to the late afternoon and evening. I have learnt from the parenting programmes on the television to ignore his insults and I tell myself that he doesn't mean what he says. But after weeks and weeks of coming under attack I gradually start to crumble. One day, as I am trying to prepare tea, Harlee tips all her pencils on the floor and then whines for food. As I pick up the pencils from amongst the crumbs of dried up mashed potato on the floor Jamie starts up again, 'I hate you you nasty Mummy and you go live in *Africa* in a van and I stay here with Daddy cos Daddy is a nice daddy not like you...'

And that last little bit of control I was keeping back finally and dramatically perishes. I throw the pencils I had collected up back on the floor and then I throw the pencil tin, which crashes against the kitchen cupboard. Harlee freezes and watches me. I march over to where Jamie is sitting. I put my face right into his and I scream,

'Just shut up, shut up!'

I feel the words 'shut the fuck up' rise up but manage just enough self-control to keep them back. Jamie looks scared for a fraction of a second and then squares up to me. 'Go on then, hit me,' he says.

'*Is that what you want me to do?*' I screech.

'*Hit me then!*' he shouts, presenting himself with an antagonistic smirk.

'*I'm not going to hit you, because I love you and care for you and mummies don't hit their children. Now go up to your room and leave me alone!*'

For a moment he looks as though he is going to resist, but then he gets up and runs upstairs. I sink on to the floor and put my head in my hands.

'Mummy?' says Harlee tentatively.

'Mummy's alright,' I say.

*****

My parents look after Harlee while I visit the doctor. It is inevitable that I will go into his consulting room and be unable to explain the finer points of parenting adopted children, the anger and disruption that is endured on a daily basis. I hold out a little bit of hope that he will know what I am talking about and save me the ordeal of explaining it from first principles, but he doesn't and so I cry and render myself unable to communicate. He has me down as any other mother of young children – tired and unable to cope. He offers me antidepressants but I still have enough of myself left to turn them down and I leave with a handful of tissues. When I get home the health visitor rings.

'I hear from your doctor that things might not be turning out quite how you were expecting,' she says in a weak, quivery voice.

It is more a statement than a question: a statement that makes it clear she thinks I am labouring under some grand delusion about parenting because I haven't done it the proper way. If I were feeling stronger I would perhaps try to educate her but I am becoming sick of being in need and of having to justify why I am in need. The all-pervasive assumption that children shake off their neglect and abuse as though recovering from a cold is marginalising Jamie and me; he is naughty and weakly parented and I am someone who rants and wails and whom no one believes. The frog needs to come into the fucking pond, my son shouts abuse at me every night, my daughter's appetite is insatiable, I am exhausted and no one seems to want to believe me. I am like a madwoman, ranting about nothing, seeing ghosts, imagining darkness. Unnervingly I sense that I need to demonstrate my sanity and my grip on reality robustly and undoubtedly. I will not have 'nutcase' written on my file.

'I was just having a bad day. I'll be fine,' I say to the health visitor, with a calm and clear tone.

'It is difficult looking after two small children,' she mithers on, 'and you are still quite new to it.'

And with that I know with complete certainty that I will never be going to her for help.

Rob comes in that night, having worked late again, looking grey and exhausted. He dumps his briefcase in the hall and we give each other a hug.

'That's it for now, back to normal working hours for a while,' he says. How is everyone?'

I don't have the energy to recount the day.

'I'll tell you tomorrow.'

Even with Rob recovering from his long hours, his presence around the house immediately takes some of the pressure off me. The pleasure of going to do a little task and finding it has already been done is out of all proportion to the size of the task. Having to perform the bedtime routine for one child instead of two, not having to spend much of the evening clearing up the kitchen detritus, having someone else to talk laminated frogs with is blissful. We gradually re-establish our routine.

*****

Anna rings, full of excitement,

'There's a new pre-school opening in the church, opposite the school. They're taking children from the age of two and a half. That means Harlee could start.'

I contemplate the prospect.

'I know the woman who will be running it – it sounds really good.'

I still don't make a sound.

'Do you want the phone number?'

'Yes, of course I do,' and the realisation starts to sink in. Some time on my own.

*****

Everything about the pre-school is lovely. On her first day Harlee appears to roll up her sleeves and dive in. She tries everything very quickly and then tries it all again. There are a series of workstations laid out around the church hall. Harlee heads for the water table, fills a watering can and waters her arms. Within a moment she has moved on to a sandpit on legs and drives a digger over a rubber snake. Although the other children are playing in a more relaxed way, the pre-school teachers don't seem worried by Harlee at all. After a couple of weeks they report back that she is a joy to have in the group – that she is always happy, plays well with the other children and is always first in line to 'get involved'. It is an utter relief to hear something positive. We are welcomed each morning with smiles and sent off at the end of each session with waves and 'goodbyes'. And there are no laminated frogs.

For the first few weeks that Harlee attends pre-school I return home after dropping her off and try to relax in a wound up, nervous sort of way. If Jamie's send-off to school has been particularly difficult I come back to the house, quiet now, the scene of the crime and I rattle around reliving the shouting and the insults, then I catch myself pairing his little socks or clearing up his Bob the Builder plate and feel a clear, straight love for him and a regret that I can't make things right for him, that I struggle to be the kind of parent he wants me to be – that I want to be. Sometimes I race into town and then revel in a walk around the shops, taking the time I need to look at things, swinging my arms, unencumbered by little hands, toys and pushchairs. I have time to think about how I'm going to stage-manage the return from school, the activities we will do together, the mealtime. I rehearse the demeanour and the expression I will hold when I stand waiting for Jamie in the queue at school. I find it better to try and extract him from school quickly, avoiding the teacher. Sometimes she mouths something to me like 'bad day today' and after a really difficult time she will usher me into the threshold of the classroom and reel off the day's naughtinesses, distractions and disruptions. Jamie is usually next to me, avoiding eyes, pulling on my coat, desperate to get home. I'm never sure what I am supposed to do with this information. I suppose I am meant to sit Jamie down at the kitchen table and give him a stern talking to. Usually I do my best to brush it off, not wanting the misery of the school day to infect our home. But sometimes my head-girliness gets the better of me and I march Jamie home and over his biscuits and milk I lecture him about how he shouldn't distract other people, how he should listen and pay attention and stay away from trouble. Even though I know intellectually that the lectures go over his head, sometimes I can't help myself. I stand on the moral high ground, because it makes me feel temporarily better. I wag my finger and shake my head as though it is going to make a difference, as though the frog is going to magically jump into the pond.

*****

After a few weeks of dropping off and collecting Harlee from pre-school I start to chat to some of the other mothers and then one cold, lifeless winter's morning, one of them says, 'Does anyone fancy a coffee after this?'

There are some appreciative sounds and then a, 'That would be lovely,' and soon there are six of us making our way to the small steam-filled cafe next door. We pull up wooden chairs, shed our hats and gloves, consult menus and self-consciously order teas, coffees and cakes. We chat about tiredness and chores and the pre-school, which everyone seems to like. Inside I am jumping up and down with happiness. I am sitting in a cafe, without my children, with grown-up women and they seem nice. By the time we leave I only just about have time to go home and sort out the kitchen before it is time to go back and pick up Harlee. As we wait for the doors to be opened and our children to be released the six of us greet each other and tentatively agree to meet up again.

The next time we meet the conversation turns to childbirth. I try to ride it out, keeping quiet, laughing in the right places, looking concerned when it is appropriate. As I listen a little worry bead rolls around inside my head. There has not so far been a right time to tell them that I did not give birth to my children. I wonder if they have guessed, if I have betrayed my status somehow. I sometimes wonder if I don't seem like a real mother to the outside world, if I don't do things properly. And it's surely only a matter of time before someone asks me why Harlee is called Harlee. No one seems to notice my silence and eventually we touch on breastfeeding and then land up talking about the need to raise some money for the new pre-school. We agree that we need a full evening to decide upon a plan. Helen, one of the more confident members of the group, invites us all to her house the following week. I write it in my diary and circle it several times. This could be the start of something new.

*****

After lunch one day as Harlee and I are settling down to watch some children's television programmes together, the phone rings and it is Mel. It is a nice surprise to hear her voice again and yet I sense all is not well. After the niceties have been dealt with she lands the punch:

'Trudy has been causing a few problems, turning up outside the social services offices with posters and other material, claiming that we have stolen her children. I need you all just to be aware of it and to be sure to keep yourselves safe.'

'Oh god,' is all I can manage. I step out into the hallway to avoid being overheard by Harlee.

'Be sure not to travel anywhere near where she lives. And you need to remind the school and the pre-school not to publish any pictures of them, or to let anyone else collect them from school.'

'Have any threats been made against us?'

'No, not that I'm aware of. I think it's more about expressing anger towards social services.'

'Mel, I worry about Harlee's name. I think it's too identifiable.'

She pauses. Then, 'I understand your concerns.'

There is a simple solution and yet it only now comes into my mind.

'I think we need to consider changing her name.'

And I say it, just like that, confidently, without rolling it over and over in my mind, without worrying about what Mel will think.

'She is still very young, so it might not be too much for her to take in.'

'And the internet scares me. What if her name appears on some school-related thing in the future, even if it's just the school choir or an award or something?'

'I think you might be right. Why don't you talk it over with Rob and then ring me if you need any more help?'

I go back into the sitting room, put the phone down and snuggle up next to Harlee. She wants me to sing along to Big Cook, Little Cook.

'Welcome to our cafe…' I sing and she laughs and joins in, rocking from side to side in time with the music. She twirls her little, chubby fingers in the air. I wonder how much her name is woven into her two-year-old sense of herself. Ideally I would not be thinking about changing a child's name, but we are not living an ideal.

That evening, whilst the children are in the bath, I manage a snatched conversation with Rob in the hallway. I tell him about the phone call with Mel and float the idea with him of changing Harlee's name.

'We should just do it. She's young, she'll get used to it and it will ease a lot of the worry about her being tracked down. And I don't like the name "Harlee" anyway, and I'm fed up of being asked to explain it.'

'So I suppose we should go for something common,' I suggest.

'Mabel, that's my favourite name.'

'There's only one problem with "Mabel".'

He raises his eyebrows.

'She's not an old lady. I like Fleur.'

'Absolutely not.'

Later that evening we spend half an hour on the internet looking at the 'most popular names of the year' list and eventually we decide that as we chose Rose as her middle name all those months ago, that it would suit her as a new first name. We feel an immediate sense of relief that our children will both have common names. There must be lots of Jamies and Roses in the population. I catch myself wondering what it must be like to be able to choose a child's name without restriction. Couples spend hours discussing and agreeing upon their baby's names, they buy books full of suggestions and derivations, they mull over meanings and sounds and initials. We've discussed our child's name briefly in the hallway and then pulled it off the internet. It's a fit-for-purpose name, it does the job. In the heady days of planning our family, this is not how I had envisaged it.

The following evening we are on the internet researching how to change a name and downloading Deed Poll forms. I fret over how to explain the situation to Jamie. I don't want to frighten him with the harsh truth but to lie to him wouldn't feel right either. And he has an ability to see right through an adult's attempts at softening the hard edges of the world. So I tell him that it is important to Rob and me that we keep the two of them safe and that Harlee's name is very unusual. Jamie appears to take it on board as though it is something quite usual for families to do although he needs reassurance that we are not going to change his name too. Rob asks him what name he would choose if he could be called anything.

'Fred Bob Jim,' he says without hesitation, 'or Rocket Boat Boy.'

Within a week the forms are completed and we have told everyone who needs to know that henceforth, Harlee will be known as Rose.

I decide not to announce the big story to all my new pre-school friends at once in case it feels too much like a broadcast. ('And in shocking news, we've changed our daughter's name to avoid her being tracked down by her violent birth family.') So I tell individuals and small groups and tick them off like names on a Christmas card list. For many of the pre-school mothers I have to deliver the news as a kind of double whammy.

'Helen,' I say, catching her on the walk back home, 'I just need to tell you something.'

I can tell from her expression that she is preparing for something along the lines of a pregnancy or a house move.

'I don't know if you know that Jamie and Harlee are adopted?'

'No, no I didn't know that, wow, I, you look so alike,' she struggles.

'Well, Rob and I have decided to change Harlee's name to Rose – it's for security reasons.'

I am pleased with my choice of 'for security reasons' as it closes off debate and I decide I will use it again.

'Well, um, Rose is a really lovely name, I think it will suit her.'

When we all meet up for the fundraising meeting in Helen's kitchen I arrive knowing that I'm no longer holding this gigantic secret, that I'm not going to have to lie about my childbirth experiences or blag about difficult months of breastfeeding.

My sense of relief chimes with everyone else's need for a good night out and we drink and drink and get very drunk and very, very noisy. We cackle and guffaw and share secrets and gossip. Some are quieter and some are louder. I'm one of the loud ones, on temporary release from worry. I am buoyed up for days afterwards.

CHAPTER 14

I am slumped on the sofa marvelling at how quickly a child-free morning can pass, counting down each minute before I will have to collect Rose from pre-school, when the phone rings. The voice is bright and positive with a soft lilt. It is Aiesha, our new support worker.

'I've just started my job and I'm ringing adopters in my area to find out if there is any help I can offer. You have Jamie and Rose, don't you? How's it going?'

I'm not sure where to start.

'Jamie is up and down, with his temper and rudeness which is a bit of a struggle. He finds school very difficult.'

'In what way?'

'The teachers seem to think he might have a learning disability and he really doesn't produce much at school. I don't see him like that at home. He gets into trouble for not being able to focus, he's constantly distracted. He doesn't have any friends either, well other than a couple of boys who really aren't good for him, if you know what I mean.'

It pours out in an unsorted tangle.

'Yes, yes I do, these children are often attracted to other vulnerable children and it can create a lot of complications. And Rose?'

'She carries on around him – she plays happily enough and is generally content. She does get into things a lot though. She draws on furniture, cuts her clothes and she flooded the bathroom recently. I have to keep her close to me.'

'Could I come and see you?' Aiesha suggests tentatively. 'Perhaps I could give you some support?'

'That would be great.'

We make a date for the following week. I put the phone down and don't know if I dare hope that things are looking up.

Aiesha is petite and young, and radiates energy. Her bright headscarf brightens the room. We sit at the kitchen table and she gets a large notebook and a DVD from her bag. The events of the previous three years spill out of me. She nods, agrees and winces in the right places. She adds things that show she understands what I'm describing. I don't feel a need to convince her. My skills as a mother are not under scrutiny. Instead she accepts me and sees the issues for what they are.

'I don't expect you have time to read very much, so try and watch this,' she says, passing me the DVD. 'It is about parenting children with attachment difficulties – it's by an American.'

I take it gratefully. I haven't read a book for a long time, but I could manage to watch a DVD.

'And tell me about school. How does Jamie present himself?'

Again I reel off my worries and frustrations.

'His inability to focus – is he distracted by what's going on around him?'

'Every time someone leaves or enters the room he has to look around and needs to know who it was and where they are going. He has to make sure that everyone has a pencil and spends ages handing them around.'

'It sounds very much like hyper-vigilance to me, and a need to be in control. It comes from being in a violent place and not being cared for. The child learns that they have to look out for danger and that no one will be there to look out for them or comfort them. Where does he sit in class?'

'On the table with the other children who can't focus or have learning difficulties, near the door.'

'With his back to the door?'

'Yes, I think so.'

'You need to ask the teacher to move him near to her, facing the door. Then he'll have the comfort of being near an adult and he can see who is coming in and out of the room. It is all about helping him to feel secure and until he does, he won't be able to concentrate.'

It sounds so obvious, but I am already wondering how I will broach this with the teacher.

'You said to me on the phone that Jamie is in trouble a lot. What systems does the school use?'

'They have all the children's names on a board. This year their names are stuck under either a picture of a sun, a sun poking out from behind a cloud or a black cloud.' Last year outcast frogs, now we have stormy gloom.

'And where is Jamie's name most of the time, would you say?'

'Under the black cloud.'

'That's not going to help. Would you like me to come into school with you and talk to his teacher?'

The prospect of having someone else with me – a professional – to help put across what I struggle to, who can operate without the emotions that I am tied up with, is exactly what is needed, not for my benefit, but for Jamie's. We chat some more. Now I know that Aiesha gets me, I tell her about Jamie's difficulties making friends. I feel a sense of shame on Jamie's behalf if he hasn't been invited to a birthday party or to play at someone's house after school and the drama around the event is being displayed in front of everyone in the playground. And I know I should just not care about it. But I do. And I may see his cheeks flush just for a moment, or feel him dragging at my coat for us to leave and I see his shame too. The unpopular kid in the class.

'He seems to be attracted to the very children who are the worst for him. And I am not proud of saying this because those children are struggling in their own way. I'm sure one of them has some social services involvement. And his mother is desperate for her son to be friends with mine. I don't want Jamie going to their house because I'm not sure he'd be safe there. But this woman stalks me. I have to get to school early to avoid her and then run out at the end of the day. And Jamie thinks I'm being mean – he doesn't understand at all.'

'Sometimes these children don't think they deserve to have nice friends, so they sabotage friendships at the early stages.' She pauses. 'You need to keep in mind that Jamie is a very vulnerable child. You are there to protect him and that means you are going to be put into difficult situations that other parents are not. You are doing the right thing.'

Just hearing that gives me courage.

'Would you like me to meet the children? I could introduce myself and do some fun activities with them.'

I need to get as much help from Aiesha as she is offering. We agree to meet again the following week and in the meantime I will organise a meeting with the school.

When I approach the head teacher Mrs Jenkins, she is not all that enthusiastic and I sense defensiveness. She asks me to explain several times who Aiesha is and why she wants to come into school. Then the hammer blow, 'How long has Jamie been with you?'

'Three and a half years.'

I hear it coming.

'That's quite a long time. He should be alright by now.'

And so the klaxon has sounded. Your time is up, little boy. You have used up your quota of sympathy and understanding.

*****

The meeting is awkward. Mrs Jenkins and Jamie's teacher are there and listen to Aiesha explaining about the long-term effects of early neglect and abuse on the brain. There is a chill in the air, which I notice takes some of the edge off Aiesha's confidence. Much goes unsaid, particularly by the staff. Then Jamie's teacher starts to talk about how Jamie performs academically. She repeats her view that Jamie is not, as she puts it, 'ever going to be the sharpest tool in the box'. She doesn't meet my eyes but I know this is aimed at me. I am the alpha-mother who hasn't accepted that my son is not going to be a lawyer or a doctor. Maybe she is right. But I'm not ready to lie back and accept a future of low expectations mapped out for him by someone else.

'You saw the story that Jamie wrote at home, didn't you? It was well written, interesting and long. And he reads well, above his age. I know he struggles with numbers and he finds it hard to express himself verbally but this is common in children with Jamie's background.'

There is a grudging acknowledgement. Still no eye contact.

Then we move on to the black cloud. Aiesha explains why these types of behaviour systems don't work well with children who feel a crippling sense of shame. The meeting starts to feel like a negotiation. The school is clearly not going to move on this one but the teacher agrees to move Jamie's name around the weather system more quickly so that he doesn't languish for too long in the shadows.

The meeting comes to its stilted end. Aiesha and I walk the short distance home in the sunshine.

'That was a struggle,' she says and shakes her head.

'I was hoping for better, but I'm not surprised. I'm glad you were there with me.'

'You're doing a great job,' she says, 'never forget that.'

*****

It is the end of the summer term – Rose's last one at pre-school – and instead of dreading the long holiday I am looking forward to having a break from school, from being the awkward and deluded alpha-mother with the dysfunctional child, who has to avoid twice-daily ambush in the playground.

On Rose's last day at pre-school a little show is put on by those heading off to school in September. The children dress up and sing songs. They have all iced biscuits, which they hand around. Rose's are loaded with icing and packed with sweets. Then at the end each leaver receives a teddy as a reminder of their time at the pre-school. Amongst all the difficulties it has shone out as a special time. Rose has been happy here and has looked forward to going. She has made friends and is known as a confident and artistic child who will have a go at anything. This is the end of our time at home together and although I am pleased and relieved that she is happy to be going to school, I will miss our time together. 'That's my girl,' I think proudly as I watch her standing up dressed in a gauze veil and performing Twinkle Twinkle Little Star. She loves dressing up and is usually a mermaid or an animal of some kind. She comes shopping with me in eccentric get-ups, unaware that she is attracting the attention of lonely old ladies and shop assistants. Her vocabulary is good but she still struggles to make herself understood and so the old ladies look to me with puzzled faces when Rose tries to tell them her name. She hasn't mastered the sound 'ffff' and so cannot say her age either.

'Or,' she says insistently.

'Four, she's four,' I have to say.

At home she plays constantly. Anything she has to hand becomes animated and is given a voice, whether a couple of spoons or some old lolly sticks.

'Hello, what your name?'

'My name Bobby.'

'Bobby, you like to come to beach with me?'

'Yes, I like beach.'

And off the objects walk together, 'La, la-la, la-la.'

She arranges her animals and Barbie dolls in great, dramatic scenes where they act out songs and rhymes. There is action, often an event that requires the telling-off of one character by another. Then some comforting and perhaps some plastic food will be passed around. Sometimes I happen upon these scenes when I am putting away laundry or changing her bed sheets – the Barbies with arms outstretched and wild hair sit semi-naked around a tyrannosaurus rex. He has a pink beret on his head and stands on a quarter of plastic birthday cake with a candle stuck in it. What appeared to be a scene of fright and danger is in fact a tea party and when I look more closely I notice that some of the Barbies sit alongside giant teacups on saucers. It delights me that this imaginary world is being played out, that here in our home this childish innocence can flourish, has remained intact and has not been driven out.

There is no doubt that Rose has been less damaged by their earlier experiences than Jamie. Her play is freer and less crowded by anxiety. She seems untroubled by frustration and anger and still has a strong inner determination. If she sees an older child perform some physical feat in a playground she watches that child very carefully. I see her absolute certainty that she too will climb to the very top, teeter on one foot and launch herself down from the top rung. This is the great difference between the two of them – if Jamie sees another child demonstrating an ability, his default position is 'I'll never be able to do that – there is no point me even trying.'

The time Rose and I have spent together whilst Jamie has been at school has allowed me to start teaching her to read letters and words. Although she struggles to sound the letters, she has started to recognise simple words such as 'boy', 'girl', 'dog' and 'ball'. We do a little bit of reading every day on top of her usual bedtime storybooks and as she enjoys doing it, I continue. I regret not having had the space and experience to do the same with Jamie and I think it would have helped him to have started school with just a kernel of confidence. I remember my mother teaching me to read before I started school and clearly recall feeling proud that this skill enabled me to sit on a special table, with the other children who could read too. My mother gifted me the belief that I can do things at least as well as everyone else and I would like to pass on this gift to Rose.

*****

I enter the playground on the last day of the school year with a plan of attack. I am spotted immediately and cornered by the stalker mother and tell her with confidence that we will be away for most of the holidays but that I will ring her if we have some free time. I know I have sounded brusque and perhaps rude. It is for the greater good. Jamie comes out of class with carrier bags full of pictures and exercise books. I take them from him and notice that in his hand is a squashed chocolate cupcake.

'This is for you and Rose.'

I bend down and take it from his sticky outstretched hand.

'Thank you very much. It looks lovely. You are very kind.'

He looks pleased.

'Shall we go home now?'

'Yes.' And he puts his sticky hand inside mine and the three of us walk home. Rose is troubled by the cake and pesters me for it. Jamie and I are burdened with school bags but we share the relief that the school year is over.

'Shall we have ice lollies when we get home?'

'Yesss,' they both cheer.

Our trudging turns to skipping and chatting the nearer we get to home.

We eat our lollies and I give them sweets: 'Friday sweets'. Rob and I have introduced Friday sweets to try to mark the end of five days of toil and unhappiness and the beginning of a weekend of fun. This small ritual has become important to them both and if I am forgetful and Friday sweets become Saturday sweets then there is much consternation. They like to close their eyes, hold out their arms and have me place the sweets in their palms. There is whooping and cheering as they open their eyes. Rose will eat hers at speed. Jamie will savour his and always offers me one and puts one aside for Rob. As Jamie carefully finishes his sweets, the three of us sit at the kitchen table and draw a calendar for the summer holidays. It is something that Aiesha has suggested as a way of helping Jamie through the daunting prospect of six weeks of unstructured time. We draw a row for each week and a box for each day. Some days have plans written into them, other days have question marks. One of the rows contains the words 'Holiday in Cornwall' and Jamie draws a bucket and spade alongside.

'We go seaside?' asks Rose.

'Yes. We are going to stay in another house near the sea.'

'How many sleeps?' asks Jamie.

'Seven sleeps and then we come home again.'

'I come home with you?' He looks at me and his expression is one of genuine puzzlement.

The prospect of a holiday, even though we have been on holiday before, is unsettling him.

'We all go together, in the car, we all stay in the holiday house for seven sleeps and then we all come back home again.'

'I have ice cream?' says Rose.

'Oh yes, lots and lots of ice cream.'

Jamie looks preoccupied.

'Jamie, you and Rose are with me and Daddy forever.'

He doesn't really respond and I wonder if 'forever', such an abstract word for a young mind, means anything to him.

'You will always be with me and Daddy, always.'

I lift them both on to my knee and put my arms around them, pulling them into me.

'And Mummy and Daddy love you so much.'

I kiss them all over their faces and necks and they screech and struggle to get away. They smell sweet and earthy and familiar.

*****

We wallow in the summer holidays. We play a lot. We are police officers with walkie talkies. We host a sports day, which involves me being timed to run around the garden, skip and throw a beanbag into a hoop. Rose spends much of her time on her hands and feet, barking and asking me to throw things for her to fetch. We cycle around the lanes and we go swimming. We have a big family gathering in a pizza restaurant. The children all want to sit together. We are noisy and messy but no one minds. My nephews Luke and Harry come back to our house for a sleepover. I start to feel like a part of any other family.

But as we tick off the boxes on our homemade holiday calendar and the new school year moves closer, a dread comes over Jamie. Rose is looking forward to starting school so I try hard to mask my own feelings of dread. She tries on her uniform and admires herself in it.

On the first day of every school year Rob and I take a photograph of Jamie and Rose in the garden, in the same spot, standing to attention in fresh, new uniforms. This will be the fourth photograph in the set and the first when Rose is wearing school uniform too. The morning sun shines on their clean faces and on their auburn hair, lightened by the summer. On the face of it they both look a picture of health, they are beautiful, but when I look back at the picture weeks later I see something I hadn't noticed before. They smile with their mouths but their eyes say something else entirely, particularly Jamie's. He is preoccupied, blank even.

*****

It is not many days into the new term before his teacher, Mrs Watts, is signalling to me after school. Most days she catches my eye, rolling hers, tilting her head to one side. A list of misdemeanours, lacks, failures – Jamie by my side looking sheepish, Rose charging around the playground uncontrollably. The ritual takes place almost daily and my store of energy and confidence built up over the summer takes a battering. One day after school I hear about how Jamie cannot stay away from the troublemakers. I suggest that he has some help with that, but am told it is something he must start to learn for himself – to make the right choices. We rush from school to the hairdressers where summer-bleached curls are lopped off. I look at them strewn across the floor with an unexpected sadness.

The school suggests that Jamie see someone – someone who may be able to help with his 'issues'. There is talk of play therapy. It sounds promising. Various referrals are made and an appointment arrives for him to see a Dr Darling at the disconcertingly named Child and Adolescent Mental Health Service.

The health service building is crumbling and faded. We are buzzed in by a lady sitting behind glass panels. The door snags on thin carpet tiles curled up at the corners. We head to a seating area, which looks more like a dumping ground for broken toys. There is no obvious feeling of welcome or warmth. We try to play table football but we can't find a ball anywhere so we look at a pop-up book, which has seen better days.

Dr Darling appears. He is a short, slight man. He wears an expensive, dark wool suit, a waistcoat and brown Italian brogues. But, as I stand up to shake his hand the first thing I notice is his bow tie; it is a bow tie with cartoons on it. I ask if I could speak to him without Jamie present. He looks put out as though I have made an outlandish request but agrees. I tell Jamie I will be a short time and follow Dr Darling to his room. He sits back, arms up, hands meeting behind his head, one leg outstretched, the other crossed wide and confidently. I know the body language.

'So why did you want to speak to me alone?'

'Because I need to talk candidly about some things that I don't want Jamie to hear.'

('Obvious,' I think, 'isn't it obvious?')

He kind of sighs as though this is all going to be far too tedious for words. So I tell him a bit about Jamie's background and the problems at home and at school.

'So what sets these episodes off?' he asks, leaning forward, too far forward.

'It's never really anything significant.'

'Well, it must be something, it's always something,' he says, leaning back further, reaching to the side and fiddling with a fountain pen on his desk.

('I've told you, it's nothing significant.')

'Let's get Jamie in, shall we?' he says.

I collect Jamie from the waiting room where he has been sitting quietly driving some cars along a table. We enter the room holding hands.

'Over here, young man. If you could just take your things off, we need to do some quick weighing and measuring.'

('You are kidding.')

I am speechless. We are here for clear psychological reasons and yet Jamie is being asked to take his clothes off.

Jamie starts to get undressed. I go to help him.

'No, Mum, let's see if Jamie can do this himself.'

I feel my face flush, for being called 'Mum', for being put down, for being shut out, for not having the confidence to put a stop to this right now.

('Idiot little man, stupid joke bow tie like this is some kind of joke.')

Jamie is weighed and measured and has his heart listened to. Dr Darling asks him some questions, which he struggles to provide clear answers to, of course.

'He is still receiving some speech therapy,' I offer.

I am ignored.

'I am going to speak into this Dictaphone so that my secretary can make the necessary notes for me,' he declares.

He then proceeds to relay weights and measures and other details as I dress Jamie. As I finish he brings some sheets of paper out of a drawer.

'Have you ever considered Ritalin?' he asks, like a threat.

'No.'

'Why not?'

'Because he's not hyperactive.'

My courage takes me by surprise. He raises his eyebrows and looks at me over his wire-rimmed glasses.

'If I were you I wouldn't be so quick to judge.' He hands me two pieces of yellow paper. 'I want you to fill these in and then make another appointment to come back and see me.'

My eyes flick over the sheets. They contain questions and statements, the answers to which will go towards determining whether Jamie is hyperactive.

'We could start him off on a small dose and see if it makes any difference,' says Dr Darling, looking up at the ceiling, as though the answers to the questions will be irrelevant.

'No.'

'Well, have a look at what I've given you and we'll discuss it again.'

No, we won't 'discuss' it again. A discussion indicates that a degree of listening has taken place and it has not. I am never coming to see this man again. And just to top it all off and as a final act of power over me, Dr Darling then picks up his Dictaphone again and, looking me straight in the eye, recounts all that I told him whilst Jamie was out of the room.

Jamie puts on his t-shirt ('abuse').

He puts his legs in his trousers ('multiple injuries').

Does up his button ('adoptive mother finding behaviours difficult to manage').

He searches for his socks ('have concluded ADHD, adoptive mother disagrees').

Sock, and shoes go on ('back for a further assessment, Mum will complete ADHD forms').

I think I know that science is on my side. This man is a doctor, a man of science. I am a mother, whose intelligence and life experience is washed away by the very act of being a mother. I have read that modern brain-scanning technology is showing what social workers, foster carers and adopters have known all along – that the baby brain is severely impacted by poor early care. But has this all been a figment of my imagination? Am I just being hysterical?

'What were you hoping for in coming to see me?' he asks.

'I was led to believe that there may be some appropriate therapy on offer here.'

'There may be something like that here, but there's a very long waiting list, so we won't bother with that.'

He stands up and this is the final act of the power play, our signal to leave. I take Jamie's hand. He looks up at me, quizzing me. He reads my expressions competently and today I am not hiding my feelings well. Together we walk out, through the crappy waiting area with its crappy toys, out through the security doors and into the open air. It is a clean blue autumn day and I fill my lungs with the clear air. I am shaking with anger and frustration.

'You alright, Mummy?'

'Yes, I'm alright,' I say with a big breath out, not convincing either of us.

'I not like that man.'

'No, I didn't like him either.'

'I not want to go to him again.'

'Jamie, we will never be going there again, ever.'

I take Jamie back to school, take him into his classroom and kiss him goodbye. I march the short walk home ranting and swearing under my breath, tears in my eyes. If Dr Darling could see me now it would confirm everything he thought he knew about me.

I think I have calmed down so I ring Aiesha to tell her about the appointment. Within seconds my throat is straining with the effort of holding back tears. Her kindness only makes it more difficult to keep back the weight of emotion and anger in my chest.

'Sally, I've worked with children with ADHD and Jamie is nothing like them. When he feels safe he is able to sit quietly and play, or read, or watch a film. It's about anxiety and fear for him, not about ADHD.'

She knows of Dr Darling and evidently I am not the only parent who has been subjected to his charms.

'I hadn't expected you to be referred to him – I thought you would end up with one of the therapists. I'm really sorry.'

She has organised another meeting at Jamie's school as a follow-on from the last one. We run through what she wants to cover. I struggle to engage.

*****

I need a short break from my washing machine of a mind, some distraction. Trivia jars and irritates me more than it should. I put on the television. 'Is the A-line flattering to the pear shape?' 'What do *you* do with leftover chicken? Send us in your recipes.' 'Would *you* consider teeth-bleaching?' 'What *are* the risks of too much coffee?' Don't care. Don't care. Shut up. Get lost. I am irritable with other people too. I try to hide it, but it blows around and screeches in my head. Our neighbour Jean often spots me on my way home from school in the morning. She wants to chat. Were I living a normal life, I would probably want to chat too. She is dissatisfied with much of modern life, particularly 'young people', who play too many computer games, like awful music and have a tendency to leave litter in her front garden. All this is said through pursed, disapproving lips and with arms across sweatered chest – a barrier between her and failing society. I nod and 'mmmm' and try the occasional subtle disagreement when I feel up to it, before excusing myself, citing the many chores that need doing.

'By the way, how's Rose doing at school?'

'Really well, thank you, she enjoys it.'

'And how's Jamie doing? I heard him talking to you outside here the other day,' she says, suddenly engaging full-disapproval tone, 'testing you out. He was being very rude.'

I fix the smile I keep in the bag for these situations.

'Mmmm, he can be like that.'

'It sounded as though he needed some firm discipline.'

Forgive her, I think, for she knows not what she says. My exit from the conversation is rather hasty but necessary to protect good neighbourly relations. I try to listen to Radio 4 whilst I scrub at a scrambled-egg pan ('was Aristotle the father of modern thought and what about…'). I find it hard to give a shit. Like a glutton for punishment I flick through the daytime television offerings and settle on a repeat of Frasier. It takes me back to the lazy Friday nights of my past – a glass of wine and a takeaway after a week of work. Our Friday nights are now planning sessions washed down with exhaustion. Rob and I have noticed that, unlike us, Jamie and Rose find the prospect of two days at home, devoid of any structure, unsettling. So we plan who will lie in on which morning, who will take which child for a walk; if there are homework or birthday party obligations we build these in; we consult the weather forecast and then hash together a plan for something we can all do together.

*****

Even though I enjoy meeting up with my new friends from the pre-school I still retain this sense of dislocation that I can't shake off. Husbands never bother to put the corkscrew in the correct kitchen drawer, recyclables are sorted badly, beer cans not washed out. Sometimes I have to physically stop myself from oozing rude uninterest. And this is turning me into a horrible person – impatient, with too little interest in other people. I worry that I am incapable of having a normal human relationship now. And I know that I am being unreasonable and crabby and unkind.

*****

Aiesha and I walk into the school together for our meeting. Mrs Jenkins and Mrs Watts are already seated when we enter the staffroom. It is as though we have interrupted something and there is a bristly atmosphere; there are more arms across chests and pursed lips. We start with a summary of Jamie's behaviours over the past few weeks and something new: associated parents' complaints, of which there are quite a few. I start to wonder which parents have made the complaints and whether it is anyone I know. The tone is noticeably more accusatory than it has been before, although when Aiesha uses the word 'neglect' in relation to child development, expressions turn to concerned understanding. But when we are back on to what, in other parents' eyes, is basic bad behaviour the mild accusing is turned back on again. 'We are terribly sorry for what happened to him but we wish he would just learn how to behave,' is the overriding message I receive. 'Child neglect is a terrible thing that we can all wring our hands about,' say the playground parents publicly, 'but we don't want our own children being taught with the victims of child neglect: my goodness no, they are just so disruptive.'

After the meeting we walk a respectful distance across the playground before I dare look at Aiesha. She takes a deep breath and shakes her head and I see something in her expression that gives me a little pinch of dread.

'That wasn't as positive as I was hoping,' she says. 'There seems to be a certain amount of lip service.'

We walk on in silence. I have a horrible feeling that we have come to the end of the road.

Rob calls from work to find out how the meeting went and when I recount the whole depressing tale he goes straight to the point.

'We need to think about moving Jamie to a different school. We should consider a private school.'

'Private school?'

'Let's talk about it this evening.'

*****

Private school. Somewhere for the fortunate to educate their children away from the less fortunate. I wonder where we fit into that picture. Or should we start looking into other nearby state schools – big town primaries or small village schools? I need a crystal ball so that I can see the degree of support Jamie will need, whether he would shake off his problems if the education were expensive enough or good enough – and what constitutes good enough? I cast around on the internet and find several schools located in former stately homes in grassy settings. There is much emphasis on rugby and big oak trees. The 'family atmosphere' is trumpeted; so are the happy, thriving children. There are overblown written statements from head teachers about their own personal visions for education, which are all remarkably similar. Then there are the more budget private schools in nearby town centres, where school fees are less expensive. They deliver lots of sport and religion. There are photographs of families on benches in the grounds. None of the family members look like us. The mothers wear chunky necklaces over polo neck jumpers and have sensible haircuts. The fathers look confidently professional, but not in an office job kind of way. The children are all having the most enormous fun. I know that Rob would feel as out of place as I would, but he has come over all 'doing the very best I can for my children,' echoes of his family's working-class values. He has some money from the sale of his dad's house and, of course, would like to see it put to good use.

From my internet search I come up with two possible schools – one leafy, one towny. I ring both. The head teacher of the leafy school has a confident, charming, slightly smarmy way about him. I give him a bit of background, but not too much, and he delivers me a marketing pitch and stitches me into a visit.

I put much consideration into my attire and my demeanour and when I pull into the gravel drive in front of the house and park beneath the climbing roses, still carrying a few late-season raggedy blooms, I have to suppress the feeling that this is the sort of place where I should be weeding the borders, not having my child educated. The large panelled doors are open and I step over the threshold. To one side is a small office where a slim middle-aged lady is on the telephone. I wait awkwardly. Trying not to look as though I am eavesdropping, I check in my handbag for my list of questions and readjust my scarf. The telephone conversation ends and I attempt to catch the lady's eye. She fiddles with some papers and makes it clear she is not ready to attend to me. Finally I crack.

'Excuse me, I am here for a tour of the school.'

She looks up as though she had not noticed me. And then turns on the charm.

'Oh hello, very pleased to meet you. You must be Mrs…?' She pauses.

'Mrs Donovan.'

I hold out my hand, which she shakes without enthusiasm. Hers is so small and bird-like that mine feels large and ungainly in comparison. She shows me into a large, oak-panelled room, with shelves of books and a low table with copies of Country Life artfully arranged on it. She brings me a tray of tea, which she delivers with a slight chill. I try to ease my nervousness by flicking through one of the magazines. The property section distracts me for a moment. These are properties in the true sense of the word – not just houses with a garage and a shed if you're lucky, but land with many buildings, stabling, cottages for employees, orangeries, sporting facilities. I wonder at the subtle message being played out here, in this oak-panelled room with its dark floral drapes and its rows of old books and grandfather clock ticking out a slow wash of boredom.

Then in a whoosh of noisy confidence the head teacher is in front of me, holding out his hand. I barely have time to stand before his hand crushes mine. He is loud and large and wrapped in a sage-green sweater in the manner of a captain of industry on a day off. I gather my things and follow on behind him. There are several rooms of students' work; art and technology, see how wonderful it is. Some have won prizes. There are certificates and cups. Prizes. More prizes.

'A boy you say, you have a boy?' His eyes flick around, his mind is on something else.

'Our adopted son. He is struggling at school, finding it hard to concentrate and sometimes gets into trouble.'

A bit of honesty but not too much.

'Boys, yes we have lots here for boys.'

Then I am marched around sports pitches where hockey is being played.

'Rugby, we do lots of rugby. Morning, Travers.'

'Morning, Sir,' says a boy in a stripy shirt running past.

'Walk, Travers, walk.'

'Sorry, Sir.'

'Pastoral care, excellent pastoral care,' he trumpets as I am shown into a boys' dormitory. It is crammed with bunk beds. On top of one bunk is a boy lying in bed, looking sleepy and ill.

'Doing alright there, Henry? Matron been looking after you?'

'Yes, sir,' says the boy, maybe 12 years old, looking embarrassed at our intrusion.

He looks lost, as if he needs his mother.

Then along gravel paths we march, to classrooms full of faces. There is talk of woodwork and more rugby.

I ask what would happen if Jamie were to need some help, some extra tuition.

'That would have to be paid for on top of our fees. Mr Wilcox, how was your test yesterday?'

'Fine, sir,' replies a tall boy with a mop of dark hair, as he dashes past us.

And then we are back to the front of the house where my Ford Focus is parked.

'Jamie will need to come in for a trial day. Next Wednesday, is that convenient?'

'Yes, that's fine.'

'Just to see if he likes it here and if we all can get along.'

He is walking me towards my car.

'How much support is he receiving in his current school?'

'Some one-to-one help, and we have a new support worker who is trying to get him some therapeutic work.'

'Therapeutic work, from where?'

'Well, we've tried CAMHS, you know the Child and Adolescent Mental Health Service…'

And he cuts me off with a brisk handshake and an air of many more things to attend to.

I sit in my car for a moment and take a breath. Through the window of the office I can make out the head teacher standing across the desk from the lady I had met earlier. He is giving her some instructions.

I drive home along the wide gravel drive, through the narrow, muddy lanes and into the outskirts of town. I pull up outside our house, get out of the car, wave and mouth 'hello' to Jean, turn the key in the lock, go into our hallway and kick the sprawl of shoes into a neater pile. The red light on the telephone is flashing. I hang up my handbag and press 'play'.

'Mrs Donovan, this is Manor School. We are very sorry but the head has informed me that we are completely full for the next year and anticipate being so for quite some time, so it really isn't worth you bringing your son to see us next week. Many thanks. Bye now.'

*****

I take Rob with me to visit the town school. It is an open day. We are given ten minutes with the head teacher. We have heard he has taught in an inner-city comprehensive, so we are hopeful. We needn't have been.

He leans back in his reclining chair and folds his hands behind his head. I am reminded of Dr Darling.

'It will be one strike and he's out here – that's the way we run things, that's what the parents expect,' he says, his friendly tone not matching his words.

We nod like stupid donkeys, both knowing the absolute impossibility of this policy for Jamie.

'We have had adopted children here before. In fact one has just had to leave but she had quite severe problems.' He says this with not an ounce of compassion.

When Aiesha heard that Rob and I were coming to visit the school, she told us about this particular child. Social services considered her problems to be relatively mild. Nevertheless she was not thought to be suitable for the school and was asked to leave.

We exit the school, walk into town and sit in a cafe.

'What the fuck do we do now, then?' I say, shaking my head.

'You need to stop swearing, Mrs Donovan.'

'Swearing is about all that helps right now.'

We drink large cups of expensive, weak tea and hold hands across the table.

PART 7

A Time for Healing

No Matter What

CHAPTER 15

Head down, hands in pockets, I make my escape from the playground, just before most of the other parents and children arrive. I am congratulating myself on a well-executed school drop-off when I hear my name being called to the background beat of the 'clip clip' of grown-up shoes. It is Helen.

'I've been trying to catch you for a few mornings now.'

She is dressed for work in smart grey trousers, little pointy shoes, a white shirt and a red mac. Her hair is long, brushed and immaculate.

'I spend as little time in the playground as I have to.'

'I know. Anna mentioned that you were having some problems. I just wanted to talk to you about my sister Justine,' she pauses to catch her breath from running. 'She has adopted children, a bit older than Jamie and Rose. They've both been to a primary school that has really worked out wonderfully for them where the staff have done a marvellous job with the children. My sister said that you can ring her any time, if you want to talk to her about it.'

Sounds promising.

Helen opens her black, leather handbag and retrieves a silver pen and a small notepad in which she writes her sister's telephone number. She is the very picture of efficiency. She tears out the page of heavyweight notepaper and hands it to me. I thank her and she dashes off again, 'clip clip clip'.

I walk the rest of the way home wondering what Helen made of me – unshowered, clothes on from yesterday, a wreck of a person, avoiding perfectly nice people. In the house I ignore the dried clumps of mud on the hallway floor, the pile of double-glazing leaflets on the bottom stair, the dirty dishes in the kitchen sink, and fill the kettle and unlock the back door. It is the beginning of October. The garden looks like me – scruffy and unkempt. The perennials loll around, brambles wind through the shrubs and the grass is creeping into the borders. No one would believe this was a gardener's garden. Maybe I can't call myself a gardener anymore. The grass is littered with childish detritus – a broken seaside bucket, a plastic teacup, a dirty foam ball nibbled at by rodents, a lone beanbag. The bird feeders are empty and a collection of petals and leaves that Rose has put together blow around the paving. I need a job like Helen. I need to be rushing off somewhere, with things to do, important things. I need a wardrobe of ironed blouses and pencil skirts. At the very least I should get a grip of the garden, tidy the house and sort out the children's bedrooms.

I should ring Helen's sister Justine. I should do it now, before I lose my nerve altogether. I imagine ringing this person I don't know and she will say, 'Sally? Sally who?' and I will have to explain who I am and then she will be frosty and I will wish I'd never had rung.

I know of the school. It is called St Mary's. It is maybe ten miles from here, across the county boundary. It would mean almost an hour round trip twice a day to transport Jamie and Rose to school and back. I've rung schools nearer to home, but all have been full.

Gathering up my scraps of confidence, I take a deep breath, go back indoors and ring Helen's sister.

'My name is Sally, your sister Helen…'

'Sally, how are you?' she trumpets before I have time to trot out my rehearsed introduction. 'You're trying to find a school for your two, is that right?'

'Yes, the eldest, Jamie, isn't really doing too well so we need to find somewhere more suitable for him and we'd prefer that Jamie and Rose went to the same school.'

'I expect Helen told you our children went to St Mary's. It's been fantastic. The staff have been so patient and understanding and they all know about the difficulties children like ours have. You must at least visit. I think you'd like it.'

'It's just so far from us.'

'It will take you probably 20, 25 minutes and it will be worth it. Ring the head teacher, Mr Andrews.'

We chat some more about our shared experiences. Speaking to a fellow traveller I realise how much we have in common. Our children display similar behaviours, which we don't have to explain to each other, we both know the reasons why and we get to the point without having to go through the nausea of the 'all children do that', or the 'surely they should be alright by now' conversation. We agree to keep in touch.

I busy myself with diversionary tasks for far longer than I should. Finally, I decide I have to do it; I have to ring this school and speak to the head teacher. I rehearse again, make some notes and then stand up to make the call. The head teacher picks up.

'I am looking to move my two children from their current school. They are our adopted children and the eldest in particular is having some problems…' I run out, worrying that I have put him off already.

'What school years are they in?'

'Jamie is Year 3 and Rose is in reception class.'

'We have space to take Rose and we have one space in Year 3. Would you like to come and have a look around and we can talk in more detail? I could see you tomorrow at around half past ten?'

My heart thumps in my chest. That soon.

'Yes, tomorrow. And I just have to tell you, in case it makes a difference, we would be coming from out of county.'

'Not an issue for us at all.'

Then I am alone in the kitchen, listening to the buzz of the fridge and the quiet sound of obstacles being removed.

*****

The next morning I am up early, showered, dressed and mentally prepared. I have a list of questions about behaviour policies and reward systems – questions to test how much the school really does know about managing children like ours, questions to bring out attitudes to children with additional needs. Had I known the difficulties that Jamie was to face at school, this is what I would have done before he started. I must get it right this time.

It takes me 23 minutes to drive to the school and I arrive 20 minutes early. It is situated in a small, rural village, the kind of place that people might holiday or retire to. I wander up and down the short high street and buy a newspaper from the village shop. There is a feeling of calm and order. Several ladies chat outside the shop. They are sensibly and expensively dressed in the dark colours of country wear. One carries a wicker basket over her arm.

I go back to the car and sit flicking through the newspaper. I am shivery and unsettled. Then, just a few minutes early, I gather myself and take a confident walk through the school gates and into the playground.

The school secretary buzzes me in and I am met by the head teacher, Mr Andrews. He is younger than I had been expecting, younger than me. We go into his small office and I am shown to a wobbly, wooden chair. The secretary brings two mugs of tea. She seems friendly, welcoming. Mr Andrews starts by asking me lots of questions. How long have we had the children? How long had they been in care? What had their early experiences been like? He then asks how Jamie presents himself at school. I explain that he is like two different children – at home, despite some challenging behaviours, he reads, writes stories, plays and is funny and at school he doesn't produce much work at all, gets into trouble a lot and won't comply with the teacher's demands. It is clear from his questioning that Mr Andrews understands and there is an absence of judgement. He talks about acceptance, not pushing things and focusing more on well-being and encouragement than on general behaviour.

'These children need approaching differently to other children – above all they need to feel safe and valued and only then might they start to learn.'

I share my belief that Jamie is more capable than he shows himself to be, that he has more inside him that just can't show itself right now. I half expect the 'alpha-mother' alarm to sound and my chair to collapse spontaneously. Mr Andrews doesn't flinch.

'If Jamie started now then we have got three and a half years to work with him and you before he would be off to secondary school. And it would be useful to have some contact with your agencies too. Do you have a social worker?'

'Yes, we do.'

'We would be looking to work with them as well, to do the best for Jamie that we can.'

'Yes,' I think, 'I want my children to come here.'

The tour of the school takes about ten minutes. We dip in and out of classrooms. The younger ones are busy outside chalking pictures on the playground; some are constructing a den from blue tarpaulin and milk crates. Older children are gathered around desks covered in newspaper clippings, discussing headlines.

'They are learning about different writing styles,' says Mr Andrews.

They all look up at me; the teacher smiles and says 'hello'.

'These are Year 3s and 4s, the class that Jamie would be in.'

The classroom is large and light with big windows that look out over the school playing field. I look around for charts. There is a chart with reading levels on and one showing the register and tidy monitors for the week. No clouds, no frogs.

Another class are sitting on the carpet around the teacher. They are doing words with 'oi' in. 'Soil' they all shout, 'boil', 'oil'. Mr Andrews tells them all I am visiting the school.

'Good morning, Mrs Donovan,' they chorus.

We head off through the hall and back to the entrance.

'Take some time to think about things and give me a ring when you've decided,' says Mr Andrews. 'The places won't be available for long, though.'

I thank him and leave. At the school gate I stop for a moment and look back. I try to imagine whether I could see Jamie and Rose here, whether they would belong. I wonder if the area is diverse enough, whether they would stand out from the crowd too much. But the head teacher knows about adoption and attachment problems and the school successfully taught Justine's children. Maybe it's because the sun is out, or because the village is picturesque, but the overwhelming feelings I get from the school are happiness and calm. The children were bouncy and energetic and happy. And I felt welcomed.

That evening Rob and I go over all the pros and cons of staying in our local school versus moving the children to St Mary's. We talk about the driving, about whether we should be schooling them away from the community where we live, about where they might go to secondary school. Each obstacle seems smaller as we contemplate leaving the children in our local school. It no longer seems like a viable possibility. As usual it is Rob who cuts to the chase.

'Ring Mr Andrews in the morning and tell him "yes", then arrange for Jamie and Rose to have a visit and I'll try and get some time off work so that I can come too.'

For the next few nights I have dread-filled dreams that I have made a terrible mistake, that hidden beneath the shine of St Mary's is a place of children's nightmares.

I have told Mrs Jenkins that the children will be leaving next week, just before the October half term holiday. She doesn't say much but seems disappointed. Word gets around the playground and waiting there at the end of each day becomes even more awkward than usual. Now and again I have to catch my breath when I suddenly remember what we are doing.

We tell Jamie that he will be going to a new school; we tell him about its big playground, the football field and about his new teacher Miss Taylor. It is difficult to work out how he takes it. He seems happy, relieved almost, but then will sometimes say, 'And then I'll go back to *my* school,' and I will get that thud in the heart again and worry that we are making a big mistake. Rose doesn't seem to understand. She goes along with it all – the new uniform and book bag – but I know that in some ways it will be harder for her, leaving friends behind.

The second visit eases my concerns. Jamie and Rose seem to enjoy looking around and sitting in their new classes. Rob and I leave them for an hour and sit in the village pub and drink coffee.

'Good choice,' says Rob. 'The atmosphere is great and I like Mr Andrews.'

'It feels a bit like the second viewing of a house. I was ready to see the faults today, but I haven't seen any, except perhaps the driving.'

'Think of all the money we'll be saving on school fees.'

We sit back and laugh, savouring this precious time together and another life hurdle successfully jumped.

*****

Aiesha has asked me if I will speak at a training event for those interested in becoming adopters. She calls me to confirm the details and to tell me what she wants me to say.

'You need to be honest about what it's been like, what adoption has brought to your lives but also the difficulties. I want you to talk about the problems at school and your work situation.'

'I don't have a work situation.'

'Explain why you can't work at the moment, why childcare would not be appropriate for your children, the time it takes out of your week going to appointments, the time you've put into finding the right school. Don't pull any punches.'

'I don't want to put people off either.'

'I'm sure you won't, not the right ones anyway.'

When I walk into the suite in the hotel where the course is being held, everyone is milling about with tea and biscuits. Aiesha greets me and introduces me to the other social worker who is leading the training. Again I am given the lead that I must be honest.

The session starts. Aiesha and I sit at the front, wrapped by a semicircle of people. My part of the training runs as a question-and-answer session. Aiesha poses either commonly asked questions or things that she wants to draw out and I try my best to be balanced. Her final question floors me for a second.

'Do you have any regrets?'

Regrets. How could I say I have regrets?

'Parenting our children has been far harder then I had ever thought it would be and yet I couldn't imagine my life without them now. It sounds trite to describe adoption as a journey, but it is – it's a long and often arduous journey, but it has taught me a lot and I'm a far better person now. And

I know that my husband Rob would say that adopting our two has been the best thing we've ever done.'

There are maybe 20 people in the semicircle. Some are nodding. Some thank me. I think I can tell which people I've scared and which I've encouraged. There are a few questions at the end, which are mainly to do with the adoption process – how long it took, what the approval panel had been like. I try to put myself in their shoes. Many will have been waiting a long time for a family, just as Rob and I had, and they don't want to hear that appearing in front of the approval panel would now rank as a good day out compared with what many days at home can be like.

There is another break for sandwiches. A professional-looking woman approaches. She asks if the reason I have found parenting Jamie and Rose difficult might be because I had had no prior experience of being a parent. It is clear that this is what she believes – second-rate parent, not match fit. Perhaps my account of what a bad day in the office can look like did not explain things clearly enough. I politely disagree and wonder how badly she needs adoption to be the end of the journey and not the beginning. Then I notice a couple standing behind her, looking eager to speak to me.

They introduce themselves as Sue and Nigel, foster carers who want to adopt their foster child. They are friends of Rose's foster carers who had told them I would be here. Awkward small talk clunks between us and they seem uneasy. Nigel looks like he is gathering courage to tell me something and then he starts to recount an Easter morning five years ago. He was awoken by the telephone; it was a social worker. A mother, well known to social services, had contacted the office. Two of her boys were out of control, wrecking the house, had spread food everywhere and she threatened to leave them unless someone took them away. Nigel and Sue were asked to collect the children from the house and care for them for a day and a night, after which a social worker would collect them and take them back to their home. They left immediately and were met at the door and then invited in by the mother. They describe her as aggressive and angry and she referred to her children as 'little bastards who are fucking out of control'. Nigel recalls that the house was crammed with piles and piles of indeterminate rubbish, that it stank of animal faeces and that 'it wasn't fit for animals to live in'. A toddler was crying in an upstairs room. The mother said that the child had an earache but could not be soothed so she was leaving him there. That child was Jamie.

Although the recount has been horrifying enough to listen to, when the connection is made with Jamie – my sweet boy – my guts twist. My son in a rubbish tip, crying, in pain, alone. 'He was left alone for long periods of time,' said the information on his form. This is the reality behind that statement. Was he hungry, dirty? Why didn't Trudy ask for him to be taken for the day along with his two brothers? Was he showing signs of abuse? How did he spend his day? In a room full of hopeful, smiling couples, I struggle to maintain my composure.

The two children were dirty, tired and hungry. They had a lovely day with Sue and Nigel, who said that they had been delightful. They were returned back home the following day. I wonder what they made of their day out. Knowing that their mother had asked for them to be taken away, spending the day with strangers, being returned back to the mother that doesn't mother.

I notice another couple waiting to speak to me. I mentally zip myself back up and quickly thank Nigel and Sue and wish them luck with their adoption. I hope that my body language conveys how grateful I am to them for giving me a piece of the jigsaw. They showed me they understand how difficult it is to come to terms with the suffering of not only our own adopted children, but their brothers and sisters too, children that we may never meet, but who are the flesh and blood of our flesh and blood.

On the drive home I am haunted by images and sounds of Jamie as a baby, alone. The words 'not fit for an animal to live in' worm around in my head. The forms don't really go into detail about the living conditions. They use the word 'neglect' frequently but I've avoided thinking in any depth about how neglect plays itself out. It is often used to refer to life's minor infringements. I've neglected to put the rubbish out. I've neglected to file my tax return. Neglecting a child can sound like ignoring them a bit. It doesn't get across the visual impact, the smell, the sound of a house that is not fit for animals to live in. I want to get home to Jamie, to pick him up and to show him that I understand a little bit more now.

*****

Jamie and Rose's last day at the school is difficult. There is an assembly in the afternoon, which I go to. They are given a 'Good Luck' card each, which all the children have signed. They stand up in front of everyone, looking lost and bemused. A recurring pull in my chest warns me that I could be making a big mistake with dire consequences. One of the children, a girl in Jamie's class, hands me a card. When we get home Jamie opens it. Inside is written 'Bye Jamie, now you are going there will only be Liam and Daniel'. Liam and Daniel are the two other 'naughty' boys in the school.

'What does she mean by that?' asks Jamie.

He knows what it means.

'I don't know. What a strange thing to write.'

He knows that I know too.

*****

The half term holiday is painful.

Jamie fights me over everything – every request, even if it is connected with him doing something he wants to do.

'Time to get changed so we can go to Aunty Alice's.'

'*No!* I'm not getting changed so *get lost, loser!*'

'You wanted to play with your cousins ,didn't you?'

'*No,* I never said that.'

'I think you did – that's why we're going there today.'

'You must be deaf, deaffo, fat deaffo.'

One day an argument about putting on a sock wells up and spills over.

'Let me put it on for you then.'

'*No, stupid head, get lost!*'

He says this into my face and then without blinking picks up a pile of papers – forms for school, bills, unwritten birthday cards – and drops them on the floor.

'You need to pick those up.'

'Not until you are *dead!*'

'Well, I'm not planning on dying soon so maybe you could do it now?'

'Shame cos you need to be dead.'

He runs upstairs, me stupidly shouting, 'Get back down here now,' after him. Of course he carries on and slams his bedroom door. I breathe. Rose continues to watch the television.

'Are you alright, Rose?'

She shows me her teeth through a rigid smile and gives me her eye-rolling expression which means, 'Oh dear, trouble, again.'

I hear the sound of destruction from upstairs and run up to the sound of, '*Do not come in here!*' A big scrawly sign is taped to Jamie's door. It says, 'KEEP OUT YOU ARE NOT WELCOME EVER' and 'EVER' is underlined. There are pictures of guns being pointed at heads and a speech bubble saying, 'YOU WILL BE DEAD.' In the hallway is a collection of items – his football shirt, a photograph of Rob and me in a frame, some letters that I had written to Jamie when we were playing post offices in the summer, a reading certificate from the library torn up and his '7 today' badge and birthday card that is written with love from Mummy, Daddy and Rose. All are tokens of love or achievement, all carefully selected.

I knock on his door and go in. I notice the amount of bright light first and then the curtains and curtain rail on the floor and the big holes of white plaster in the walls, next to the holes from the previous incident and the one before that.

'You are clearly very cross about putting your sock on.'

He dives on his bed and wraps himself in his duvet.

'Go away,' he says, with less conviction this time.

I sit on the end of his bed.

'Why you not going away?'

'Because I care about you and I think you need some love.'

'You are wrong, again.'

'OK, well, I'll just sit here quietly.'

I sit. He remains still under his duvet. I look across the devastation. The shelves are empty of books, the drawers are open and clothes hang out.

'You did a good job in here.'

'Go *away!*'

Silence again.

Then he lifts his duvet a small amount and looks at me. He sees me looking back and quickly brings the duvet back down. I rub his arched back and he lets me. I move closer.

'I am bad and horrible.'

I take a moment to remember Aiesha's advice – don't deny his feelings, explore.

'I don't see a bad, horrible boy.'

'You don't see right.'

*****

Towards the end of the holiday we visit old family friends for a day and Jamie is amusing and helpful and charms everyone. The charm oozes out of him, he earns admiring compliments and I am taken aside and told what a credit he is to me – what a marvellous boy he is. I watch Jamie play the room, getting everyone onside, as though his life depended on it. I know the act because I've seen it before. Like me. Love me. Don't hurt me. See how lovely I am. But this isn't the real Jamie in full cinemascope. There is an anxiety powering the charm. It is too much, spread too thickly and sweetly. Everyone is left trying to fathom why I find parenting this gorgeous boy so difficult.

*****

The night before Jamie and Rose start at their new school I lie in bed, worry looping repetitively through my brain. Awful scenarios play out, over and over. Conversations behind hands between people I know, which I can overhear, 'I can't believe she's moving those poor children/such unrealistic expectations/it will all go wrong/they'll be back here/you mark my words.'

We arrive at the school ridiculously early and sit in the car. I'm wired with worry and tiredness, but keep up a front of jolly excitement. Jamie and Rose are quiet and play along with my optimism to keep me happy. We see some children arriving and then a school minibus stops at the gate and unloads its passengers. We gather our book bags, PE kits and lunchboxes and head across the road and into the playground. Some older girls are plugging in a CD player through an open window. Other children gather in front of them. Then the music starts – Cotton Eyed Joe – and the older girls stand at the front facing the other children and perform dance moves. All the children, some of the staff and some parents join in, stepping to one side, then the other, then backwards and crossing legs. The moves are difficult and everyone laughs when they get it wrong. I stand with Jamie and Rose and see their faces full of discomfort.

'Would you like to join in?' I ask.

Without taking their eyes off the dancing, they both shake their heads, almost in disbelief.

'Hello, Jamie. Hello, Rose. Good to see you here. You're both looking very smart.' It is Mr Andrews. 'Are you looking forward to your first day at St Mary's?'

They nod, unconvincingly.

'In a moment I'm going to blow this whistle and all the children will line up in their classes. Don't worry, I'll show you where to stand.'

Jamie and Rose's class teachers both approach us and say 'hello' and I start to feel a confidence that I will be leaving them somewhere where they will be not only cared for but cared about.

After the whistle has blown and all the children have stood still, I kiss Jamie and Rose and whisper, 'Have fun today.' The whistle blows for a second time and the children line up and file into the school building, chirping and chatting. Then the playground is empty and silent. When I get back home the house feels empty and silent too, as though the breakfast bowls and cups had been left there by ghost children.

As the week goes on a sort of normality takes over. The morning drill gets easier and we get to school with a bit of time to spare but not too much. The class teachers speak to me at the end of most school days, but instead of presenting a catalogue of misdemeanour, it is all about how well Jamie and Rose are doing. I am invited into the class to see some special work or to admire a new drawer or peg. There are smiles and other children say, 'Bye, mate,' or 'Bye, Jamie, see you tomorrow.' At the end of the week both children come out full of smiles. They have something to show me, they say.

'No,' Jamie says, 'I have *two* things to show you, Mummy.'

He thrusts a party invitation in my hand. And then they both point to their chests. 'Head Teacher's Award', the stickers say.

'For being brave,' says Jamie.

'Yes, we been brave and I did get sticker,' says Rose.

'Well, I think we need to go and choose some Friday sweets *and* some brave sweets then, don't you?'

*****

I start to feel the benefit of the geographical separation of home and school. School now happens somewhere else, where no one really knows us. There doesn't seem to be the same tense atmosphere in the playground, or at least I'm less sensitive to it. And when I see friends locally, it is unencumbered by the baggage that inevitably comes with whose children have been under the black cloud and whose have been rewarded with stickers. It is less complicated, liberating.

Mr Andrews invites Aiesha and me to come to a meeting one morning at the school. First we have the chance to speak to Rose's teacher, Miss Stein. She tells us that Rose is doing very well – her reading is good, she is confident and enjoys 'getting involved'. There is some amusement around just how much Rose likes getting involved, but it isn't seen as anything unusual. Her speech makes it difficult for her classmates to understand her, so the school has made a referral to the speech and language therapist. Miss Stein is doing some extra work with Rose on sounds and letters and she feels that Rose is making good progress. Everything is laid out for me. I don't need to remind, beg, nag or convince.

Then Jamie's teacher Miss Taylor comes in. 'Jamie is doing really well. He is sociable, lovely to be with, thoughtful and kind. He does struggle to focus and listen, and I have to sit with him sometimes and encourage him. He tends to think he can't do things when he can. But he's produced some good work.'

She shows us some writing and some sums that look much more like the work he was producing at home.

'He sits near to me so I can keep him close and we reward him frequently.'

'And will he be put on to the Special Educational Needs register?' asks Aiesha.

'From what I've seen, he doesn't have any Special Educational Needs; he's managing fine academically. Clearly he does have emotional needs and it would be helpful to keep contact with you, Aiesha.'

I can tell that Aiesha is impressed.

'And I don't know if you're aware, Sally, but Jamie has told me a few things, about being adopted. He says that he has a book at home, which he would like to show me. A lifestory book?'

I am astonished. Jamie has never volunteered any information about his past to anyone outside our immediate family. He has hushed me when I've referred to it in passing, given me the 'shut up now' eyes and he's asked me to put the book away so he can't see it.

'It's important that we allow him to do that,' says Aiesha.

'Of course, I'll make sure he has his lifestory book with him tomorrow.'

'And I thought you might be interested to see this,' says Miss Taylor. 'The children have been writing down what it is that makes them special and we've been collating it and sticking it in this book, which will be on display in the reception area.'

She opens the book at the page marked with a pink sticky note and points to a square of paper.

'I am special because…' is typed in Comic Sans. Alongside it, Jamie has written in his best wobbly writing, 'I am adopted.'

CHAPTER 16

'Tea?' asks Rob.

'No, coffee.'

The caffeine may just get me through the day. We are to spend this bright, child-free, April Saturday in a conference room smelling of gloss paint and plastic furniture, learning how to therapeutically parent our children. The conference room is in a country golf club and overlooks the start of the golf course. One wall is almost entirely made up of windows and looks out over golfers, who are readying themselves for a morning of unrestrained pleasure. Neither Rob nor I are remotely enthusiastic about the day ahead.

I have been on courses run by the Local Authority before and have found them heavy on the 'why' of behaviours but rather light on practical solutions. Consequently I know precisely why Jamie throws his shoes at me whilst shouting, 'Go crap yourself, loser,' but as to what to do about said infringement, no one seems brave enough to advise. I am also well versed in what not to do. I must not shout back, 'No, you go crap *yourself*,' or, 'If I'd ever said that to my mother…' or, 'You are going to lose the use of the computer for a week,' because these responses are a) childish b) lecturing and c) setting up a classic control war, which I will lose.

Aiesha has organised the speaker for this training event, Patrick McKenzie. He has worked with fostered children for many years and Aiesha sings his praises. I wish I were feeling energetic, bouncy and positive about the day but I am not. The room murmurs with the setting up of equipment and the finding of chairs and the blocking of bright sunlight. We find seats at the back of the room.

I am wrung out by something subtly different from ordinary tiredness. This tiredness is a more hopeless affair – a buzzing, fried, shaky, resigned giving in. I can no longer summon up the energy to fight with Jamie. His ups and downs go in waves, although the ups are only ups in comparison to the downs, which are drawn out and dark. Right now we are in a down – a deep, deep hole, which I can't see my way out of. Not only is he trigger-happy with his anger, he argues with and tugs against every twist, turn and change in direction of the day.

'You must be hungry after your busy day?' 'No, course I'm not hungry, don't want tea.'

'Goodness, is that the time? If you go and clean your teeth I'll come upstairs with you.' 'You can't make me clean my teeth and I don't want you near me.'

This applies to every exchange we have. I notice myself starting not to care. It is a dangerous feeling. On top of everything I am hormonal – high-pressure, about-to-boil-over, don't-want-to-be-here hormonal. On a rare day with Rob and without the children I want to walk through fields, eat lunch in a pub garden and feel the sun on my face, not stew in a conference room learning how to parent a child who shows few obvious signs of wanting to be parented by me.

Rob returns with thin, muddy coffee and a rich tea biscuit. And now I must put on my happy face and not be tiresome, miserable, grumpy and ungrateful.

'I hope this is going to be worth it,' mumbles Rob, unable to believe he is about to spend a Saturday in the confines of a conference room after spending most of his working week in one.

Aiesha makes her way over to us.

'Glad you could make it,' she sings.

We are all smiles and handshakes.

'I don't know if you've met before but Martin and Stewart over there live not far from you and have two children of similar ages to Jamie and Rose.'

She points to two men on the table adjacent to ours. They are about our age, maybe younger, and shy looking. She attracts their attention and the two men move and sit on the empty seats at our table. I can feel Rob bristling at the prospect of having to be sociable. We introduce ourselves and lay the foundations of basic information – children's names, ages, ages at adoption, school years. Then Martin says, 'Bloody hard though, isn't it?' when the usual pattern is to start with something like, 'We're so lucky to have them, we are blessed.'

'Yes, it is,' I reply, heartened by this no-messing, straight-to-the-point approach.

Aiesha calls for everyone's attention and starts the session. She introduces Patrick. He is a social worker, trained in all things attachment and trauma, who provides therapeutic support to fostered children and who is just starting to work with adopted children and families too.

'We'll have to talk later,' says Martin in my ear.

Patrick introduces the day and then starts.

'One of the first things I have to remind myself of when I meet a foster carer or an adopter in need of support is that I am not seeing the person they once were. Traumatised children can traumatise their carers. I need to see beyond that trauma.'

It is as though a big finger stabs at the middle of my forehead. Bullseye. I am no longer me, the person I once was. She is lost and what remains is wreckage and distant memories. Unravelling, stitch by stitch, I feel the loosening, the giving in, here amongst this roomful of strangers. I look up at the ceiling then out of the window praying that the distraction will delay the unravelling until I'm safely at home.

Patrick explains how healthy babies' brains develop. Their parents provide constant and reliably good care. They feel safe and unstressed, their little frontal lobes grow in the first few years of life, learning that the world around them cares and values them. The neglected baby lies alone in a cot, scared and dirty, not knowing when its need for comfort or food will be satisfied, not being talked to, not seeing a loving gaze, not learning that it is good and lovable. The baby's frontal lobe – unexercised, un-nurtured – misses its best opportunity to grow and develop, and is left full of holes, where the wind blows in. The traumatised child learns that only it can protect itself. It must assume control, stay on high alert, scan the room, survive. These factory settings are not like the brightness of a picture or the volume of a television. These children are wired for danger and a few years in a loving home will not reset them. They need parenting in a different way, so that they can learn they are good and lovable, so that the shame of their early years is eased, so that they can experience calm and start to learn from new experiences. But I don't know if I have the engine power to turn the tanker around, to make it any different. The trauma has won and I am ready to take out the white flag.

Patrick talks about different ways of parenting our children – how we must reach them, show them that we understand how they see the world. The usual methods don't work – the threats and rewards – because much of their behaviour is impulsive, unplanned, wired in. They see themselves as almost entirely bad and nothing we can say or do will make them feel any worse about themselves, which is why the sanctions don't work, why Jamie couldn't drag his name from beneath the cloud and into the sun.

The remaining scrap of me whispers that Patrick is right. I need to summon up some drive from somewhere, learn how to do things differently, seize control, inject some energy. But the greater weight of exhaustion bears down.

We watch some DVD clips of various experts discussing shame and its power, and the importance of keeping shame levels right down, and then there is a break. I chat to Martin and gain a growing sense that we are sharing a very similar experience. He tells of the same battles over putting on shoes, over who sits where in the car, over who had slightly more lemonade than the other and over schools and behaviour. He fizzes with energy and talks quickly. I wonder what he makes of me – every word an effort, tears never far from the surface, in the final stages of meltdown.

In the next session Patrick turns to the practical. When a situation is brewing we must first stop and think out the strategy. Then we must employ something from our new toolbox – something playful or accepting, showing curiosity and empathy. Next there are role-plays, which, fortunately, are carried out using Aiesha and the other social workers and then a discussion about 'not sweating the small stuff'.

'Think about the worst that can happen in any situation. If your child is refusing to pick their coat up off the floor and you know they are not in a great place that day, think about saying, "I see that you are having a hard day so I'm going to pick it up for you," or do something surprising to take you both out of the confrontation – throw your own coat on the floor, say you don't feel like hanging yours up either, then see how that plays out. You may be able to play around with it a bit, make a joke.'

Don't sweat the small stuff. In our house the big stuff often starts with the small stuff so that once the dust is settling I can't remember how the confrontation started. I write the phrase down in my diary, 'DON'T SWEAT THE SMALL STUFF'.

Over lunch Rob and I talk again with Martin and Stewart. They are interested in why we moved Jamie and

Rose to a new school. They report similar scenarios with their eldest son – always in trouble, the same behaviour systems that play on his shame, the same after-school lectures from teachers recounting the day's atrocities. Martin suggests that we meet up, and we exchange telephone numbers.

After lunch there is a question-and-answer session. One question is about why a child would behave quite well at home but badly outside the home. There is much agreement and then strategising about how to build success into going out, addressing the anxieties and then dealing with potential failure. I listen and don't recognise our experience so I put my hand up.

'We find the opposite – the behaviours when we go out are generally alright but at home it is terrible, really difficult to cope with,' my voice goes over a bump of emotion, 'and then other people don't believe you.'

Patrick takes some time to think about this but meanwhile a man sitting near the front turns around to face me and says, 'What's the problem with that? It sounds much easier to cope with. You don't have the public scenes and the difficulties being out.'

There is general agreement and then someone else adds, 'I'd much rather have it that way round,' and some laughing. There are some noises of disagreement from somewhere but all I can focus on is the laughing. I shake my head slowly, unable to defend my position. I recognise this man, an attender of events, a self-appointed doyen of adopters. He enjoys playing the competitive game of misery top trumps, needs to have a winner and a loser.

I can feel Rob looking sideways at my reddening face.

'Don't get upset by it,' he whispers to me.

I have to get out of this room, right now. Tears boil up in my throat and I concentrate very hard on the table whilst Patrick gives his response. I hear none of it. Then as soon as the attention moves from me I get up and leave the room, ignoring the 'Are you alright?' from Rob. I run to the toilets and lock myself in a tiny cubicle. There are others within earshot, chatting golf handicaps, so I silently cry, leaning against the cubicle wall, doubled over in two. It is physically painful, animalistic, unstoppable. I feel utterly, utterly alone, stranded, washed up. Way up above I sense a small protected part of me looking down, watching, reassuring.

Eventually I force the emotional tap to close. There are noises in the corridor outside indicating that the course has finished. I wait for some of it to pass by and then leave the cubicle and splash myself with cold water. I look in the mirror. A red, swollen, blotchy, broken person looks back. Then I leave the toilets, keep my head down and go along the corridor back into the conference room. It is almost empty. Rob is alone looking anxious.

'I was worried about you – where did you go?'

'I've been in the toilets.'

He sees my distress.

'Let's go home.'

Aiesha calls out from the front of the room, 'See you soon.'

I wave. I dread what will come out if I speak.

When we get home I go to bed and sleep, for 14 hours.

The bedroom door opens very slowly. The room is alight with bright, late morning daylight. A wobbly little hand carries a big mug of slopping tea into the room.

'Mummy, I have made you tea, sit up.'

Jamie just about gets the tea on to the bedside table before it spills. I hold out my hand from under the duvet and he takes it.

'Thank you. That's so lovely.'

'You had a very long sleep. I've been up for *ages*.'

'What have you been up to then?'

'I have played Lego, I have watched Police Camera Action!, I have had hot chocolate that Dad made me, I have had toast with jam.'

He recounts his morning with such enthusiasm, like it is the best day ever.

*****

I sit in Martin's garden with my face to the sun, its gentle warmth melting the edge off my rawness. His garden is beautiful; a small oasis packed full of exotic plants and running water. I am not in the best place to make new friends, but I need to reach out to someone who might understand. When he appears with drinks I start by apologising.

'I'm sorry I took off towards the end without saying goodbye. It's been an emotional time and the reaction to my question just tipped me over the edge.'

'I wondered where you'd gone. Don't worry about it. I feel the same way. No one believes how bad things are at home and I can't describe it well enough. I seem to suffer some kind of memory loss after a big blow up. Anyway, we've decided to move the boys to a different school,' he says. 'It's just not working out where they are now, for much the same reasons that your local school didn't work out. How are your two now?'

'Doing so much better. There's a professionalism there. The staff know what they are doing and they accept Jamie and Rose. There's no blame, that's the biggest difference.'

'How long have they been there?'

'Two and a half years. Jamie still doesn't really love school but he seems happy enough there and he is starting to produce some good work. Rose is doing well. She just seems to get on with it.'

We share in the frustrations of behaviour charts and after-school lectures from classroom teachers. We talk about how deeply life has changed, how relentless the behaviours become, how we feel guilty about the younger child living in the shadow of the elder, our shared sense of isolation. We talk for four hours. I find a relief in not having to explain situations from first principles, not having to describe strange behaviours, not constantly having to preface everything with, 'Of course I love them and I'm lucky to have them'. I find I can be gritty and spiky and honest and it's alright. I share with him my moments of despair, when I half plan an escape from everything. He has the same moments, the same frustrations and exhaustions. We agree to meet up again.

*****

I take Jamie and Rose into the school playground and Rose's teacher makes her way over to me.

'Can we talk?' she says, looking trepidatory, flushing a little.

'Yes, sure.'

'Just follow me inside.'

We walk into her classroom. She takes a deep breath.

'The thing is, Rose has been rather wild, not all the time, but at certain times she is all over the place, off-the-wall really and the other children are starting to find it a bit weird.'

I can't believe this is Rose we are talking about.

'I'm sorry to have to tell you,' she continues. 'I've left it a while to see if things improved but Mr Andrews said I should let you know.'

'Yes, yes. Don't worry about telling me things – I need to know.'

'If you make an appointment in the office we can talk at more length and sort out some strategies. But in the meantime, don't worry.'

The whistle blows signalling the start of the day and we head back outside. The children are lining up in their classes. I search out Jamie and Rose, wave them goodbye and walk back to the car. The drive home is crowded with disorganised thoughts. I knew I hadn't been paying enough attention to Rose. And now she is struggling and I hadn't noticed. There have been signs at home, like the constant battle between them for love and attention, her need to touch, bend and feel everything, but nothing extraordinary for our family. All sorts of fears pass through me. I'd been keeping my fingers crossed until now, thinking that Rose had got away relatively unscathed and now this is it, the end of the illusion. I imagine her at school. Her 'off-the-wall' behaviour will be down to anxieties – not feeling safe – that much I'm sure of. But what shakes me is imagining the reactions of the other children to her, how hurt she must feel, how she hasn't talked to me about it. And I've had to drive away and leave her there. I start to plan what I need to do. First, ring Aiesha. I can't think beyond that. A desperate lethargy comes over me. I know I have to and I will, but right now I don't know how I am going to pick myself up again and fight another battle. As I get near home my throat tightens up.

Aiesha says and does exactly what I need. She expresses surprise that Rose is struggling at school, which eases my guilt that I have been caught napping. She empathises with the fear of having to fight the fight all over again. And she throws around thoughts and ideas – lack of security, something has thrown Rose off kilter, we must try to work out what it is, we must work with the teacher. Finally she suggests that the teacher record when Rose is unsettled during the day to see if a pattern emerges.

I mull over the Rose situation all day. I'm not often preoccupied with issues around Rose. I have been swayed too easily by who shouts loudest, and that is Jamie. His anxieties are all out there, on display, demanding to be noticed. Rose is much more difficult to read. She has a distant look when conversation gets too personal. She can't say the word 'adopted'; instead she says, 'because I'm, you know'. I fill in the missing word and she swipes it away. Any talk about birth family or foster care – even in the most general terms – and she will put her fingers in her ears. I realise now that she is blocking out this reality about herself, that the root is probably shame. And she avoids having to confront it by being the malleable one – the smiling, sweet-natured one, the onlooker, the busy, the preoccupied. I am becoming better practised at the loud and angry, but I am all at sea with the hidden and secretive. Jamie has started accusing her of hiding his things, of going into his bedroom and taking his torch or his teddy. He will then claim to have found the missing item under her bed or in her wardrobe. I wonder if at least some of the time he might be telling the truth. Love is something limited in supply – it must be fought for, jealously guarded and it is of more value if the opponent is perceived to have less. If one cuddles up to me on the sofa, the other must cuddle in more closely. If one engages me in conversation, the other must shout louder, or be funnier or more extreme in some way. If one compliments me, the other must be more complimentary. I tell them in words and demonstrate with my actions that there is enough love to go around, that there isn't a finite supply, but they don't get it at all, not deep down where it matters.

When I speak to Rose's teacher she has already concluded that there may be a pattern to her behaviour and she has set up a system of recording for each lesson. She reassures me that most of the time Rose is behaving normally.

I can't get anything out of Rose other than, 'fine'. How was school today? Fine. How was playtime? Fine. Who did you play with? Fine. She squirms and fidgets and changes the subject.

Aiesha rings again to see how things are going and to offer to come into school to talk to Rose's teacher.

'It might help if I can talk about the anxieties that Rose will be feeling and how school can help bring her anxiety level down.'

'It would be better coming from you – it gives it more weight.'

'I've got another suggestion. Do you remember Patrick McKenzie who led the course you and Rob attended? We are offering adoptive parents sessions with him. He's worked with foster carers up until now. What do you think?'

'I think I'll take anything on offer right now.'

'I'm sure you will find the sessions very helpful. You can describe the behaviours you are seeing and Patrick will give you strategies to help deal with them.'

Something has landed, rather than being chased and fought for. And the course was helpful, what I can remember of it.

*****

Martin and I meet up and again talk without stopping for hours. The similarities between our children are astonishing – the strains of keeping the basics of a family going let alone managing the anger, the fighting and arguing, the anxieties and the fears. Neither of us feels the need to justify our mental state against the tide of popular misconception that all children are the same, that we are just inexperienced parents, that we are looking for causes in the past when we needn't be. It is a marvellous relief to laugh at how bad things can be. And also to admit the darkness. Gradually we both gain the confidence to share the worst, the same monstrous imagining – driving along a fast, single-lane road, psychologically numb, seeing a lorry in the distance, an invisible string connects the car with the oncoming vehicle, unblinking, the promise of blissful oblivion. The end. Rescued by an inner kernel of what's left, to return home to a silent house filled with breakages and echoes of another day, another trauma. Sitting amongst the scenes of the crimes, fearing the future, guilty for flirting with a horrible escape.

I know I will never make that game-changing tug on the steering wheel, but I've tasted the sweet attraction and it helps to know I'm not alone.

*****

After school, Rose's teacher indicates that she wants to speak to me so we grab ten minutes whilst the children play outside. She shows me sheets of tables, coloured in with highlighter pens.

'Here's the record we've been keeping of Rose's behaviour. Look, she is fine, until there is an unguided lesson.'

It is as plain as day. A structured lesson results in a four or five out of five for behaviour, an unstructured lesson results in a one or a two.

'And what happens in unguided lessons?'

'The children will have a number of tasks to complete, in any order, and they will have to move around the room completing a task at each table. It might be experimenting with different materials – like paper or sand or water – and then writing about it, or tasting different things and recording the tastes, something like that.'

'And you think it's the lack of structure?'

'Yes, all our other lessons are much more firmly led. What I'll do is make sure we direct her more clearly, reduce the choices, and then hopefully she will be less anxious.'

'And in September, when she moves to the next class?'

'The next class up is much more desk based and although I couldn't say this for all children, I think it will suit Rose much better. So don't worry. We'll sort this out.'

I feel like hugging her for her patience and confidence.

*****

It is Friday and on the way home from school we stop at the newsagents to buy Friday sweets. Jamie chooses quickly, a Sherbet Fountain. Rose takes forever. She picks up one sweet after another, needing to maximise her choice. She tries me for things she knows are too big – a giant Aero, a large tube of jelly beans – and works her way down. Eventually I give her the countdown from five and she quickly picks up a packet of Rolos. Both children eye up the other's choice, hoping they have the most, the best. I silence my concerns over sherbet and car upholstery and they eat in the car. I glance in the rear-view mirror and see Rose emptying one Rolo after another into her mouth. Jamie watches her. His expression is one of jealousy and disappointment. The Rolos are looking good compared with his Sherbet Fountain, which is now damp on the end and blocked. He growls and goes red with boiling frustration. I step in.

'Jamie, give it to me and I'll sort it out at home for you.'

'I *hate* this stupid thing!' he shouts.

'I'll have it if you don't want it,' says Rose, quick as a flash.

'You have it,' he says, throwing it at her, 'you won't get nothing out of it anyway.'

Unperturbed and with her hands on unimaginable riches she bites into the liquorice and unblocks the hollow tube inside. She proceeds to noisily and enjoyably suck out the sherbet.

'*I want it back now!*' shouts Jamie.

I look around for a lay-by to pull the car into.

'Rose, give it to me,' I say, reaching into the back of the car, quickly hatching a sharing arrangement at home.

Sensing she is in danger of losing the sweet entirely she starts to consume it with haste. Jamie explodes with red rage, shouting, kicking, punching himself, lashing out at Rose.

Still there is nowhere to stop the car, so I brave the last mile home.

We pull into the drive and just as Jamie is readying himself for an almighty showdown, he notices Jean and her daughter and new baby in the front garden next door. Jean waves as we pull in. He zips up his rage, gets out of the car, slams the door and marches around to the back garden.

'You remember my daughter Penny? And this little angel is my new granddaughter.' Jean holds up a small, white bundle of baby. I walk over to the fence. Rose pushes in front of me, touches the baby's hand and then casts me a victorious glance.

'She's Grandma's little darling,' says Jean, touching her nose to the baby's nose.

'She's beautiful. How is it all going?' I ask Penny.

'Fine but tiring – she's awake in the night for feeds and up really early in the morning.'

'She's the apple of Grandma's eye,' says Jean.

I make my excuses, go inside and settle Rose with a drink before going into the garden to find Jamie. He is sitting on the grass throwing stones at the shed.

I avoid mentioning stones and windows (don't sweat the small stuff).

'Do you want to come in and we'll find a lolly or something?'

He shoots me a dark look, gets up and walks past me. I hear him stamp up the stairs and slam himself into his room. Lego is thrown against Lego, something hits the door. I decide to leave him and see if he will calm.

I sit next to Rose on the sofa. She is watching something on the television about fearsome animals. She looks at me and pats my arm, then continues watching. I take her hand and hold it. She squeezes mine. I slouch, staring at nothing in particular, listening to the crashing from upstairs, knowing which way this is heading. An almost imperceptible dark cloud passes over me, like a cool crush of disappointment. I put it down to it being a Friday, which should welcome in the rest and fun of the weekend, instead being anything but.

I can ignore the sounds from upstairs no longer and drag myself into action, mentally preparing myself. Empathise with his feelings, don't get angry, stay regulated.

'I never liked Sherbet Fountains. I find they are always a disappointment.'

'I hate everything about you,' he shouts before head-butting the pillow.

I am composing my next playful epithet when he looks up briefly to deliver, 'You get out of here now, *loser*, go on get out, get out, why aren't you getting out, go on, go on, now, *get out now, I said now!*'

'*How can you say that?!*' I yell back, with no empathy, no playfulness, just pure anger.

'*You want only Rose to have sweets not me!*'

I try a smattering of logic, but his head is buried and he can't hear me. Eventually I sit on the top of the landing, head in hands, and pray for Rob to get home.

Later that evening, the children are in bed and a fragile, tense peace creeps over the house.

'I forgot to tell you, we saw Jean's new granddaughter today,' I tell Rob.

He looks up from his laptop and expresses a mild interest. The same darkness creeps over me again and I nail it: it is the cool shadow of grief. It is both familiar and unexpected and it is about the baby. I should not be in the market for grief; I should be counting my blessings. I try to trap the shadow and examine it. The new life is not something I begrudge, nor do I begrudge Jean and her daughter their joy. The bitter taste of jealousy isn't present. But there is something about the fresh-out-of-the-box, crisp, new hope of the baby I wish for. The grief is not a real loss; it is the dashing of a vision of a hoped-for reality, an imagined future I had projected for all of us. Not even a gold-plated future, just an averagely dull, averagely problematic future would be fine. I had been hanging on to the false hope that after these few years of love, structure and extra parenting we would be out of the woods by now. Jamie is ten years old, another eight years at least of trudging this relentlessly steep road. And I can't be certain I have the resolve, the energy, the fight to see it through.

With the next morning comes a mini-revelation. I clear up the breakfast dishes and Jamie mutters, 'Sorry 'bout yesterday.'

'What was that?'

'I am sorry for being rude to you. I don't mean those things I say. I was just angry.'

'I know you don't mean it.'

'I love you, Mummy.'

I sit and pull him on to my lap and put my arms around him. I breathe into the crook of his neck, 'And I love you very, very much, no matter what.'

'Can I do something with you today?'

'That would be lovely. How about we finish clearing the vegetable patch and plant some seeds? You can use the big spade if you like.'

'Yes and I can make us a tea break.'

'Great, I like a tea break. Why don't you go and get some old clothes on?'

'OK, Mummy,' and off he goes upstairs, without complaint, without confrontation.

Rob takes Rose out and Jamie and I spend a lovely few hours together. He is helpful and eager to please me. We prepare a large area and then he brings out drinks for us both.

We sit on the bench side by side.

'I think maybe I should pick your Friday sweets next week. I'll get you and Rose the same and you can eat them at home. I think I made a mistake yesterday and you found that hard.'

'Yes, you choose next time.'

'Because when you are angry you say things that are hurtful.'

'But Mummy, I already told you I don't mean it.'

'I know you don't, but I think there may be better ways of feeling angry. It's OK to feel angry, but it's not OK to break things and say hurtful things. Can you think of something you can do which might help you to calm down?'

'Digging might help.'

'Yes, I find digging helpful too.'

'I could go into my room and play Lego to calm down.'

'That's a good idea too.'

'Can I put the seeds in?'

'Of course you can. Do you want to start with the peas?'

I show him how to rake out a shallow trench and then how to sow the seeds in patterns of five.

'That pattern is called a quincunx.'

'What?' he asks, looking up and rolling his eyes.

'A quincunx.'

'You are so posh,' he laughs.

That evening we all sit around the table after dinner and play Yahtzee. Rose is on a personal mission to add up the spots on the dice before Jamie, which she often does and which she over-celebrates with air punches, which winds Jamie up to the point of meltdown, which is, of course, her aim. Then he throws three fives.

'*Fifteen!*' Rose shouts.

Jamie is about to throw in the towel and stamp upstairs.

'And does anyone know the name for the pattern that five spots make on a dice?'

Jamie almost bursts with the effort of trying to remember. Then, '*Quincunx!*' he says.

'Well done,' says Rob, 'I didn't know that.'

'I know something that Daddy didn't know,' he says proudly.

As he basks in glory, Rose picks up the dice and won't give them back to him. Between us Rob and I damp down his irritation. Then she takes four throws, instead of the allowable three, claiming that the first one didn't count as one of the dice bounced off the score pad. She throws a Yahtzee, thus securing her winning position. It is all too much for Jamie. He grabs the dice, throws them on the floor and runs upstairs. The three of us sit and listen to his steps and then the slamming of his bedroom door. I notice Rose looking pleased. Rob catches my eye.

'Don't sweat the small stuff, remember,' he says.

Over the next few days the still-functioning part of me gains ground and takes control. I set myself an objective: to go on a night out. I compose an email to an assortment of local friends.

Just wondering if anyone would like to come and see Mamma Mia at the cinema with me, either Wednesday or Thursday. No worries if you can't as I'm planning to go anyway.

I read it through. The right amount of casual, not too needy. I'm not planning to go on my own as that would require buckets more fortitude than I've got at the moment, but I think it sounds better. I worry over the choice of film. There have been some bad reviews. But I have prescribed myself fun, sun and happy, not slow and artistic or horrific. I press 'send'. Within a day I have five responses. Everyone wants to come.

We all squeeze into my car and then squeeze into the cinema, which is packed overwhelmingly with women. There is a strong sense of release, like we are all out on parole. From the moment the film starts I sink luxuriously into an alternative reality. I am Meryl Streep. I live in Greece with a beautiful daughter who can dress herself and avoids steep drops. It's sunny every day. I laze around with interesting friends who visit. We swim in the sea to cool off. We drink alcohol not having to care about the school run in the morning. My only obligations involve a bit of DIY. Then men appear, who fight for me. There are fantastic parties, with singing and dancing, outdoors. In real life I'm ambivalent about Abba music, but in this cinema – this pot of frustration and tiredness – I love it. We all sing along unselfconsciously. As the film nears the end, I feel a happy sadness at having to go back to the real world, my real world. The real world of shitty pants, unflushed toilets, bottomless laundry baskets, impossible-to-scrub scrambled egg pans, bins that always need emptying, toothpaste on walls, soap cut up into bits, lidless pens, crumbs in toy boxes, single socks under sofa cushions, a Barbie head, a legless giraffe, clean laundry that still smells of pee, biro marks on tablecloths, unidentified stains on carpets, scribbles in my books, Lego in my slippers, an empty pack of marzipan stuffed behind a radiator, cup rings on best furniture, my lip gloss on a flannel, banana skins under the chair, nits, spellings to learn, forms requiring a doctor's phone number (again), a fancy dress outfit to assemble, cakes to make for a cake stall, holes snipped into school sweatshirts…

I lie in bed that night unable to come down from the success of the evening out. I had never really understood the value of escapism before, maybe not really had anything to escape from, but a part of me had got away and recuperated a little bit. And the mended part knows that this mini-grief has to be processed and stitched into me. And I have to wake up to the new reality – Jamie and Rose are not going to be magically healed, we have to get more professional and better educated about early trauma and about brain science; parent them in an almost entirely different way to the ways Rob and I were parented – to the ways our friends parent their children.

CHAPTER 17

The tiny car park is full, but in order to discover it is full I have to drive to the end of a long, narrow cul-de-sac of cars with no turning circle at the end. I reverse back out and get caught up with other drivers optimistically looking for spaces. I had left home in plenty of time to get to our appointment; I always arrive at hairdressers, doctors' clinics and dental surgeries in time to read at least a couple of back issues of Country Living. A swell of panic. To be late would send out the message that we are not desperate for help. I find a barely adequate space on the main road and try to blank out the traffic building up behind me as I make multiple attempts to parallel park.

I leave the car at an angle to the pavement and push in the wing mirror. Walking up the hill to the centre reminds me of my last visit here: Dr Darling and the ADHD fallout. I hear my name and Rob is walking up behind me, out of breath.

'I've parked miles away.'

'I'm just there.'

I point to my car, its front end sticking out into the traffic. He raises his eyebrows.

'I was panicking I was going to be late.'

There is a buzzer and speaker system at the glass double doors. We are buzzed in by a sullen woman sitting behind a glass screen. She makes no eye contact as we walk into the waiting room. I half expect police officers to appear, to be fingerprinted and bundled into a cell. Aiesha is sitting in the far corner and she stands up and smiles when she sees us.

'Patrick won't be long.'

We sit together. The room has been refurbished since my last visit, although the new toy box contains the old broken toys and the atmosphere of hopelessness still clings to the low tiled ceiling. There is one newspaper on the table: a free local paper that's three weeks old.

'How have things been?' asks Aiesha. 'Or daren't I ask?'

'Difficult,' says Rob.

Patrick appears and shakes our hands, and we follow him into a small room containing four chairs, all of differing heights, and a beanbag. We arrange ourselves self-consciously and I find myself in a ridiculously low chair.

'I don't know if you've ever been to CAMHS before?'

'Jamie and I saw Dr Darling once, about four or five years ago. He suggested the problem was ADHD. I didn't agree and we never went back.'

'We'll give you more constructive help today,' he says, looking not all that surprised. 'Tell me about your family. You have two adopted children?'

'Jamie who is ten and Rose who is seven.'

'Aiesha, we know that they have had a history of neglect and some physical abuse?'

Aiesha briefly describes their histories. 'I don't need to go too far into that. What we know for sure about children who have suffered early neglect and abuse is that they have missed out on nurture and care, which all children need in order for healthy brain development to take place. What is the most challenging thing about parenting them?'

Rob and I are lost for a moment. Where to start? We had expected to have to go into the past for most of this session.

'For me, it's the anger and the aggression,' says Rob and I agree with him.

'Talk me through how this looks. A recent incident.'

Rob describes the latest incident in freshest and rawest terms. It resulted in Jamie punching and kicking a wall with such force we feared he would smash his bones to pieces. Neither of us really knew what to do; our uncertainty and fear were evident. Jamie ended up in his bedroom and the curtains and curtain poles were torn down again. No words seem to adequately communicate the intensity – the trauma of the incident.

'I know what this anger looks like. I know it isn't anything like a tantrum. I understand how explosive it is.'

I sink further into my chair. All the pressure of needing to describe these angers is gone. I badly needed to hear someone say that.

'This is what you do next time there is another incident like this. First, you need to warn him that you are going to hold him on your knee to keep him safe. Calmly but firmly. Then you sit him on your lap, facing away from you, and hold him in a firm hug. While you do this you say, "Jamie, you are safe, I am keeping you safe and that's what mummies and daddies do for their children. I'm going to help you to get calm. You are safe." And you repeat this. How do you think he would react if you were to do this?'

'I think he would shout, "I hate you, I'm going to kill you," and so on.'

'So you might like to add in, "I get that you are angry, but I am here to keep you safe." What do you do once his temper has calmed?'

'We all recover quietly for a bit and then I guess we just get on with life.'

'You revisit the incident with him afterwards, calmly, without blame and in narrative form. So it would sound something like, "Earlier on you were playing really nicely and then something made you angry; just remind me what that was. Oh yes, it made you so cross and then you tried to hit your sister and tried to hurt yourself and Mummy had to hold you and then you calmed down and we enjoyed playing with cars together." You're helping him to see that his anger doesn't make him a bad person, helping him to make sense of it. And do you give a consequence for pulling down the curtains?'

'No. We've run out of consequences. We take things away but it doesn't make any difference to him. He ends up with no television, no pocket money, no treats at all.'

'It's important there's a consequence so he learns, something like a chore which he does to make up for whatever has happened and he does that chore with one of you, so it is time in – time spent with him. Taking things away from these children doesn't work.'

'Why not?' asks Rob, 'It seems like he just doesn't learn from anything, he repeats the same mistakes over and over again.'

'It has a lot to do with control. They are used to having to look after themselves because no one is caring for them and they find it hard to relinquish control. And also, these children are used to having nothing, so what kind of punishment is taking things away? It just reinforces the message that adults are bad and not to be trusted.'

I think of all the times we have taken things away to try to defeat him into behaving, only to be faced with a smirking, victorious child saying, 'Take all my money then, take my games, take all my Lego, go on, be quick about it.' There is nowhere to go when he seems to be surrendering but somehow still has complete control.

'I know how hard it is – parenting children who have missed so much.'

The empathy stings and I can't speak.

'It's really hard,' says Rob, 'harder than we ever imagined it would be.'

'It will get better,' says Patrick.

The sting again. I daren't speak.

'Let's organise another few sessions.'

'How many will there be?' ventures Rob.

'As many as you need. I don't offer a fixed number of sessions after which you go off on your own. I'll be here to support you for as long as you need.'

I force down a geyser of emotion.

*****

That evening Alice rings to see how we got on with our appointment and to invite us to her 40th birthday party.

'It will just be family and a few friends.'

'Can we make a cake?'

'Yes, if you like. But I don't want any embarrassing surprises.'

'Cancel the Dreamboys then?'

'Hold on a moment. Dreamboys, you say?'

Jamie and I make a cake together and he sets about decorating it with coloured icing and sweets. Rose eats the remainder of the sweets and then makes a birthday card with a giraffe holding a birthday present. Snails with wings circle the giraffe's head.

'You've both done a really good job,' I say. 'Alice is going to be so pleased.'

'Can I wear my new football boots to the party?'

I am not sweating the small stuff and so I say, 'Yes, of course.'

Rose wants glitter painted into her hair and purple lip gloss. Again I ride with it but have to say 'maybe not' to the suggestion of eye shadow.

Party guests sit around the edge of Alice's conservatory. I chat to a few I recognise and haven't seen for years. Several I was at comprehensive school with. We indulge in some, 'Do you remember Mr So-and-So?' banter. We recall the smoking in the toilets, the regular fights in the playground, the 'copy-out-the-next-50-pages' style of teaching, the rat dissections. The inevitable question, 'What do you do now?' is hard to answer. What do I do? I can talk about what I used to do before child trauma came to stay and narrowed life down. The evening goes on, some of Alice's friends go home and things loosen up. I see my nephews Luke and Harry coming towards me giggling. Clearly a plan has been hatched.

'Aunty Sally. Could you come and watch this YouTube video?' says Luke with a big grin across his face. His younger brother is giggling behind his hands.

'Mum, Mum, Aunty Sally is going to watch the advert on YouTube.'

'Wait for me,' she sings, draining the rest of the wine from her glass.

We gather around the computer. Luke clicks on the advert. An expansive, wild, sandy beach. A cow gallops along the waterline. Then a woman perched on a rock comes into shot. She has long fair hair flowing down her back and tendrils are blown artistically across her face. She holds a teaspoon and carton of yoghurt, which she looks at longingly. She takes a spoonful of the yoghurt and enjoys it tremendously. The boys watch me watching the advert. I have clearly missed something.

'Aunty Sally, that is so you on that rock.'

'What are you on about?'

'That lady looks exactly like you,' and they laugh again.

I notice Jamie and Rose looking at me carefully, measuring how I will react.

'She's nothing like me. Is she?' I look at my sister.

'Every time that advert comes on the boys say, "Oh look, there's Aunty Sally sat on a rock eating yoghurt.' I can see the likeness."'

'Well, I'm quite flattered. You could have told me I looked like the cow.'

'No, it's Mum who looks like the cow,' the boys squawk in adolescent out-of-control voices.

'I know what we can do. You can be the lady on the rock, Aunty Sally, you be the cow, Mummy, and I'll film you acting out the advert,' says Luke. 'Harry, get Aunty Sal some yoghurt and a spoon.'

Alice and I have had enough alcohol by this time for this idea to present itself as both hilarious and quite everyday in terms of family entertainment. I am given the wheelie computer chair, a yoghurt and a teaspoon. The boys play the soundtrack from the computer. Alice, on all fours, lollops across the carpet in front of me laughing and mooing. I load up the teaspoon then put it into my mouth, making sure I achieve a good-quality yoghurt moustache. The assembled audience screech and guffaw and there is clapping.

I hear someone say, 'Come and look at this,' and through the haze of alcohol a tiny voice in my head whispers 'What *are* you doing?'

We watch the film back on the computer.

'Aunty Sally, you are sooooo funny,' says Harry.

'I can't wait to tell my friends about this,' says Luke.

I notice Jamie and Rose looking intently at me with a vague, distant amusement, perplexed that some part of me other than the sensible parent has been revealed. Then Jamie says, 'Luke? Have you got Tik Tok, by Ke$ha? Put it on and clear me a space.'

Part of me thinks, 'Oh my goodness, what is he going to do?' but then he has just seen his mother and his aunt re-enacting a yoghurt advert. Luke puts the music on and gets the camera ready. The audience reassembles. Rob casts me a worried look. Jamie stands within a gathered circle looking ahead, seriously. As the music starts he springs into action as though this is part of a well-rehearsed routine. His feet apart, one arm by his side, he looks up to the ceiling as his other arm moves out in front of him. One knee starts to flex with the rhythm and then the music shakes through his whole body. He introduces bits of robotic dance and then runs his hands down his face and chest. He turns to the side, keeps one foot on the ground but curls up the rest of his limbs into a ball. Next he's on his knees and then spinning on his back. His comic timing is tremendous and he maintains a faux-serious expression, staring off into the middle distance despite the torrents of laughter around him. I look across at Rob and he mouths, 'Where did this come from?'

I shrug, just as surprised as he is. The audience are completely captured. I look on, dislocated from the scene. The clapping fades into the background and I watch Jamie, so rarely at home in the world, at ease with himself. He displays a confidence maybe gained by putting on a persona, but it is a confidence nevertheless. The song wraps up and I wonder how Jamie will manage the potentially awkward transition between performance and reality. He bows, raises one hand, high-fives his cousins and says, 'Thank you, bros. That's all for tonight.'

He walks out of the circle of admirers and into the kitchen as though he has done this many times before.

*****

The car is the perfect place for children with rocky attachments to communicate difficult stuff to a concerned parent. Lack of eye contact (check), no chance Mum is going to want to cuddle me (check), no chance Mum is going to get distracted (check), we'll be at school soon and that will naturally end the conversation (check).

'How did I get the scar on my face?' comes the question from nowhere when we are halfway to school one morning.

A mental deep breath (a physical one might be interpreted as 'Mum is not strong enough to talk about this').

'You were hit by your birth father and it cut your face. When the cut healed over it left a scar.'

'Did I go to hospital?'

'Yes, you did. You were in hospital several times.'

'When else was I in hospital?'

'Well, you were badly burned. I think some hot water spilled on you.'

Rose looks at me. 'Poor Jamie.'

'Yes, poor Jamie, he was hurt when he was a baby when he should have been cared for really well like other babies are. And he deserved to be well cared for.'

'How do you know what happened to me?'

'I have lots of information which I can show you when you are older.'

'What sort of information?'

'Some letters and some forms. Also some photographs the police took of you when you were taken from the house.'

'I want to see all of that when I get home from school, today.'

He is insistent and yet he is only ten years old. I try to compute the scenarios quickly, but go with my gut. I pull into a parking space outside school.

'OK. I'll get the files out and we'll look at them together.'

'Can I go into school now?'

'If you want to. Or we can sit in the car for a while?'

'No, I want to go in now,' and he gets his bags together, opens the car door, gets out and waves. 'Bye Mum, love you.'

I watch him cross the road, go in through the school gates and high-five a couple of friends. I look across at Rose and take her hand.

'I know it's hard to hear about what happened to Jamie and to you.'

'I want a fish tank with fish in it,' she says.

'If you ever want to look at your information, or ask me questions too, that's fine. I'm always ready.'

'I want fish with googly eyes.'

The drive home is, not for the first time, coloured by the enormity of what Jamie and Rose have to come to terms with. The ultimate rejection: those bound by blood to care for them have not done so. These children have looked into the eyes of the parents who bore them and seen at best ambivalence and at worst hate and disgust. It has robbed them of a babyhood and continues to rob Jamie at least of a happy childhood. The longer I parent them, the more I connect with Jamie's anger. Sooner or later he is going to want to know why, and there is no adequate answer. Because your parents didn't know how to care for you? Because they hadn't been taught how to care by their own parents? They couldn't put your needs over their own? They hit you because they were angry? It sounds inadequate. Nobody's fault.

*****

Jamie puts his school bags down, kicks off his shoes, refuses a drink, sits at the table and starts reading. He is focused and businesslike.

'Do you want me to go through it all with you?'

'Just show me where to start.'

'This form on the top. Most of your information is in there.'

'You go with Rose and I'll look at this on my own.'

Rose stays close to me as we watch children's television.

'I love you, Mummy.'

'I love you too, both of you, very, very much.'

After half an hour has passed I put my head around the kitchen door.

'Are you alright in here?'

'Yes, I haven't finished yet.'

I leave him again and after another half an hour has passed I hear him.

'Mum. Mum.'

'Are you alright?'

'I want to see the police photographs now.'

'Are you sure you want to see those? It might not be too easy for you to look at them.'

'Yes. I want to see them now.'

They are at the back of the filing cabinet. I retrieve the three A4 black and white photographs – the earliest pictures we have of Jamie. Head and shoulders portraits, at first glance similar to the pictures parents commission from a photographer in a supermarket and yet the face that looks out is damaged, haunted and lost. The eyes look off-camera, not focusing on a colourful prop but seeking out removal from the unbearable world they find themselves in. The face is puffy and bruised. There are cuts to the beautiful chubby cheeks, the little neck and the chest and shoulders. It is unmistakably Jamie's face that looks off into the far distance, but much younger. The photographs were taken at the time when Rob and I were starting to doubt whether we would ever be parents. I put the pictures down in front of Jamie. He looks at them, almost forensically. He asks me questions for which there are no adequate answers. Then he looks into my face.

'Are your eyes watering?'

I consider denying my emotions, putting on a brave face.

'Yes. It makes me feel very sad to look at these pictures.'

'Why?'

'Because I can't bear to think that someone hurt you like this. It makes me want to reach into the photograph and take you out and hug you and look after you.'

There is a silence between us as he looks again at the images of himself as a toddler, covered in the evidence of his mistreatment.

'I am old enough to see these, Mum.'

'I know. And I'm really proud of you. It's a very brave thing to do.'

'Did they go to prison?'

'No, they didn't. They should have done.'

'Why didn't they?'

'Because the evidence wasn't strong enough. The police wanted to charge them. There were no witnesses and the judge needs witnesses.'

'Weren't these photographs evidence?'

'They were, but they are not enough.'

The truth, the inadequate truth.

'I want to take my files into school and show my teacher.'

I pause. I hadn't seen this coming.

'Let me mention it to her in the morning, just to make sure it's alright with her.'

'Why wouldn't it be alright with her?'

'I'm sure it will be, but it's polite to ask her first.'

I hope she is able to take this next important step with him. Later on that evening he comes to me for a hug and I rock him and stroke his hair.

'I must have been a bad boy.'

'Why do you think that?'

'I must have made them hurt me and not want to look after me. I must have been really annoying.'

'Jamie, you are not a bad boy and none of it was your fault.'

He doesn't believe a word of it.

*****

Jamie's teacher agrees to look at his files with him and I pack him off to school with them carefully wrapped in the bottom of his school bag. He comes home at the end of the day looking tired but cheerful. His face looks somehow more open – a gentle light shines from it, which I haven't seen for a while.

'Did you show your files to Miss Taylor?'

'Yes.'

'And how did it go?'

'Fine.'

The next morning Jamie says,

'I feel less heavy after talking to Miss Taylor.'

He has shared his burden and the shame is drying up in the sunlight.

At our next session we tell Patrick about Jamie's wish to find out about his past. He is pleased and thinks we've dealt with it correctly, although he warns about potential ongoing problems as Jamie makes sense of the information he has acquired.

'Does he ever say anything like, "I am bad"?'

'Yes, he said, "I must have been a bad boy," like he must have somehow caused the abuse.'

'And what did you say?'

'I said, "You're not a bad boy".'

Patrick visibly winces.

'If he says anything like that again you must be sure not to disagree with him, because for him this is his truth and he needs to be able to trust that you can hear these highly shameful things he feels about himself. You need to employ curiosity and empathy. Try something like, "I wonder why you would think you are a bad person," or, "Do you think babies are born bad?" and go from there.'

I think I knew this, that I've read it somewhere, but Jamie had caught me off guard and the urge to convince him of his goodness was overwhelming.

It is not long before the opportunity arises for me to tackle the 'I am bad' differently. There is an argument over a Playmobil vet's car. I intervene and the end result is not to Jamie's liking. Rose and I watch as the pressure builds inside him. First he tries to argue. When this doesn't work he is rude, then his face reddens and he growls and kicks the sofa. He casts around for something to throw, his anger now gripping him.

'Jamie, you need to calm down,' I say stupidly.

'I fucking hate you!'

He throws a cushion at me and then picks up a toy dog that belongs to Rose. He smashes it into the floor and the batteries fly out.

'You can either calm yourself down or I am going to hold you and help you to calm down.'

He stands in front of me.

'*Fuck off!*' he shouts and then runs upstairs.

I hear his bedroom door slam and some banging and crashing. Rose looks at me.

'He did break my dog.'

'I know. I should be able to mend it.'

I hold her into me.

'Why is he like this?' she asks.

'I think he gets angry that he wasn't treated well when he was a baby. But it's still not acceptable to break your dog.'

'No, it isn't.'

The crashing sounds diminish. I decide not to go into his room for now but to see if he will calm. We collect up the batteries and put them back into the dog. It raises a paw pathetically and silently barks in slow motion. We sit together and half watch a cartoon on the television but both our minds are monitoring the sounds from upstairs. I am primed and ready to avert destruction.

After maybe 20 minutes I creep upstairs. All is quiet. Jamie has wrapped himself up in his duvet. I sit on the end of his bed.

'Go away,' he says without the usual force of meaning.

I stroke the curve of his back and we sit in silence. Then, 'I told you I was bad.'

It cuts me to hear him say this. I forget what I am meant to say.

'Is that how you see yourself?'

'Well, I am.'

'It must be really, really hard thinking you are a bad person.'

There is silence and I don't know where to go from here.

'Perhaps I can tell you how I see you, with my eyes.'

Again, silence.

'I see a lovely, kind, funny boy, who I love very, very much and who wasn't cared for properly when he was a baby.'

'They didn't care for me because I was bad.'

'Are babies born bad? Is that the way it is?'

'Well, some babies are born bad.'

'Like you?'

'Yes.'

'So when you were a tiny baby, wrapped in a blanket, just like Jean's granddaughter, you were bad?'

Silence. A thinking silence.

Slowly he unfurls himself from the duvet. His face is red and tearstained. His lips are swollen. He looks at my face but in a disconnected way.

'Have you got tears in your eyes?' he asks, incredulously.

'Yes, I have.'

'Why?'

'Because it makes me so sad that you didn't get the care you deserved. I wish you had been my baby and then I could have cared for you.'

He fixes into my eyes with disbelief.

'You are my best boy, the boy I love the most in the world.'

I hold out my arms and he rolls into me, head first.

'I love you, Mummy.'

That evening I go out with my friends to the pub. We chat about our week. I cannot begin to explain.

*****

During our next session with Patrick I get better marks for my part in the 'I am bad' conversation, and my ad-libbing goes down well too. We have come to talk about the next most important thing on our list after the anger.

'It's like living with gremlins,' says Rob. 'They constantly take food from the cupboards, they take my stuff and hide it in strange places, they cut up things like tea towels and flannels with scissors; at the weekend I found a shit under the climbing frame.'

He could run on and on with this theme, as could I. It drives us both completely crazy.

'This would be a good time to talk about close supervision as a way of starting to increase feelings of safety in Jamie and Rose. By close supervision I literally mean, go everywhere with them. So when you get home from school, play with them or sit and watch the television together. Show them that you enjoy all these moments with them. Take them to the bathroom, sit with them whilst they have a bath, go out in the garden with them. This way, you will also be dramatically reducing the failure rate. They will make fewer mistakes and their shame levels will reduce.'

Pure exhaustion oozes out of my pores.

'You have to think "toddlers", which emotionally they are. And once they start to feel safer and less anxious, you will experience fewer of these behaviours.'

So now I have a ten-year-old toddler and a seven-year-old toddler, and the elder toddler can look me square in the eye and tell me to 'fuck off'.

'You might be wondering how you are going to fit the usual chores into the day.'

Too right.

'Eat baked beans on toast or ready meals every day if you have to. It won't kill you. Don't fret about dust and mess.'

He's got me down as a tidy-freak mother but as I am not, this is music to my ears. A professional person is ordering me to be more untidy and to up my provision of nursery-style teas. I am already planning baked potatoes, boiled eggs, bigger and better dust bunnies, recyclables in with the main rubbish, increased use of the tumble drier. Yes, I'm going to kick back and be a slob. I'm going to be great at it.

'And remember not to sweat the small stuff.'

Our new ways of being bring about a growing sense of calm. But just as the green shoots of recuperation appear and there is the energy and space for fun, Rob starts to withdraw from me, the children and from life. I notice it on Mother's Day. He is quiet and distant and for a while I think I have done something wrong.

'I'm fine,' is his refrain although everything else about him says that he is not.

The children become unsettled by his emotional absence and start to come at him louder and stronger. He goes to bed later and later into the night and spends the days suspended in tiredness. I try to find out what is wrong, but all I get is, 'I'm fine.' I start to worry that he has had enough of our extreme life and that he is considering leaving. He says this is not what he wants. I find myself getting jumpy when Jamie and Rose are irritating him, and I whisk them away. The weeks go on like this and I realise that he is enveloped in a dark cloud of depression. He becomes like a passenger in our lives. He sits in the corner of the sitting room, always in the same spot. His presence sucks the joy and the energy out of me. I tentatively suggest that he visit our doctor and I print off some information from the internet on depression. The papers stay on the windowsill where I left them.

Then one Monday he entirely folds in on himself. He takes the day off work, lies in bed and barely engages with me at all. I get the children to school and bring him some breakfast.

'I'm fine,' he says although his head shakes.

The significance of the day only dawns on me later that morning. It is his late father's birthday.

'What is wrong with Daddy?' the children ask in the car on the way home from school.

'I think he is feeling sad that his mummy and daddy have died and he can't see them anymore.'

They know too much about grief and loss to be patronised by adult lies.

'Poor Daddy,' they say with concern.

'Even grown-ups miss their mummies and daddies sometimes.'

'I would miss you so much if you were dead,' says Rose, and Jamie agrees.

'I would miss you too, so much,' I say.

'Would you?' they fire back. 'Really?'

'It would feel like the end of my life if either of you died.'

They are taken aback. It comes as a complete revelation to them that I, their mother, would be destroyed if she outlived them, that they could mean so much to another person. It is a reminder to me that despite our years together, they retain a doubt that they are truly loved.

After weeks of floating about in helplessness, I confide in Aiesha.

'It is not uncommon for adopters to suspend emotions like grief while they get on with the job of parenting traumatised children. But grief cannot be held back forever. Family life is calmer for you right now and grief has seen an empty space and crept in.'

She advises me to try to be mum and dad to Jamie and Rose – to take them out and do family things together as normal and hope that Rob emerges. But what if he doesn't emerge? The prospect is frightening.

'I just don't know where I will get the energy from.'

'Try it and see how you go. I'm sure that Rob will come out of this. Ring me if you need to vent.'

There is no magic wand that will soothe away the grief.

*****

The following week is the half term holidays. We leave Rob in bed and visit the gardens where I used to work. It is the first time I have been back since I left. During the journey I explain to Jamie and Rose that I used to be a gardener there and they struggle to equate me with a person who had a job, another life before I became their mother. From the moment we park and walk into the visitor's centre I feel as if I have come home. The ladies in the shop welcome us and introduce themselves to the children. We are waved through and amongst the vast expanse of straight green lines and billowing clouds of colour I spot Andy edging the top lawn. I wave and walk towards him.

'Sally, how the devil are you, stranger?' he calls, putting down his edging shears.

'Very well, thank you. How are you?'

'Oh you know, rolling on. Are these your two?'

'Yes, this is Jamie and Rose.'

He bends down and shakes their hands.

'Do you drive a tractor?' asks Jamie.

'Yes, I do sometimes. Did you know your mum used to drive a tractor?'

Jamie's eyes nearly drop out of their sockets.

'Would you like to sit in our tractor?'

'Yes please.'

'Jon is using it down by the walled garden. I'll radio ahead and tell him you're on your way.'

Andy calls up Jon on the walkie-talkie. Jamie watches intently, deeply impressed.

We head down a path and spot Jon.

'Sally, what a nice surprise. Have you brought some workers with you?'

'Some trainee tractor drivers.'

'Luckily I have a tractor right here. Would you two like to sit in it? Maybe you would like to move the bucket?'

Jamie climbs into the seat first. He bounces up and down in it and twists the steering wheel. He is trying to look as though this happens every day, but an enormous smile escapes and lights up his face.

'Mum, look, this is the indicator.'

'If you let me sit up there with you I'll start the engine and we can move the bucket up and down.'

It is all his birthdays wrapped up together. Jon shows him how to tilt the bucket, how to move it towards the ground and back up again and then how to empty it. As it shakes, the tractor judders and Jamie looks at me as if to say, 'Just take a look at what I am doing.'

'I don't think I will have a turn, Mummy,' says Rose.

'Are you sure?'

'Sure.'

Jon shows Jamie how to turn off the ignition, declares it to be about tea break time and invites us to the bothy.

'I like tea breaks,' says Jamie.

'You'll make a good gardener then.'

Going into the dark, dusty bothy is like opening a drawer of half-forgotten objects. I rediscover things I had forgotten about and there is a comfortable familiarity about the dirty mugs, the plastic swing bin stained with tannin, the ancient chairs that leak little cubes of disintegrating yellow foam. The children sit close to me, Rose on my lap.

They look around the old, stone building with big eyes. Two separate parts of my life touch. It feels good to be back and in the comforting arms of the camaraderie, the beauty of the gardens, the simplicity of life here, the quietness. I chat to the gardeners as they come in, but the children tug at my arm and interrupt. They are not comfortable with this glimpse into the unknown part of me. In my naivety I had planned to come back to this world, thought I could maintain it in parallel with parenting, but the parenting swamps me, takes up all of me to the exclusion of almost everything else. Grief briefly brushes my face.

On the way out we walk through the shop.

'Can we get something for Dad, to cheer him up?' asks Rose.

'That's a really lovely idea.'

They choose a box of fudge and a pencil.

'I'll give Dad his present,' says Jamie.

'No, I want to,' says Rose.

'I am the oldest, you know, and you gave Dad his last present.'

'It was my idea. Muuum?'

That slight sense that their mum has edged emotionally out of their immediate proximity has unnerved them. They argue all the way home. Don't forget us. Don't forget us. Don't leave us.

*****

The school year rolls on and the prospect of Jamie's last few weeks at his primary school loom. There are visits from older children who talk about how great life at secondary school is and how much bigger it is. Jamie and I are invited to visit the school several times together and then he visits with his class. It is not a huge school but to Jamie it appears enormous and frightening. He says he is looking forward to 'big school' but his behaviour deteriorates and I know he is already starting to grieve for his safe little school and the teachers there who have nurtured him so well. Events that spell the end of the school year fly past – a school play, sports day, moving-up day.

During the last few days of term I prepare as best I can for the long summer holiday: the chasm of unstructured time, which will open up and swamp Jamie and Rose. I buy activity books, reading books, plenty of flour for baking, new footballs and cricket balls and some DVDs. I box it all up and hide it under my bed. My summer holiday toolbox. To break up the six weeks and give the expanse of time some structure, I make a calendar on the computer showing each day and write in all the plans we have made: our holiday in Cornwall, a visit to relatives, tennis court bookings, a possible trip to the cinema. It is a route map of sorts – some scaffolding for the holiday wobbles. While I run around gathering booking forms and checking diaries, the computer lapses into lethargy and shows random photographs from our collection. The mishmash of randomness lends the pictures a distance from the now. Jamie and Rose standing on top of a windswept peak in the Lake District looking impossibly small, playing in a river, building dams by the sea, going down a slide, standing in front of the Christmas tree, drinking lemonade in a pub garden, in fancy dress, at a birthday party. They wear clothes I had forgotten about, pull faces that had made us laugh, clutch treasured toys long since gone. Rob and I carry them, hold them on our laps, hold their hands, then struggle to capture smiles as they stand unaided in front of the camera. Some of the more recent pictures are taken by them: odd snapshots of views important to them – a Barbie's face, the cogs of a bicycle, a snail. It strikes me that over the past seven years we have built a family and despite the hardships it is glued together by the days out, the family celebrations, the traditions that have grown up around us and knitted the four of us together.

CHAPTER 18

We arrive first and sit side by side in the front row. This is a gateway moment and we want to experience every drop of it. I sit on my hands. The grey, plastic chairs are clammy in this heat and my skirt sticks to the back of my legs. More parents come into the hall and find seats. They seem relaxed. A ball of nerves bounces in my stomach.

Jamie's face appears around the door of his classroom.

'Mum, Dad,' he calls and waves.

He smiles, seems to light up.

Children file in class by class and sit cross-legged on the parquet floor, each in turn. They bob around searching out the reassuring smiles of parents. It is common at these school events to share in the disbelief that our older children were ever that small. I can connect with Jamie's infant years vividly – little boy lost – and I feel no sense of a backwards yearning for those times. He has become part of this village school family, woven into the fabric of it. It has held and nurtured him, faced down the challenges with patience and kindness. He doesn't want to leave here and despite all the best intentions of both his current and future schools to ease his transition, he is being shadowed by the worry of moving on to secondary school.

Rose's class file in and I spot her, her eyes flicking around the hall trying to locate us. I wave and she sees us, her face relaxing. I watch her line up and sit down in her row and am struck by the familiarity of the bounce of her auburn bunches and the shape of her shoulders. The invisible cord connecting us pulls deep inside.

Jamie's class enter the hall last and they have the older children's privilege of sitting on the old wooden PE benches in front of the parents. Jamie places himself in front of Rob.

'Hello, Mummy, hi, Daddy.'

'Hello, Jamie.'

'It's a secret, what we're doing. It's going to be *really* good.'

The small group of leavers are dressed in their costumes for the play they have devised – some in formal white shirts, some in a jumble of coloured tights, stripy trousers, hair back-combed, sprayed with glitter. There is a gathering hush as Mr Andrews walks to the front of the hall.

'May the peace of the Lord be with you.'

'And also with you,' the children sing-song in response.

He stands alongside a table covered in trophies and cups and in front of a projector screen. He welcomes parents, carers, families to this momentous day in the lives of our Year 6 children – the leaver's assembly, after which they will take the next step in their lives. He indicates to a child who presses 'play' on a CD player and tinny piano music struggles out of the speakers.

'One more step along the world I go,' we all sing.

The notes go up high for, 'And it's from the old I travel to the new' and Rob's voice changes down a gear. We both stifle a laugh. Jamie looks around and puts his fingers in his ears. The music finishes and as Mr Andrews moves towards the trophy table a clenched expectation rises in the room. The individual class prizes are awarded first. Tiny children step up to the front and are given enormous cups on wooden plinths. They stare at the silverware and are prompted to go back to their places.

Rose's class. A build-up and then her name is called: 'Rose Donovan'. She stands, cheeks flushed, shocked. She steps between children to the front and shakes Mr Andrews's outstretched hand. Her eyes search out ours ('Look what I've got'). I feel a rush of pride and happiness for her. She carries her trophy back to her place and shows her friends. Another child receives a cup and then,

'The final class trophy, to make a matching pair on the mantelpiece, goes to Jamie Donovan. Jamie, where are you?'

'This is very well deserved,' says the head teacher as he shakes Jamie's hand.

We all clap. I clap until my hands sting. As he sits back down he immediately turns around to show us his trophy.

'Rose *and* me,' he says with disbelief, as though it was given to him by some mistake.

There are quiet rumbles of disagreement as the sports awards are announced and then:

'The final prize is the Art Prize. It goes to someone who has a great talent for drawing…

(That could be Rose)

This person uses every available moment to draw…

(It sounds like her)

they are particularly good at animals…

(Got to be Rose)

The prize goes to Rose Donovan.'

She stands up quickly, face crimson, a huge smile breaking across it. She receives an envelope. A voucher to spend on art materials.

There is more rumbling in front of us and the older children get up and make their way to the front. Jamie and his friend put headphones around their necks and pick up clipboards. They are Ant and Dec introducing Teachers Have Got Talent. The children have dressed up as their teachers and put on little comedy acts. In between each act Jamie and his friend ad-lib a commentary and then introduce the next. Jamie oozes confidence and the audience laugh along with him. I hear someone behind say, 'Who's that boy? He's so funny.'

A girl wearing high heels trips on her way to perform her act. Quick as a flash Jamie says, 'Careful there, Lady Gaga,' and the room erupts.

I watch him in wonderment. The boy who not so many years ago struggled to string a sentence together, who sat on the margins of school, who had few friends, is the star of the show. A few of the girls on the stage start to giggle.

'Come on ladies, pull yourselves together,' he says, effortlessly playing to the audience.

It is remarkable to see him like this, to see him differently; it is a bright glimpse of a future of possibilities. His eyes sparkle and I see in him the captivating little three-year-old whom we brought home with us. More than the trophy and the academic achievement, I wallow in watching him holding the stage, confident and so at peace with himself. During the clapping at the end, Rob leans over to me and whispers, 'Unbelievable, I didn't know he had it in him.'

The children gather in a group at the front, each with their arms over the next child's shoulder. Music starts and then the screen lights up: 'Year 6 Leavers'. A montage of photographs flashes up. Image after image of happy children: rock-climbing, at the beach, in school plays, at sports day ('We are not what you think we are' comes form the CD player), in fancy dress, gardening, holding insects, painting ('We are golden, we are golden'), building models, measuring each other, larking around, swimming ('No giving up when you're young and you want some'), cooking, the end-of-year party ('We are golden'). The children sway and chant, 'We are not what you think we are.' I look at Mr Andrews, standing watching his film, perhaps quietly making a point about childhood and education, even in the lyrics of his chosen song. Several of the girls sob. It has indeed been a golden time – for Jamie a time of recovery, blossoming and finding out good things about himself.

Mr Andrews makes a short closing speech about moving on to new chapters of life and how he hopes they will all look back on their time at St Mary's with happy memories. There are louder sobs. He wishes us all a good summer and then it's over. Within moments the room is a melee of children and parents and teachers, all trying to collect belongings and locate each other. Jamie comes over to us.

'You were fantastic in your play.'

'I know.'

'You kept that a secret.'

'Well, I wanted it to be a surprise. Anyway, I'm going to give Miss Taylor her card and then I want to go home.'

The evening before, unprompted, he had sat quietly at the kitchen table and written a 'thank you' card to his teacher. It read:

> To Miss Taylor,
>
> Thanks for teaching me well and helping me through the hard. I think you should teach in a big, posh comedy school. I will miss you loads and it's going to be hard without you. Your obviously the best and only proper teacher I've had, the only teacher who understands where I have been and my background. I feel so much more confident about speaking about my past and now you've come into my world it's going to be hard to say bye.
>
> Keep this on the fridge. If you feel down get it down and it'll remind you of me.

He would only let me see it when it was finished. The writing was small and neat and filled the card. Its honesty and depth astonished me. Whilst I knew that he was fond of Miss Taylor, I had not realised he appreciated her so deeply. Now I knew how much he was going to miss her.

When I go to find him, he is standing over Miss Taylor who is seated at her desk. She is reading the card, wiping away tears. She looks up and mouths to me, 'Thank you.'

'Jamie wrote it himself.'

I walk towards her; she stands and I give her a hug.

'Thank you so much for everything you've done. You've made such a difference.'

'I wasn't going to cry.'

'Neither was I.'

Jamie looks up at us both, perplexed and puzzled.

'Can we go home now?'

'Come on then, let's go.'

We drive home, a car full of tired-out excitement. Eight years ago I wouldn't have dared to hope Rob and I would have lives bubbling full of family, let alone be spending a hot July afternoon witnessing our children's hard-won successes. Jamie and Rose have been gifted to us and they have changed everything; they have filled that empty, gaping hole in our lives and so much more – their uniqueness, their love, their pasts and their futures. They brought with them the bumps and scrapes to their selves and we have been charged with learning to accept and soothe them, to coax the damaged parts back to life, to calm their fractured nerves, to show them a life that they deserve and have a right to. They have shaped us just as radically as we have shaped them. We have had to shed so many expectations, to learn to do things differently, to be brave, not afraid to stand away from the crowd – the only way to create the right growing conditions to allow Jamie and Rose to flourish.

I am not a believer in magic, nor in destiny, but from the moment I met Jamie and Rose I felt they were meant to be mine – had been kept aside so we could be together. They have waited patiently for us to catch them up and in many ways we've always lagged behind them as we've fought to understand the deep harm that was done to them.

Compared with many of the families in that village school hall, the future will be different for us. We will always need Patrick and Aiesha and the other experts in child neglect; we will never be able to stand back from school; we will always be battling the misconception that children are robust and bounce back and what they can't remember won't affect them. We are always going to have to do that little bit extra, but we are up to the job now.

'Shall we go out for tea tonight?' says Rob as we pull into the drive.

'Yesss!' they chorus and Rose punches the air.

'Can we have pizza?' asks Jamie.

'I want fish and chips and I never get to choose,' says Rose.

Rob turns to me and laughs. 'Oh no, what have I started?'

'We can go to the pub and everyone can have what they want,' I suggest, my mind nimble and well practised at negotiating crisis-aversion.

We unload the car of school bags, lunchboxes, PE bags and trophies and dump everything in the kitchen.

'Who wants an ice-cream smoothie?'

'Group hug first,' says Jamie, holding out his arms.

Rob and I each put an arm around him and fold Rose between us.

'Well done, you two,' says Rob, 'the Donovans done good today.'

'I love you, my mummy and my daddy,' says Rose.

'You're the best mum and dad in the world,' says Jamie.

And we hold each other tightly.